Becoming
Coastal

Becoming Coastal

25 Years
of
Exploration and Discovery
of the
British Columbia Coast
by
Paddle, Oar and Sail

Alex Zimmerman

SEAWORTHY PUBLICATIONS, INC. • MELBOURNE, FLORIDA

Becoming Coastal
25 Years of Exploration and Discovery of the British Columbia Coast by Paddle, Oar and Sail
Copyright ©2020 by Alex Zimmerman

Published in the USA by:
Seaworthy Publications, Inc.
6300 N Wickham Rd.
#130-416
Melbourne, FL 32940
Phone 321-610-3634
email orders@seaworthy.com
www.seaworthy.com - Your Bahamas and Caribbean Cruising Advisory

Library of Congress Cataloging-in-Publication Data

Names: Zimmerman, Alex, 1952- author.
Title: Becoming coastal : 25 years of exploration and discovery of the
  British Columbia coast by paddle, oar and sail / Alex Zimmerman.
Other titles: Twenty-five years of exploration and discovery of the British
  Columbia coast by paddle, oar and sail
Description: Melbourne, Florida : Seaworthy Publications, Inc., 2020. |
  Includes bibliographical references. | Summary: "In this collection of
  narratives Victoria technologist, environmentalist and writer Alex
  Zimmerman tells stories not only of self-propelled travel and adventure
  but also of nature, the magnificent environment and of interesting
  people that he meets on the coast of British Columbia. Zimmerman is not
  the first to paddle and write about the BC Coast, but he brings a fresh
  and personal perspective as he details how he learns the necessary
  physical and mental skills of solo traveling. His encounters with the
  non-human inhabitants of the coast, the whales, wolves, bears and a
  super-pod of dolphins, are brought to life with a thrilling immediacy.
  Zimmerman's writing evokes vivid visual imagery and he conveys to the
  reader a strong sense of being there. You will share with him the
  wonder, joy, fear and awe he experienced as he discovered the coast's
  geography, its ecology, its people and his own growing capabilities in
  the process of becoming coastal"-- Provided by publisher.
Identifiers: LCCN 2019033756 (print) | LCCN 2019033757 (ebook) | ISBN
  9781948494274 (Paperback) | ISBN 9781948494281 (eBook)
Subjects: LCSH: Zimmerman, Alex, 1952---Travels. | Sea kayaking--British
  Columbia--Guidebooks. | Sailing--British Columbia--Guidebooks. | Boats
  and boating--British Columbia. | Coasts--British Columbia--Guidebooks..
  | Natural resources--British Columbia. | Physical geography--British
  Columbia. | Voyages and travels--Anecdotes. | British
  Columbia--Description and travel. | British Columbia--Guidebooks.
Classification: LCC GV776.115 .Z56 2020 (print) | LCC GV776.115 (ebook) |
  DDC 797.122/409711--dc23
LC record available at https://lccn.loc.gov/2019033756
LC ebook record available at https://lccn.loc.gov/2019033757

Acknowledgments

This book benefited greatly from encouragement, advice, comment and criticism of its several drafts, in whole or part, by many people. I would like to thank Rick Searle, Bernie Gaudet, Jack Meredith, Lori Garcia-Meredith, Dave and Rosemary Lesser, Debbie Quigg, Norris Weimer and Susan Conrad for their helpful and insightful comments. Mike Higgins very kindly volunteered to edit the first chapter and pointed out some glaring faults and bad habits I had allowed to creep in. Chastened, I strove to eliminate them and I looked at and revised the remainder of the manuscript with a much more critical eye.

Any remaining faults in the book are mine alone.

Thanks to Dave Lesser, Tad Roberts and Ryan Masson for their permission to use photos that are included in the book.

I would especially like to thank my friend and fellow adventurer Peter Freeman for his generous time, encouragement and guidance in helping me when embarking on the publishing journey, which in some ways is as arduous as the writing process itself.

In this, my first foray into the book publishing world, all the people at Seaworthy Publications were immensely helpful in explaining the business and what is required to help make a book successful. It was a pleasure to work with their straightforward and transparent style.

Finally, I would like to thank my wife Kathleen, whose forbearance and tolerance throughout the years as I embarked on the many solo journeys, leaving her to mind the home fires, I deeply appreciated.

Beginnings

Fire-Drake on Inside Passage north of Klemtu

A thousand years the cedar stood alongside its companions on the slope of Vancouver Island's outer coast mountains and slowly grew taller before falling, decades ago, to the loggers saw. Then rough weather broke the log loose from the tug's boom as it was being moved south to the mill. Before it could be recaptured, a storm of unimaginable fury drove the massive log in on a king tide, over the myriad outer reefs and rocks and past the outer guard islands of the Broken Group. Now it slumbers here, half-buried in the fine sand above the normal high tide line, in the sheltered cove below the campground on Turret Island.

Spared from being rendered down into roofing shakes, that log now serves generations of kayakers as a beachside seat, and this evening, at dusk in early August, it is a perch for my wife Kathleen, my daughter Carla, and I. We have not lit a fire against the evening's chill. We don't want to spoil our night vision, as tonight is the predicted peak of the annual Perseid meteor shower. Clear skies promise a good view, unspoiled by city light pollution. The afternoon's wind has mostly subsided, leaving tiny wavelets lapping at water's edge. As the light fades and stars begin to appear, a blanket of low cloud sweeps in from offshore, completely mantling the sky. We are disappointed to miss the meteors, but only a little. The meteor shower would only have crowned an already rewarding week of paddling and exploration in the Broken Group. The week has been a revelation for us in this small corner of a fabulous jewel of a place we now call home.

How does a Prairie boy, born and raised in Winnipeg, 550 miles from the nearest ocean, and knowing nothing of it, become transformed into a zealous coastal sailor? Growing up I was immersed in family genealogy and stories that told me I came from many generations of people grounded on the land through farming and homesteading. I learned of lives governed by the seasons of planting and harvest, of survival through the bitter Canadian winters. While these stories were compelling, they didn't resonate with me. Instead, I was always drawn to the water, although I haven't a single sailor ancestor among the nine generations that I could trace. As a young teenager I salvaged a derelict old Chestnut canoe that washed up on the riverbank. I patched it, learned to paddle it, and with it explored the rivers and lakes of southern Manitoba and the Canadian Shield.

We had lived in British Columbia before for a couple of years in the mid-70's when I joined the Navy. The coast of British Columbia was utterly foreign to my experience the first time I saw it. In some ways, though, it felt like coming home. The basic seamanship that I learned in the Navy felt natural to me and I felt that I belonged on the water. Because I was at sea much of the time, there wasn't much time for exploration of the coast outside of the Navy, but we were struck, almost smitten, with what little we did experience. When I left the Navy, work forced a move to Alberta, but thirteen years later when the chance came to move back to British Columbia, we took it. When we moved back, I sensed that the coast defined this place. Nevertheless, there was a vast amount to learn about what it meant to live on and embrace the coast. What did it mean to be a coastal person now that I had moved back? What had it meant to the original inhabitants of the coast - the First Nations? How had the coast shaped the lives and outlook of the Europeans who had settled here? How will it change me?

I knew that the coast was shaped by its waters, islands and shorelines. I knew that the people and the plants, fish and animals that sustained them, are bound up in the complex intersection of land and water - where the sea meets the shore. I felt that this coast could only truly be understood by accessing it from the water, and I wanted to understand the coast.

I had heard about the Broken Group islands, which are part of Pacific Rim National Park Reserve. We knew little about them except that they seemed like a wonderful destination for a family holiday. However, getting there on our own seemed daunting. A cursory look at the chart shows there are several nautical miles[1] of open sea that must be crossed from the nearest access by road. In Alberta we had bought a canoe to paddle the rivers and lakes there and we brought the canoe with us back to Victoria. It seemed inadvisable to make the crossing in that small canoe. Then I learned of the *MV Frances Barkley*, a coastal freighter based in Port Alberni. This small freighter drops you off in sheltered waters within easy paddling distance of the islands. I realized that this was the answer to accessing the islands with our canoe.

That first trip was just a start. What about the rest of the coast? A good road runs up the sheltered east coast of Vancouver Island, but most of the outer west coast is not accessible by road at all. The British Columbia mainland coast is even less well served by roads. The coast road north of Vancouver extends less than a hundred miles. A couple of other threads from the interior of the province stretch out to the coast. There are ships and ferries that traverse the coast, to be sure, however, they have only a limited number of stops. The question was, how to see and experience the sections of coastline and adjacent waters between those stops? It seemed the only recourse was to acquire some kind of boat other than a canoe. The cost of a full-sized cruising boat, either sail or motor, was then beyond my means.

However, the week in the Broken Group convinced me that a small boat of some kind is entirely suitable, maybe even ideal. A small open canoe is not the safest of craft for the open ocean. A sea kayak, in skilled hands, can be very seaworthy. A sea kayak can also be taken by car to put-in points close to the area you want to explore. To reach areas not served by roads, a kayak can be loaded on to larger boats. At your campsite, a kayak can be lifted out of the water beyond the reach of wave and wind. A kayak can carry enough gear for relatively comfortable camping. With closed-over decks and a spray skirt, kayaks can cope with surprisingly rough conditions.

However, even off-the-shelf sea kayaks were too expensive. With the arrival of the summer 1993 edition of WoodenBoat magazine, the answer presented itself – a design for a simple plywood sea kayak designed for extended journeys. I persuaded a couple of friends, Jack and Lori, to join me in a boat-building project. Over the next year, we met several times a week in my garage workshop and built three boats. We learned how to scarf together pieces of plywood to get the required length, to lay out hull panels and cut the pieces with a jig saw. We learned the ways of epoxy - that marvelous and forgiving glue. We learned how to use copper wire to stitch the panels together into hull shape. We learned how to apply fibreglass tape with thickened epoxy to solidify the temporary shape. We learned how to scribe bulkheads to fit the hull and deck. We learned how to steam bend wood to form the cockpit coaming. We learned about sanding, painting and varnishing.

For old hands at boatbuilding, this is simple stuff, but when you have not done it before, the transformation of a pile of plywood and lumber into a boat, an object of both beauty and utility, brings both pride and confidence. At the end of the year, we had three identical boats, ready for a life of exploration and adventure.

As it turned out, the three of us made only a few trips together in those kayaks. This was partly due to circumstance and partly because of differing inclinations. My boat, though, started me on my unplanned and unrecognised (at least initially) journey of discovery. I had no grand plan as I began to explore the coast. Early, safe trips became more ambitious ones in more challenging and less accessible waters. Mostly, I felt a need for adventure that was not provided by my land-based day job. I was driven by an urge to get out there to see it for myself, to become part of the coast.

A journey cannot be separated from the mode of travel and my journey continued over the next twenty-five years in a series of home-built boats. These included two more kayaks and two rowboats with sails. The latter were lightweight open boats that can be sailed when the wind is suitable and rowed when it is calm. They also can be drawn up on a beach when camping ashore or they can be anchored offshore for sleeping aboard. These versatile craft also are known as camp cruisers. All my boats helped me to understand the coast and what it means to be coastal.

Another imperative gradually emerged as I traveled this journey, through it was harder to articulate to those who have not made similar journeys. It is akin to the immortal reply given by George Mallory when he was asked why he wanted to climb Mt. Everest: "Because it's there!" For me it comes down to wanting to be alive when I die, not just putting in time until the machine winds down. Self-propelled exploration provides that sense of immediacy that affirms to you that you are living your own life, not just going through the motions. So much of modern life in the western world is experienced indirectly through a mediator that diminishes reality. Whether the mediator is the windshield of a car zooming along at sixty miles an hour or a screen of some kind, where the virtual is substituted for the real, increasingly we live lives separated from the actual world.

Paddling or sailing your own boat, riding your bicycle, running or hiking along a trail, you live life first-hand. When you are out there doing it for yourself, the time that you experience does not unwind itself at the rate that a clock measures. Time expands so that your experience grows beyond the cognitive space of day-to-day life. Memory becomes more intense. I can easily recall details of a week-long back-country trip from twenty years ago but can hardly remember what I was doing the other fifty one weeks that same year. Travelling under your own muscle power or using the wind also attunes you to the nuances of your surroundings in a way that you can't experience when powered by stored energy. You may be tired, cold, wet, hungry, sore and sometimes scared, but you are intensely alive. Life is a richer and denser experience.

With this book, I hope to share with you some of the wonder, joy, fear and awe I experienced as I explored the coast over the past twenty-five years. The book is a chronicle of the voyages I made, both outer and inner. The chapters are organized loosely by geography and then within them by chronology. The boats that I built, and the voyages I made with them, became portals to experiences that would deliver adventure, introduce me to engaging people, revitalize my life and reveal additional facets of the coast while I was learning how to become coastal.

"We were not pioneers ourselves, but we journeyed over old trails that were new to us, and with hearts open. Who shall distinguish?"

J. Monroe Thorington, The Glittering Mountains of Canada

Table of Contents

Acknowledgments v

Beginnings vi

Nuggets 1

Broken Group 16

Brooks Peninsula 25

Quatsino Sound 44

Clayoquot Sound 53

Hakai Pass 61

Gwaii Haanas 78

The Broughtons by Kayak 119

Vancouver Island East - Shipyard Raid 132

Gulf Islands by Sail and Oar 158

Broken Group by Sail and Oar 182

The Broughtons by Sail and Oar 203

Inside Passage South 218

Inside Passage North 273

Endnotes 324

Bibliography 334

Author 337

Nuggets

The camping gear is loaded into the various bags, packs and containers and stowed in the family VW Golf. The canoe, the last item to be strapped on, otherwise the back hatch won't open, is lifted up onto the roof rack and strapped down. One last check to make sure we haven't forgotten anything, we lock the house, climb in the car and set off up the highway for the long drive to Port Alberni. It is a typical hot, sunny summer on Vancouver Island and Kathleen, Carla and I are excited to be embarking on a week-long adventure in the Broken Group islands. It is new territory for us as a family, both literally and figuratively. As a sailor, I am confident of my navigation and seamanship on the ocean, but I am more used to much bigger boats. What we will encounter with an open canoe, albeit in relatively sheltered waters, is still an open question. Anticipation mixes with trepidation but I am certain we will experience aspects of our new coastal home in a way that we have not been able to before now. We arrive at the dock early next morning, well before sailing time, to get our gear and canoe transferred from the car to the ship. The trip out to the Broken Group on the *MV Frances Barkley* in the bright morning sunshine that morning is one of wonder. The dark green forested mountains unfold one after the other around each reach and bend as we wind down the length of the Alberni Canal. Excitement builds as we talk to kayakers about the upcoming week.

The scene at the Sechart Lodge drop-off point, the site of the old whaling station, is one of apparent chaos. The *Frances Barkley* crew unloads the boats onto the crowded dock. Kayakers and canoeists pull their gear from the ship's large grey plastic fish totes and stow the dry bags and stuff sacks in their boats. People mill about seemingly at random among the heaps of gear.

1

Alex and Carla in the Broken Group

Gradually, at differing paces, paddlers pack their boats, don and snug down their spray skirts, climb in and paddle away. Finally, the dock is empty.

We camp the first day on Nettle Island above the beach on the northeast aide. On returning to camp from an exploratory walk along the beach, Kathleen says "What are all those crows doing by the duffel bag?" "It looks like they've pulled out a bag of trail mix," Carla says, "and pecked a hole and eaten most of it." We didn't zipper the bag all the way," I say, "Who would have thought they could get at the food through that little gap? The devils." We won't go short of food, but it is a good lesson to keep gear tidy and packed.

We discover an off-lying ring of rocks by one of the small islands alongside Imperial Eagle Channel. The ring is awash at low tide, the interior is shallow, and it encloses a fecund tide pool. We ease the canoe through a gap in the rocks into the pool and eat lunch while we sit, held fast by the eel grass[2] and kelp. We marvel at the diversity of plants, corals, algae and animals below our keel. On another small island on the opposite side of the group, we stop for a break and discover a perfect little white

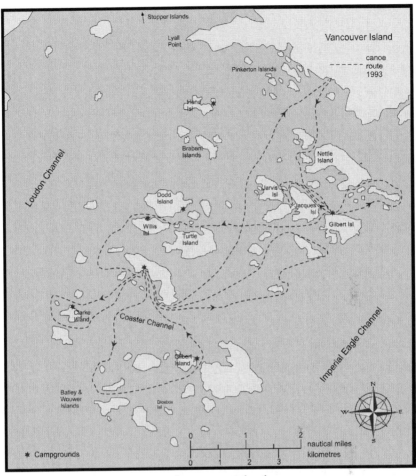

Broken Group Islands

beach. It is white because it is ankle-deep in small bleached shells of tiny sea creatures that we have not yet learned to identify. Carla is fascinated and spends an hour picking through and examining the shells. "You have to mark this beach on the chart, Dad," she says, "so we can find it again if we ever come back."

In the lagoon in Jacques Island, we are amazed at the profusion of life that we can see below us as we float through. There are many different kinds of seaweed. There are clams, oysters, tube worms, hermit crabs and sea cucumbers. The shallow bottom is covered with different coloured bat stars, blue, red and purple.

There are dozens of egg cases of moon snails, which look like tires sliced in half around their circumference then abandoned here by some careless nautical wrecking yard.

The sea lion rookery on the exposed, swell-battered rocks out past Batley and Wouwer Islands is full of the big animals hauled out in the sun. They declare their territory with hoarse barks and bellows that get louder as we approach. We get too close, the animals become agitated and several of them dive into the water. Within seconds, a big male about the size and weight of a small car swims to within a boat length of the canoe. He pops his head clear of the water and eyes us suspiciously. Suddenly this doesn't seem like a good place to be. We quickly paddle away and leave the sea lions to their territory.

We run back across Coaster Channel to the campground on Turret Island in the sunshine and brisk afternoon onshore wind. The run turns into an exhilarating and slightly anxious downwind paddle. We are just about at the limit of our skill among the white horses of the breaking wave tops. Carla sits in the middle of the canoe and is fortunately oblivious to the anxiety, sightseeing and occasionally trailing a hand in the water. We are relieved to arrive safely back at the campsite. At the end of the week, we load the canoe back on to the Frances Barkley for the scenic trip back up the canal to Port Alberni. The ride on the ship allows for a gradual re-compression back to land life with its bustle and demanding schedules.

* * * * *

Kathleen and I have come to Tofino for a weekend getaway. I loaded my recently built kayak on the car on the off chance that some opportunity would present itself for a little paddling. In talking to people in the town, we learn that a Grey Whale has been feeding for the past month in Grice Bay, east of the peninsula Tofino is located on. The whales haven't been seen in these inside waters for many decades.[3]

I have never seen a Grey Whale and am excited to get a chance. Kathleen drops me off at the boat launch in the bay and

I paddle out under cloudy skies to see what the bay might hold. Within fifteen minutes I see a whale's blow ahead and the sound of it reaches me a second later. I stop paddling and wait. A minute later, the whale surfaces and exhales again, nearer to me this time and now I can see its mottled skin and barnacle patches. It dives again and a minute later it comes up again even closer. Now I can see a muddy brown patch of water where the whale expelled its mouthful of bottom mud with its load of bottom-dwelling creatures. I am mesmerized! For the next four hours I paddle slowly around the bay, watching the whale determinedly feeding. It must put on enough weight here to see it through the winter fasting period down south. The bay must be rich grounds for the whale if no whales have been feeding in here for thirty years or more.

I stop on a small gravelly point to stretch my legs and eat lunch. I find, to my delight, a Chocolate Lily[4]. I have heard about these flowers, with their dark purple-brownish flowers with yellow mottling, but have not seen one before. It is a treat to see these flowers, so emblematic of the coast.

There are other boats in the bay too, commercial whale-watching boats who have a sure-fire sighting for their clients. I expect that the power boats will disturb the whale feeding, but after observing the whale today I think it is just the opposite. The bay is never without a power boat, except for one short period of about twenty minutes. During that time, the whale stops feeding and begins spy-hopping and looking around. It is hard to avoid concluding that the whale has gotten used to the sound of power boats and is nervous when they are not there. Sort of a "What's this lack of noise all about?" behaviour. I am convinced that the whale is used to locating the boats sonically, and, with that knowledge of where they are, gets on with its feeding. On one of these spy-hops, the whale surfaces quite near me. I have the distinct impression I am being scrutinized and judged by that enormous, intelligent eye. I must be judged harmless as the whale does not either come any closer or swim off any further.

* * * * *

On a Saturday morning in mid-September I unload the kayak from my car alongside Lochside Drive in Sidney, BC and carry it down to the adjacent gravelly beach. It is calm and sunny out on the water and the ten-mile paddle I have planned should be good, but I have mixed feelings about the day. It's not going to be just a recreational day paddle. I am going to witness the sinking of the first ship that I served on, in the Navy. When I joined her for my basic seamanship training, *HMCS Mackenzie*, the first of her particular class of destroyer escort, had been in service for thirteen years. In her I learned how to handle lines large and small and how to tie knots for various purposes. I learned how to launch, handle and retrieve a small boat in a seaway. I learned how to keep a sharp lookout from the wing of the bridge on a black middle watch of the night. I learned how to keep a mess deck clean and tidy and how to get along with wildly diverse shipmates. In short I learned how to become a sailor in a modern navy[5].

Now, *Mackenzie* has been decommissioned and sold out of the Navy after thirty-one years of active duty. But, rather than being purchased by a scrap dealer and melted down for razor blades, she has been bought by the Artificial Reef Society. She has been stripped of her gear, has had any hazardous materials removed and has been readied for a second, much longer life as a reef. Her hull, decks and bulkheads will become an armature for the marine algae, sponges, corals, plants, animals and the fishes that will make up the supporting structure for a reef and subsequent dive site.

When I arrive at the site of the sinking, *Mackenzie* is sitting, anchored over her final resting place, on the 20-fathom line north of Gooch Island. There are already dozens and dozens of other boats there to watch, sailboats, power boats, skiffs, other kayaks. Some are anchored, some are drifting and others are under power. Coast Guard Zodiacs buzz in circles, trying to keep everyone back at a safe distance. The ship herself is looking rather forlorn, to my eyes. Much of the equipment that made her a functioning warship has been removed. Even the main armament, the twin 3-inch forward guns, are gone, with two steel mock-up tubes mounted in the gun turret in their place. The hull identification number, 261, has been painted over. Many large holes have been cut in the topsides of the hull to allow both easy colonization by marine life and easy access by divers. One hole is in the topsides exactly where my bunk was, in the forward port seaman's mess deck.

I ease my way towards the south inside of the circle of boats surrounding *Mackenzie* as the time draws near for the sinking. There are many other kayaks and rowboats ranged alongside me. They have set explosive charges at various points on the bottom of the hull. The intention is to set them off at the same time so that the ship will settle on the bottom evenly. The appointed time for the sinking comes and goes. Nothing happens. Official boats are still tethered to the ship's side. Time passes. Finally, people clamber down into the boats and push off. The atmosphere is tense. With no warning, there is a mighty bang and puffs of white smoke shoot out of the holes in the sides of the ship and a larger black cloud of smoke erupts straight up. The slight breeze from the south blows the smoke over the boats to the other side, away from me, giving me a clear view of what is happening. Slowly at first, the ship begins to list to port and then settles down more by the bow than by the stern. Now the foredeck is awash.

I have a sudden flashback to the daily drills we conducted aboard, firefighting, damage control, flood control – all to keep the ship afloat and operational – and now here the ship is sinking before my eyes. Now air trapped below decks is bubbling up as the ship sinks further below the water and both the foredeck and the forward gun are completely submerged. Now the ship is listing heavily to port, perhaps twenty degrees, and is submerged bow down, stern up, and I can see into the mortar bay aft and onto the signals deck behind the bridge. The bridge is completely sunk now and only a corner of the stern is showing, when, with a last gout of trapped air, water fountains up and the ship is gone, leaving only a swirl on the surface. It only took forty-five seconds.

There is a kind of stunned silence as all of us in the surrounding boats absorb what has just happened, but only for a few moments. Then there is a roar as boats start up or throttle up and begin to manoeuvre. It is a chaotic scene. Being low on the water, I am afraid I will be a mere speed bump to the larger boats who seem to be in an awful hurry to leave. Dodging the big boats as best I can, I quickly paddle over to a small gravel beach on the south side of nearby Comet Island and land to wait for power boats to clear the area. I'm joined by a number of other kayakers who also see the wisdom of avoiding the big boats. While, strictly speaking, engineless boats such as kayaks have the right of way over power boats, I learned long ago that in situations like this, it's better to get out of the way that than to stay and be "dead right." When the coast is literally clear, I paddle slowly back to where I left the car, in a contemplative mood. I reflect on the transitory nature of things that seem so permanent at the time. It is a reminder not to take anything for granted, because all things must change, and to immerse yourself in experiences of the moment because they will never come again.

* * * *

It is one of those calm breaks between winter storm systems and it coincides with the Christmas break. I launch my kayak from the park behind the marina in Oak Bay for a day paddle out and around the Chatham and Discovery Islands. The day is cloudy and cool, but there is little wind and no rain. I am dressed for the water, with my wet-suit and a couple of fleecy layers on under a waterproof paddling jacket, life jacket and spray skirt. I have my neoprene paddling gloves to keep my hands warm from immersion in the cold seawater, which is only about 7-10 degrees Celsius[6] at this time of year. Paddling out past Mary Tod Island, which protects the marina, I am thrilled to be on the water. There are few other boats out but I see lots of bird life. Many of the pelagic seabirds move closer inshore in winter. In addition to the usual gulls, I see Common Murres, Cormorants, both Double-Crested and Pelagic, and a few Pigeon Guillemots. As I paddle closer to the small islands that make up the Chatham group, I see Oyster-catchers and even a few Surfbirds, with their distinctive wing patterns as they lift up, fly and settle back down. There are also Harlequin Ducks in their colourful paint-by-numbers plumage, which migrate the other direction, from inland mountain lakes in the summer, to the coast in winter.

I paddle past the yacht outstation dock on the largest Chatham island and wave to a couple of people standing there. I approach the rocks that make up Fulford Reef, intending to go out and around the island to the east. The flood tide is running strongly past the reef and there is a distinct shear line in the water between the calm among the rocks and the moving water beyond it. I don't have much experience with strong currents in my kayak and approach this line slowly, with caution, sensing danger. It is exactly the wrong thing to do.

As soon as I poke my bow across the shear line, the kayak immediately capsizes, although it doesn't roll completely over. The boat is floating on its side, leaving my torso immersed in the water, and my life jacket allows me to just keep my head above water. I am totally surprised, shocked even, as I expected my caution would keep me out of trouble. Time slows right down, almost congeals, but I am not paralyzed into inaction. I don't understand how this has happened but don't have time to figure it out just now. The water feels cold on my arms and shoulders but I am not numbed as I am wearing my wet-suit. My first reaction is to try to roll the kayak back upright, the way I had learned in the lessons I had taken a couple of years before. My first attempt fails. My second attempt fails and I am still hanging sideways in the water with my head barely above water. I just can't get enough leverage with my hips to flick the boat upright.

I exit the boat altogether and go to Plan B, a wet exit and paddle float re-entry. I right the boat and extract the paddle float, which was tucked under bungee cords behind the cockpit. I stick one end of the paddle into it. Holding the other end of the paddle across the cockpit, I heave myself into the cockpit. The boat, which is full of water, is so unstable because of it that I roll right over and out the other side. I set up the paddle float and try again – same result. Third attempt and this time I manage to stay in the cockpit. The kayak is still very unstable, but by keeping the paddle float held in place with one hand, it stays stable enough that I can get the pump out and begin to work it. I gradually get the water level down to where there is just an inch or so left in the bottom. While I am working the pump I think about what happened. I conclude that the strong current beyond the shear line must have both yanked the bow to the left and at the same time grabbed the hard chine of the kayak and generated an overturning force.

The pump is sucking air at the bottom of the cockpit and I re-fasten the spray skirt and look up and around to see where I am. I have no idea how much time has passed. It can't have been too long, as the current, fortunately, has pushed me back into the calm water and I have drifted back towards the yacht outstation dock. I paddle over to the dock where the two men that are there are just climbing back out of their boat. One of the men says "We were just coming to rescue you, but then we saw that you didn't need it." "Yes" says the other, "We were impressed that you didn't appear to panic at all." "Well," I say, "Slow-witted people usually don't!"

I have to admit to myself that I was a bit rattled, though. I pull the kayak up onto the dock and sponge the rest of the water out of the cockpit. I wasn't aware of feeling cold at all, although I was wet. The wet-suit and fleece layers were doing their job and of course the adrenalin from the capsize helped too. But it occurs to me I had better get back to the car as soon as I can. I thank the men for standing by, jump back in the kayak and shove off. I paddle strongly back towards the landing beach and think about what has just occurred. I realize that although I had taken some lessons in basic kayak skills, I still have a lot to learn about handling the boat in currents and surf. I vow to sign up for some lessons as soon as I get back. I also realize I need to modify my boat somehow so that I can better wedge myself in to be able to perform rolls[7].

I last visited the southern parts of Desolation Sound decades ago, in a chartered sailboat, and it was a wonderful trip. We encountered forest-bound, sheltered anchorages and long channels bordered by mountains. We experienced beautiful sunshine and heavy rain, dead calms and good sailing winds. We ended the week battling our way back to Comox against a sudden strong southeast gale in the open Strait of Georgia. With the good memories from that trip, I think it will be interesting to see the area from the perspective of my kayak.

I launch mid-afternoon of a late July day at Heriot Bay on the east side of Quadra Island. I am worried about high south winds, as Sutil Channel east of Quadra is exposed to Georgia Strait to the south. The Strait is quite windy, from what I can see of it on the drive up from Victoria this morning. Once out from behind the protection of Rebecca Spit, though, the wind is light, maybe five or six knots. Even that dies away as I paddle the couple of miles past the Breton Islands and enter Hoskyn Channel. It becomes downright hot in the afternoon sun, making the paddling hard and tedious. The whole way up the Channel the sound of generators drifts out from the fish farms that seems to fill nearly every bay. The industrial intrusion isn't what I expected at all, and, together with the heat, is an unwelcome start to the trip. My mood is sour, which is something I have never experienced before at the start of a trip.

Getting through Surge Narrows is on the agenda for the next day as the tide is against me this evening. I see a likely looking campsite behind a small point opposite the narrows and pull in to find it occupied by a tour group. Looking at the chart, there doesn't seem to be any nearby alternatives. I find a small spot out of the tour group's way and set up camp. My mood improves somewhat later as I move supper operations out to the point where there is enough of a breeze to keep the mosquitoes and sand flies at bay.

Surge Narrows is the name given to several narrow passages through the Settlers Group of islands, leading to Okisollo

Channel between Quadra[8] and Maurelle Islands. The tide tables are given for one of those passages, Beazley Passage. Peak currents can exceed eleven knots, but are not that strong this week, reaching only six and half knots. That is still too much current to paddle against. I have to wait for slack which is at about quarter to twelve. As usual, I get a little impatient and arrive about twenty minutes early. I find about a knot and a half of current and some turbulence, but although my pulse rate goes up, I come through without difficulty. Less than a mile past the narrows is Yeatman Bay on Quadra Island. I stop for lunch on the beach then walk up the trail to a small lake that feeds the stream in the bay. The sun is hot again and the water is refreshingly cool but not cold as I have a swim and a wash. Back in the kayak, I paddle slowly to cover the three miles to Octopus Islands Marine Park. I stop for a rest in the shade on a rocky point and debate

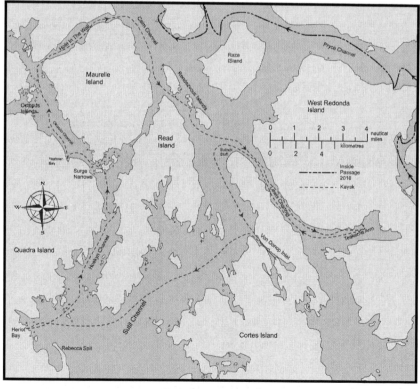

Desolation Sound

with myself whether to stay for the night. The islands are a nice little microcosm of the typical water and rock interface scenery found in Desolation Sound[9].

As a consequence the islands are very popular. There are power and sailboats anchored in every possible location in the park. Their inflatable dinghies with outboard motors are buzzing back and forth constantly. My mood, which was good during the day, is darkening again and I realize this will not be a peaceful place to spend the night. Since afternoon slack for Hole in The Wall rapids is predicted for twenty past five, I carry on to see if I can find a quieter spot. Twenty minutes before the predicted slack, when I arrive at the west entrance, there is almost no current, meaning the prediction is obviously a little off. I expect a push in my favour from the current once past the entrance, as it is changing to flood, but there is very little. Hole in The Wall, the channel between Maurelle and Sonora Islands, is actually about three and a half miles long. The centre is significantly wider than the narrow entrances. I find that once I come abreast of Florence Cove in the centre, the widest part, the current is actually against me, by about a knot and a half. How can this be, on what is clearly a flood tide? The only explanation I can come up with is that on moderate tidal differences, such as this one, the current must flow from both ends of the passage towards the middle. It is not predicted anywhere I have read, but it is an interesting bit of applied hydrography. It shows once more that the reality of the world is always more complex than we think it is.

*****

I haul my kayak up and pitch my tent next to it on a rock outcrop just west of the park boundary at the head of Teakerne Arm. The waterfall at the head of the arm is quite picturesque and popular with passing boaters. There is a dinghy dock to the left of the falls and a trail leading to the top of the falls. Docks and kayaks don't coexist well, as the dock is usually too high to easily get in and out of the cockpit. That is the case here and as I attempt to climb out of my boat onto the dock, I don't get good footing before transferring my weight and manage to slip off and into the water. It is a bit of a surprise but no harm done as I have planned to go up and have a fresh water wash in the lake anyway. Later, at camp, I think about my involuntary sea-water swim and I realize that the water isn't very cold. Curious, I dig out my thermometer and go down to measure the temperature at the water's edge. It is eighteen degrees Celsius, at least five degrees warmer than it is in Georgia Strait, and it will get warmer by summer's end[10].

*****

I am irritated. Paddling north up Lewis Channel, which is only about half a mile wide, I am continually assaulted by large steep wakes from passing power boats, and there are a lot of them. It feels like every ignorant-skippered large power yacht in this part of the world is congregating in this channel specifically to pass close by me. There are only two possible explanations, I think. The first is that they are malevolent and are deliberately trying to capsize me. The second is that they are ignorant of the effects of their boats. I have a hard time believing that there are that many power boaters with evil intent, therefore I can only conclude that they must be ignorant. It is hard to believe that so many are ignorant, too, but why else do they cruise by at speed, without regard for the effects of the large holes they are dragging through the water?

Coming around the headland of Bullock Bluff, the wind builds behind me and as the waves rise paddling gets harder. Sliding into the narrow opening of Von Donop Inlet, I am soon out of the wind and the waves don't penetrate far. The tree-fringed inlet is calm, serene and deserted, a real contrast to the channel outside. I paddle to the stream at the head of the inlet and refill my water bags. Coming back to a camping site I saw on the way in, I find a new water container of the same type as I use, full of fresh water and floating along the edge of the inlet. It must have dropped off an unfortunate kayaker's deck. As there is no way to identify who it might belong to, I gratefully add it to my collection. I sit in camp on the level ground of the old village site later that evening, nursing a migraine that has been with me for most of the last two days and I reflect on the trip. The scenery is beautiful and the weather fine, but I have encountered a lot of boat traffic, which I resent. It is not what I expected. I have been unable to let go of my preconception of what I thought the trip should be like, to fully experience it for what it is. I have been a little spoiled by the relative solitude I have found on other trips and which I have unconsciously come to expect, I think. It is a valuable lesson to carry with me for future trips – pay attention to the moment and live it fully. Nonetheless, I resolve that if I ever return to this area, it will be in a less busy season.

Broken Group

In the strengthening onshore breeze of an early July afternoon in 1786, the square-rigged ship Imperial Eagle rounded up, backed her sails and dropped anchor in a wide bay enclosed by two islands in a larger group. Her young Captain Charles William Barkley, accompanied by his even younger wife Frances, the first European woman to visit these shores, either did not ask or did not think to record the name of area that the Tseshaht First Nation of the Nuu-Chah-Nulth people, who came out to greet and trade with him, already had for the place. Instead he, like most other Europeans of the time, imposed his own names on many of the more than sixty of the islands that now make up the Broken Group, and named the larger sound after himself.

The Nuu-Chah-Nulth people say that they originated in this territory. The islands were rich in the resources that sustained the Tseshaht, including sea mammals, halibut, rockfish, salmon and salal berries. Western archeology confirms that the islands have long been occupied. The islands supported a significant population, with seventy-three shell middens and a number of village sites identified. Oral history backs this up with at least 134 Tseshaht place names in the area, although few of these names are now represented on modern charts or maps. European names do not do justice to the islands the way the First Nations names do, to their features, resources and long human history.

However, even if you don't know their history, the natural beauty and variety of geography of the islands as they are now, together with the protected waters that they provide, draws people to them. They drew me back many times.

*****

Alex, Carla and Jack on Clarke Island

After that first family visit by canoe, my next visit to the Broken Group comes five years later, when Carla is in high school. I had, in the meantime, gone on to build an additional double kayak of similar design to the three single kayaks. Carla and I drive to Port Alberni in order to put the double on the Frances Barkley again. We are joined there by my friend Jack, who brings his single, one of the original three. On the trip down the Alberni Canal, Jack rigs his hammock on deck in a shady spot, snoozing and banking rest for the week ahead. Carla and I alternate between sun and shade. We all take in the passing scenery of the Canal and watch with interest as the ship stops along the way to make deliveries to logging camps and fish farms.

We camp a couple of nights among the sand and drift logs on the beach on Clarke Island. The northeast corner of Clarke is one of the designated campsites in the Broken Group. It is an attractive place, with a small open meadow that is a reminder of a settler cabin that was once there. The only remaining trace of the cabin is a crumbling fireplace chimney and a few foundations stones. The meadow is full of the tents of other kayakers, which is why we are camped down on the sand.

Around the corner to the north is a lovely shallow bay, protected by off-lying rocks. The bay dries at low tide and provides us with a gratifying hour of beach-combing. We walk the trail across the middle of the island to the cove on the other side. On the trail in the middle of the island we find the concrete walls of the old water cistern that the owner of the cabin had built along the course of a small creek. This was necessary to store the winter's rains for the summer dry season. A sunny spot alongside the middle of the trail is crowded with tall salal bushes that are full of ripe berries. We stop for an unexpected snack and the hit of vitamin C the berries provide.

On one of our day trips from Clarke, we paddle over toward Effingham Island. As we come alongside Bauke Island we see a Bald Eagle plunge into the sea ahead of us. It surfaces again but doesn't fly off. "What's it doing?" Jack asks. "It looks like it's got too big a fish to fly with." I say. "It's swimming with it!" Carla says, "Look at it thrash and flail!"

The eagle swims to shore, flapping and flailing with its wings, with the fish clutched in one foot. The eagle reaches the beach and hops and drags the fish up to a log. It sits there looking very bedraggled from its soaking, but also looking very determined and pleased with itself. It is an amazing sight. I have never even heard of such a thing, let alone expected to see it for myself.

Rounding Meares Bluff on the southeast corner of Effingham Island, we see several more Eagles circling overhead. Jack paddles alongside and says, "There must be an eagle factory around here someplace!" We can see two fishermen in a power skiff a quarter of a mile out, drifting with their lines out. One of the Eagles that is perched on a snag high above on the bluff lifts off and floats down right over the heads of the fishermen to pluck a fish out of the water, not twenty yards past them. To compound the insult, the eagle flies back right over the heads of the fishermen, dripping water from the fish on them. After that display of fishing prowess, the fishermen start up their engine and go off in search of a spot where they won't be put to shame.

On the far side of Effingham Island, we find the sea arch that is reputed to be there. It's a tall buttress of stone thrust out from the bluff, eroded away at the base to the point that there is an opening through it at water level. The winds are still calm and the seas low as we approach it. We see that the tide is up, that it covers the mid-channel rock and allows a passage through. The passage is narrow, not much wider than the length of the paddles. The low swell surges back and forth through it, sucking and gurgling at the sides as we sit and watch. "I think we can make it through," I say," "Do you want to go for it?" Carla says, "I don't know, Dad. It looks kind of scary." "C'mon, it'll be fun. The waves are pretty steady," I say. "What do I do?" asks Carla. Just paddle hard when I tell you to," I say. Watching the pattern of the surges, we dig in and accelerate towards the arch, hearts hammering. We experience a moment's dimness, the dripping roof over our heads, the hollow sound of the reverberating waves and then the outgoing surge carries us out. We turn, stop and look back. A few seconds later Jack shoots through. "What a rush!" he says, "That was cool."

Paddling through the lagoon between Jacques and Jarvis Island again, even though it is only five years since our previous trip, we see that the lagoon is changed. The water is murkier now and there are not so many bat stars or moon snails. There seems to be algae growing over much of the bottom. Is this caused by particularly warm water this year or is the change due to some other factor and is permanent? Is it an early manifestation of climate change? There is no way of knowing.

* * * * *

A year later I return to the Broken Group in early June with my friends Debbie and Norris. This time I am paddling my single kayak and they are paddling my double. I have come back here because even the several trips I have made are not enough to see and experience everything the archipelago has to offer. I also find that even the same spots, in different weather or at different seasons, show different faces and seem like a different place. I

White Shell Bay

am pleased to introduce Debbie and Norris to this corner of the coast. We visit several spots I have been to before and some I haven't.

At just the right state of tide, we find a nearly enclosed shallow bay that is guarded by enclosing natural rock walls that leave only a narrow opening. It would be easy to miss it and we nearly do, but a gleam of white draws us in. The whole of this little bay is floored in broken white shell mixed with white sand. Low tide will leave it completely exposed. For now there is just a couple of feet of water, clear at its shallowest, then a pale sapphire, shading to a teal green-blue at the entrance and finally giving way to deep water the colour of a ripe blueberry in the channel beyond. We marvel at such an extravagant palette as we eat our lunch on a log at the edge of the beach under the cloudless summer sky. We are reluctant to leave, but the retreating water finally prods us into action and we paddle out.

We pull up to the beach at the Gilbert Island campsite to see that there are two power skiffs there, belonging to four sport fishermen. They have set up their camp at the other end of the beach. With the ability to carry more gear, they have set up an elaborate camp, with tents, tarps, chairs, coolers, tables, stove and barbeque. Often kayakers and powerboaters don't mix well, having different views about how to engage with nature. Not knowing what to expect of these boaters, we pitch our tents in the trees well away from them. We have a quiet supper and build a fire on the rocks at the high tide line. The fire is going nicely when one of the fishermen walks over to us and says: "We caught a bunch of cod this morning and we're cooking it up, with lemon and butter. It's way more than we can eat. Do you want some?" Debbie and Norris and I look at each other. "Sure, why not? Fresh fish sounds great!" Sautéed with lemon butter, the cod is delicious, tender and succulent. Half an hour later, the fisherman is back. "We've barbequed the salmon we also caught this morning. There's more than we thought. We have no ice and hate to throw it out. Do you want some?" Although we have already eaten two suppers, the thought of fresh barbequed salmon is too tempting. "Of course!" we reply. Supper number three is just as tasty as the first two.

We sit by the fire and talk and the sky begins to darken. Just as the thought of turning in begins to surface, a commercial fishing boat chugs through the pass and drops anchor in the calm bay in front of us. One of the sport fishermen jumps in one of the skiffs and rows out to the fishing boat. He is soon back and hoists a bucket out of the skiff. Ten minutes later our sport fisherman is back at our fire. "We talked to those guys on the fishing boat last night and told them if they caught any shrimp today, we'd buy some off them. We got a whole bucketful and it's boiling on the stove right now. You want some? It'll just get thrown out if we don't eat it." "Man," I say, "we hate to see food going to waste, especially fresh seafood. OK, we'll have some but we can't eat very much." Ignoring this last caveat, they heap our plates with fresh shrimp and more lemon butter. To my amazement, we finish it all. My opinion of powerboaters goes up considerably. As I drift off to satiated sleep in my tent later, I think "Where else could you eat four suppers in one night, three of them fresh seafood, courtesy of your neighbours?"

* * * * *

The May holiday long weekend seems like a perfect opportunity for a short break from the day jobs to get in a paddling trip to the Broken Group. Jack and Lori and I load up both my double kayak and my single onto my car. We drive up-island on Friday afternoon to the forest service campsite at Toquart Bay, where we spend the night. It is the second visit to the Group for Jack but the first for Lori. We are looking forward to finding out what the islands will be like at this time of year.

We launch next morning under overcast skies and a light headwind and paddle out of Toquart Bay and through the Stopper Islands at a leisurely pace. The skies continue cloudy as we round Lyall Point in a low swell and cross to Hand Island. We pull into the shell beach on the south side to stretch, have lunch and a look around. As nice as Hand is, we want to put in some more miles as it is early in the day. We push off and pass to the east of the Brabant Islands and across Peacock Channel. We paddle into the sheltered lagoon formed by Dodd, Willis, Turtle and Chalk Islands. It is a popular anchorage for big boats and one of the designated campsites is located on Dodd. We decide instead to go through the narrow channel on to the next campsite in the cove on the north side of Willis Island. This is a very pretty spot. The beach is a crescent of light sand with rocks at either end, overhung by mature trees. It is sheltered from all but strong northwesterly winds, and even in that case there are a couple of islets that moderate the worst of the wave action.

We find that the prime camping spots under the trees at the east end of the beach are occupied by a large group. Not wanting to intrude on their space, we land at the west end. There isn't a lot of room between the sand and the trees at this end. After debating whether we could flatten out a large enough patch for the tents, we think the better of it and go into the forest in search of a tenting spot. A little way in we find a small mossy clearing just past a big cedar. We set up our tents on a forest floor that is so springy with moss that we hardly need our sleeping pads. The sky grows darker and the wind increases while we set up camp and bring the gear up. We string a line between the trees and rig the tarp over the entrances to both tents, forming a kind of vestibule between them.

After supper, we listen to the marine weather forecast on the VHF radio. We learn that a front associated with a major system is headed our way. High winds and heavy rain are forecast for the next couple of days. It is too late to pack up and go back to Toquart Bay. We will just have to hunker down and wait it out. The wind increases all night and the rain begins. In the morning it is raining heavily when we get up. The tarp now seems like a stroke of genius as we are able to cook breakfast in the dry and contemplate the day. The forecast hasn't changed. If anything the wind is forecast to be higher, and will likely follow the typical pattern. It will blow from the southeast ahead of the front, with a lot of rain, then shift to the southwest as the front passes, and begin to dry after that. Down at the beach, the wind is indeed from the southeast. Looking to the north out in Loudoun Channel we can see large whitecaps and wind-blown spray marching away downwind, along with curtains of rain. We are fortunate to be tucked in to such a sheltered spot. It is one of the best places in the Broken Group to sit out a storm.

The day passes slowly, with occasional forays down to the beach to stretch our legs. In the heavy rain, even our rain gear doesn't prevent us from feeling damp. Mostly we sit under the tarp and talk and watch the rain and wind. Up here under the trees we are more sheltered from the wind than we would be had we stayed down at the beach, but the trees don't shelter us from the rain. I say "I'm glad I brought the tarp. Think what this weekend would be like if I hadn't." "Yeah," Jack says, "We'd be sitting in our respective tents a lot, talking through the tent walls without seeing each other."

As the day wears on we notice a marvelous thing. While the rain on the beach soon makes it soggy, we notice that the forest floor under us stays relatively dry. The water is there, but it is down at the bottom of the layer of moss and matted roots of the other plants. The layer is probably a couple of feet deep. It is one thing to read about, and know intellectually, how old growth forest tempers peak runoff by soaking up water, like a sponge, and then releases it slowly. It is quite another thing to sit here and watch it in action. It is a small, unexpected lesson in forest ecology, all the more valuable for being so quiet. The natural world has so much to teach us, if only we slow down and take the time to notice and listen.

The weather front is a slow-moving one. The wind switches to the southwest overnight and this morning the whitecaps and spume are still moving by in a steady procession out in the channel. It is still too rough to paddle in, nor has the rain stopped. Today is much the same as yesterday, with one exception. The beach is now host to thousands of unexpected visitors. We go down to find thousands, tens, perhaps hundreds of thousands of small jelly-like creatures that have blown into the beach. They are no more than two inches long with flat, oval-shaped, jelly-like bodies with short tentacles that hang down. The main body is an exquisite deep indigo colour. The most remarkable thing about them is a short triangular and transparent sail that sticks up vertically, running diagonally across the body. I have never seen them before, but it is clear that they are some sort of animal that floats on the water and makes their living by catching whatever comes within reach of their tentacles. When we get back at the end of the trip, I learn that they are Vellela, which are also known by the more romantic name of Sailors-on-the-Wind.[11]

Finally, on the third day, the wind drops and the rain ceases. We are able to pack up and head back to Toquart Bay. The storm scuttled our paddling plans for the weekend, but it compensated by forcing us to slow down and contemplate what was around us and it delivered a bonus viewing of an intriguing deep sea creature not normally found alongshore.

Brooks Peninsula

Uchuck III at Kyuquot

I just turned forty-five this summer of '97. I have hiked, cycled and sailed a lot in my life and have made several shorter trips in my kayak. However, I have not yet done an extended kayak trip to any place that could be considered remote. I also have never done an extended solo trip. This trip will change all that. I am resolved to kayak to the Bunsby Islands and the Brooks Peninsula on the northwest coast of Vancouver Island.

There are two ways of accessing this area by kayak. One is to drive most of the way up-island and take the long gravel road to Fair Harbour up Kyuquot Sound. This leaves you with a full day's paddle from its mouth on Kyuquot Channel. The other way is to drive paved roads to Gold River at the head of Nootka Sound in the interior of Vancouver Island and put the kayak on a freighter. The 140-foot coastal freighter, *MV Uchuck III*, serves logging camps, fish farms and the communities of Tahsis and Zeballos on Nootka Sound. Nootka Sound is a fjord-like inlet that cuts deeply into the heart of Vancouver Island. Once a week the freighter makes the trip out of the Sound along the outer coast to the remote village of Kyuquot. The freighter offers a unique wet-launch system for kayaks. Since this would avoid a long drive on gravel, since I have never seen Nootka Sound, since the wet-launch system sounds cool and since I like coastal freighters in any case, I opt to get to the paddling area aboard the *Uchuck III*.

I stay in a B n B in Gold River overnight. Last minute loading of freight and rounding up of errant passengers causes a slight delay in the early morning scheduled departure time. I count about thirty passengers, including me and six other kayakers. The other kayakers are bound for Bligh Island in Nootka Sound, because, they say, the Broken Group has become "too crowded." Most of the other passengers are bound for Kyuquot, where they are to stay the night before returning to Gold River the next day. I am the only kayaker aboard headed for Kyuquot. The cargo is a mix of supplies for logging camps and fish farms, such as fuels, lubricants, lumber, wire rope, groceries, Styrofoam fish boxes and, of course, kayaks.

It is a gloriously sunny day in the Sound with the tree-clad hills, precipitous rock faces and mountains bordering the fjord all sliding past us at twelve knots.[12] At the frequent stops, all of us passengers watch the loading and unloading with interest. The very experienced crew bring the two union-purchase type cranes into action to hoist the cargo out of the hold and swing it across to the docks or barges. It's a fine morning and I spend much of it talking to the crew in the wheelhouse between stops. I ask the skipper "How did you end up doing this?" He replies, "Couldn't stand an inside job. It would drive me crazy if I had to sit behind a desk all day." "So you're not in it for the money, then." I say. He laughs, "No, none of us are. We just keep our head above water between the commercial freighting and the subsidy from BC Ferries." "You get a subsidy from Ferries?" I say. "A little," he says. "If we weren't here, they'd have to run a ferry to service Kyuquot, which doesn't have a road. It's a helluva lot cheaper for them. But they are always trying to cut it back, saying that the commercial operation should stand on its own."

The *Uchuck III* skirts Bligh Island on its way to Tahsis Inlet. Yes, it's that Bligh, William Bligh, later of *HMS Bounty* infamy[13]. As the freighter approaches the mouth of Esperanza Inlet, I become a little apprehensive. So far it has been a pleasant cruise in sheltered waters. Now we are approaching the open ocean, with swells generated by far-off storms and weather systems making their presence felt along the coast. Although I have never been sea-sick in my kayak, I am prone to sea-seasickness in large vessels. How will I fare in the twenty or so miles north to Kyuquot? The kayak trip itself will begin once we reach Kyuquot as well. I am excited to begin, but also a little nervous about the unknown challenges ahead. The wind along the outer coast is about twenty knots. It adds wind waves to the underlying swell and sets the freighter to rolling, but it is still beautifully sunny. Watching the rocky points and beaches as they come into view distracts me enough that queasiness is held at bay. It is nearing supper-time when the *Uchuck III* pulls into Walters Cove and ties up to the Kyuquot village dock. While the overnight visitors get ready to go ashore, the crew gets the kayak launching system ready.

It is an ingenious but simple and quick system. They have built a platform that looks like a wooden pallet about four feet square, with a couple of steel bars running through the bottom. There are shackles at the ends of these bars and to these are attached four chains that meet at a fitting with a hook about six feet above the pallet. The crew lifts this out of its storage place in the hold with the crane and sets it down on deck. A couple of crew members carry my loaded kayak from its spot on the forward deck and places it onto the pallet. I climb into the kayak, get my spray skirt snapped on and hang onto the chains. The crane lifts me up over the side and lowers me into the water. The pallet sinks away from under me and I paddle out. The whole thing takes less than five minutes.

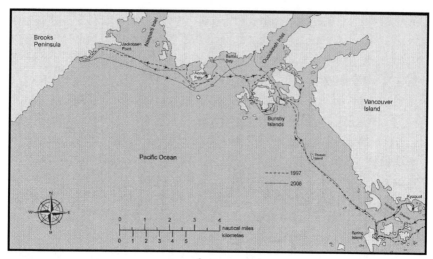

Brooks Peninsula

The northwest wind is still blowing strongly but I should be largely sheltered by the islands offshore and I don't have far to go. I paddle out of the harbour and point my bow southwest into the evening sun and across the chop in Nicolaye Channel. No sooner do I clear the harbour when I spot a sea otter, lying on its back, cracking open a shellfish on the anvil rock on its stomach. It behaves just like the animals in all the nature films! This is the first wild sea otter I have ever seen, and it is deeply rewarding to see it in its natural habitat. As I paddle past, it stops what it is doing, turns over and watches me carefully, before resuming its' feeding. I carry on to the wide northeast facing bay on Spring Island and up to the wide but steep sandy beach. I am surprised to find the shore of the bay lined with camps of other kayakers and boat campers. My idea that this area is remote and hard to access has led me to think I wouldn't see many other people. I find a vacant spot above the high tide line and set up camp. I am greatly relieved that the first stage of the trip is behind me without incident.

Next morning, I wake early and switch on my VHF radio to listen to the marine weather forecast. It scares me, frankly, with predicted northwest winds of twenty-five to thirty knots later in the day. My destination is the Bunsby Group of islands. It is an open coast crossing of seven miles to the shelter there. I think it is just too far to risk with such potentially high winds. What I haven't yet learned is the shape of the typical weather pattern on the outer coast of Vancouver Island in a summer high pressure system such as this. Typically, it goes virtually calm overnight. It stays calm until about noon and then the winds pick up, amplified by daytime heating of the land.

I launch my kayak for a day paddle around the islands inshore. At the end of the day I sit on the beach at the north end of Spring Island and stare through the binoculars at the water I have to cross to reach the Bunsbys. It doesn't look that far, but it is completely open to the north Pacific. The setting sun colours the high clouds first yellow, then pink and orange, before sinking in a haze above the waves on the western horizon. I walk back in the dusk to my tent still worried about the lack of shelter on the crossing.

This morning, my second, the forecast on the VHF is pretty much a repeat of yesterday, but it is dead calm when I get up. I decide to leave as soon as possible and attempt the crossing. My morning routine is rusty, as it always is at the beginning of the trip, and it takes me two hours to get underway. It is seven thirty by the time I paddle out of the bay. On the open sea there is a complete absence of wind and wind waves, just a long, oily, three-foot swell. Fearing that such conditions are too good to last, I dig in and paddle hard. The wind stays calm and I paddle alongside Thomas Island and its surrounding rocks within an hour. I take a water and rest break, slowly rising and falling on the swell. I look at the island to see if it would offer any shelter in a pinch, but I can't see any viable landing places. The relentless storms have eroded one cliff at the centre of the island to the point where there is a hole right through it to the other side. A couple of glossy black Pigeon Guillemots, with their white wing patches, paddle away from me, then as I drift closer, they take off, showing their startlingly red feet.

The Vancouver Island shore opposite Thomas Island is a notorious one. About a three mile stretch of this shore was clear cut logged in the 1980s. Everything was mowed down from the shoreline up to and over the tops of the steep hills more than two miles back. A US magazine called it the ugliest clear-cut on the planet. Now, more than ten years later, the short regrowth has begun to soften the scar a little with new green, but it is still a jarring sight. The history of logging in British Columbia has been dominated by one value only, that of the economic value of the wood from the trees. Values of ecosystem services, biological diversity, tourism, all took a distant second place, if they were considered at all. This attitude is extremely slow to change. In fact, both the industry and the provincial government department in charge of regulating it still routinely refer to the forest, and the trees that comprise the forest, not as trees at all but as "fibre." The talk is all about ensuring a sufficient fibre supply for the mills.

The Bunsbys are only two miles away now. I carry on at a much more leisurely pace and arrive well before lunch. I come to a south-pointing spit, with a small sheltered beach on the east side and a more open beach on the west side that gives a view out past the islands to the open sea. There is a tent already set up near the end of the spit. There are not that many good camping spots in these islands, and although I will be on the same beach, I feel I would not be intruding if I set up below a young Sitka Spruce[14] farther along. I feel a great sense of accomplishment, safety and release of the tension that I didn't realize I was carrying. That open crossing worried me more than I thought.

Tom and Anita, the owners of the tent, return later. In talking to them I learn that they have kayaked all over the world in their venerable Klepper folding kayak and are vastly more experienced than me. They bring out a tarp in late afternoon, as it looks like rain, and I help Tom rig it for a kitchen shelter. The rain arrives and I am grateful to sit underneath the tarp with them. I have not yet learned that a tarp is a key piece of gear for kayak cruising.

At supper-time, Tom gets up and disappears in the bush and I hear the creaking of a pulley. At minute later he is back with a food bag. "What was that noise?" I ask. "It's my food hanging system," says Tom. "Can I see it?" I ask. "My food hanging system takes a long time to set up and doesn't work all that well when I do get it rigged." "Sure," Tom says, and we go back to see his set-up. "It has a light messenger line with a pulley on the end to throw over a tree branch and then another line running through the pulley to quickly hoist and lower the food bag when you want it," Tom says. "That's pretty slick," I say, "How did you come up with that?" "Well, over the years I've developed a touch of 'bearanoia' and figure you can't be too careful about keeping the food out of reach of bears," Tom says. I decide that a little of that is not a bad thing and that perhaps I have been too complacent about bears up 'til now. I copy his system as best I can with a carabiner and the lines that I have.

Fog begins to drift in after supper and as the sun sets there is a spectacular back-scatter double rainbow arcing out of the water and rising skyward to the east. We light a fire and sit up talking. As the darkness settles over the beach, hundreds of beach hoppers come out, attracted by the firelight. So many of them jump into the fire that it smells like we are roasting shrimp.

* * * * *

Looking for a place to land and have lunch, I pull into a cove and ground the boat on a crescent beach of fine gravel. I sit on a log at the top of the beach in the sunshine and light wind, eating my lunch, but feeling a sense of disquiet. When I finish lunch, I get up and walk along the beach and notice a short trail back into the trees. Climbing a bank behind the trees, I start to see white shell fragments and bits of charcoal poking out of the bank. It comes to me that this must be the site of the Checleset people's village, which I have heard about. I walk back along the bank towards the kayak and find another narrow trail back down to the beach, which I hadn't noticed on the way by. Scrambling down it through the spruce, alders and salal, I suddenly come on the back of a totem pole standing in the thick bush. This is proof that it is indeed a village site.

Coming around to the front, I gaze at the pole. It is only about twelve feet high, with a bear figure at the bottom, a whale figure above that, and topped by a fearsome-looking long-toothed spirit figure on top. I am not being facetious about the description "fearsome-looking." With its crown of young salal bushes growing out of the rotting top looking like wild hair, the figure really does radiate a sense of warning - even menace. I have never before felt anything like it. I have always admired the totems I have seen in museums, as art. It is obvious now that in those settings, divorced from their original context and setting, they lose their inherent power. While I don't know what the significance of these figures was to the First Nation carver who made the pole, it seems to me that this totem, more specifically the top figure, is the source of the unease I felt earlier. I feel that it is telling me, in a wordless way, that this is a place of sorrows. It is telling me that it would not be right to linger. I heed that silent enjoinder and am glad to get back in my kayak and paddle away.

* * * * *

The outer coast of Vancouver Island is a rough southeast to northwest arc nearly 300 nautical miles long. The Brooks Peninsula is an anomaly along that arc. It is a mountainous spur that juts out nearly ten miles at right angles into the Pacific Ocean. It terminates at rocky Cape Cook at its western end. The Cape was originally named Cape of Storms by Captain Cook. Its 2,000 - 2,500-foot ridges and peaks form a barrier to the winds and weather that sweep down from the north in summer or offshore from the southwest in the winter. The weather on the north side of the peninsula is seldom the same as that on the south side. A mile offshore from Cape Cook sits Solander Island, barren of trees and open to the full force of the winds that accelerate as they round the cape. The automated weather station on the island frequently reports the strongest winds on the entire BC coast. The whole peninsula and adjacent area is now Mquqwin/Brooks Peninsula Provincial Park. The first name was added to recognize the local First Nations long history of use and occupation. The peninsula was never logged and was not glaciated during the last ice age. The geology and the weather make it a unique piece of the coast that I want to experience.

* * * * *

Leaving the village site beach, the wind is still calm. I head across the mouth of Nasparti Inlet towards the Brooks Peninsula. The chart shows a number of sand beaches both east and west of Jacobson Point on the south side. The paddling is easy in the sunshine and glittering water until within a mile of the beach. I have been fooled into thinking that the calm would last all day, but the daily afternoon wind is just delayed. Quickly the wind rises from calm to fifteen knots with gusts higher. The wind blows along the shore from dead ahead. The chop and spray that accompany it suddenly makes paddling hard and wet work. It seems to take forever, but in reality it is only a little more than half an hour before I glide into calmer water in front of a wide beach that is protected from the waves by off-lying rocks. I gratefully slide up on to a long shallow beach of the finest sand. I decide to go no further today, fearing that the winds will get stronger as the afternoon progresses.

I set up camp and carry the empty boat up above the high tide line. There is a sparkling clear spring at the west end of the beach spilling out of the trees and cutting a channel through the sand. I crouch in the cold, shallow water to wash the accumulated salt off and I air dry in the sun. I pass the rest of the afternoon in a pleasant torpor, taking in the sweeping view along the coast to the south and snoozing in the sun. After supper, the sun goes behind the mountain ridge behind me early, dropping the temperature. I spy a perfect seat tucked in a niche in the black rocks at the east end of the beach. It is still in the sunshine and I end the day reading there in the last rays of the setting sun, with the warm rocks behind me giving back the heat they absorbed during the day.

* * * * *

Next morning the wind is down but the forecast is for strong afternoon winds again. Inspecting the chart, it doesn't look like there are any good landing spots further out along the peninsula from where I am camped. I resolve to hike along the shore as far as I can get in half a day. I pack some lunch in a day bag and set out. Once past the next beach, the shore gets very rugged, with a series of sharp, volcanic jagged points and shelves, interspersed with a few small coves filled with rounded boulders and gravel. I am not certain that I will get around some of the rocky points, which are steep and offer few foot and handholds. But moving very slowly and carefully, I am never quite stopped by the terrain.

Plants are flowering along the edge of the rocks and some of the sea stacks look like overgrown flowerpots with their crowns of salal, moss and harebells. Some stacks are larger and carry trees that look like they have been trained by a Bonsai gardener. Their branches twist out and down to where they dip their elbows in the high tide and then grow back upward again. Seabirds fly by continuously on their way to and from fishing. Every little cove has its own Pacific wren which fills the cove with song to proclaim its territory. I step across a trickle of fresh water running across a tiny patch of sand in one cove and my eye is caught by a footprint. Looking closer, I can see that it was left by a cougar. I notice that the edges of the print are still crumbling. With a jolt of adrenalin, I realize that for the print to be that fresh, I must have just missed seeing the big cat. In fact, it might still be close enough to be observing me! I look around carefully but don't see it. As I move on, I look back frequently to make sure I am not being stalked.

In places along the shore, the storms have piled up great tangles of logs, smaller bits of driftwood, mats of seaweed and great rolls of eel grass. At first this seems to be only what I expected on this exposed, unpopulated coast. As I look closer, though, I can see an incredible profusion of plastic junk woven into all this storm wrack. There is plastic of all sorts and sizes. There are hawsers, ropes and lines of all sizes and colours, from pieces big enough to moor a supertanker down to fine monofilament fishing line. There are fish nets, lines attached to them, and a myriad of escaped fishing floats. There are Asian plastic round ones and torpedo-shaped ones, from finger-sized to desk-sized. There is an amazing amount of polystyrene, from intact crab pot floats to fragments of containers, to huge blocks. Bottles and other liquids containers of all sizes, with labels printed in many languages. There are packing crates, shipping boxes and pallets. There are some odd things, such as shoes, hard hats (both North American and Asian), pipe sections, lengths of hose and even a motorcycle helmet. The more I walk along and the more I look, the more plastic I can see everywhere along the shore. There is so much that it is clear that I am looking at years' and years' worth of accumulation, not just the aftermath of a single big storm. The sheer staggering quantity of it, tons and tons and tons, is deeply shocking. It brings home in a visceral way, which I have not experienced before, the monstrous scope of our take-make-waste society. I suspect that this is just stuff that has been lost off ships. I literally can't envision or imagine how much more we put into landfills every year.

Hungry, I stop for lunch at midday. I check the GPS and see that I have only come about two miles in a straight line from camp. I have not come nearly as far as I hoped I would, but with all the convolutions of the shore, I must have walked at least twice, maybe three times that distance. I reluctantly turn and head back, knowing that it will take just as long to retrace my route. With an effort, on the way back I focus my attention away from the plastic debris and onto the forest above the beach. It is irregular, untidy and beautiful, with huge old-growth, cake-forked trees and standing snags among the smaller newer growth. At the end of the afternoon, I stop at the spring by the camp, strip and have another thorough all-over freshwater wash in the bright sunshine. What luxury to be clean!

While I dry off in the sun, an Osprey[15] comes into view, hunting the shore break on the beach to the west. He hovers and stoops and hovers again for three quarters of an hour without catching anything. I am amazed at his persistence when he isn't having success, but then it hits me – he doesn't have a choice. He has a single imperative - keep hunting till you catch something or starve to death. The linkage between effort and survival for us humans is rarely so obvious or immediate, but at the base, we have the same imperative. In our modern civilization it's easy to forget that, where we are so far removed from the sources of our food.

* * * * *

At two o'clock in the morning of my last night on the peninsula, I crawl out of my tent for a pee. I look up and nearly forget why I have gotten up. It is absolutely still and quiet calm. The sea is soundless and the sky is crystal clear. The air is so still and stable that the stars aren't even twinkling. Each star is as hard and unwinking as a laser. The lesser magnitude stars are so bright that it is difficult to pick out the familiar constellations. The Milky Way is splashed across the sky like a spilled bag of diamonds. Suddenly I comprehend that I am not looking at a pattern of light against a two-dimensional background but I am seeing the disc of the galaxy, edge on. I experience a moment of vertigo as the sense of the vastness of even our small corner of the universe fills me. For an instant I am no longer standing on the surface of the earth, but I am clinging to the side of some gigantic spaceship, about to fall off and go wheeling away among the stars. The feeling quickly passes, but it is a rare glimpse into our place in the universe. Perhaps we humans aren't equipped to contain such immensities for more than a few heartbeats. The chill night air soon drives me back to the warmth of my sleeping bag.

In the still-calm morning, as I reluctantly paddle away from the beach in the early sun, I stop and turn the kayak back to look at where I have been. In that light, with the bright sandy beaches backdropped by lush green mountains, and the ripples on the sea reflecting and refracting the puffy white cumulus clouds above them, it seems to me that I could be looking at a picture of some equatorial tropical island. At this time of year, in benign weather, perhaps the comparison is not so far-fetched. This is a rare and blessed moment in my life, I think, and I wonder whether I will ever get a chance to return.

* * * * *

I am sitting on the north point of the beach in the big bay on Spring Island in the evening of the last night of the trip. I have the entire beach to myself, for a wonder, which is a total contrast from the same bay a week ago. I brought my book with me and I am enjoying the tranquility of the setting and the view north to the Peninsula. I look up now and again to see a dozen sanderlings, half a dozen Semi-palmated Plovers and a few Fox sparrows all chasing the beach hoppers. From out in the bay comes the loud cracking and crunching of a sea otter eating his supper of shellfish. I linger there until it is too dark to read and then walk back to my tent and turn in.

In the morning, I am up early, as I must cross to Kyuquot to be picked up by the *Uchuck III*. It is due to leave shortly after breakfast. I look out of the tent with a shock to find that the sea has disappeared. I now realize why I have the bay to myself. I misread the tide tables and, instead of shallow water, the tide has retreated out of the shallow bay completely. I pack everything up, put on my wet-suit, hoist my empty kayak onto my shoulder and set off through the eel grass and mud in search of sufficient water. To any observer I must look a strange sight, trudging along with a boat but no water to float it in. Finally, about 400 yards out, the water is just deep enough to float the kayak. Three more trips and all the gear was brought out and stowed. I climb in and get underway, having learned a lesson in being more careful about the tides.

Once out of the bay and past Aktis Island, I turn to head for the west opening of Walters Cove and Kyuquot. The sun clears the horizon directly over my bow, instantly blinding me, even with my sunglasses on. I pull my hat down lower, take a bearing on the opening and paddle by compass with my head down, hoping I won't run afoul of any other boats who are similarly afflicted. Soon the sun rises a little higher, I gain the opening to the bay and I turn towards the dock. The *Uchuck III* is there and the crew is busy on deck. I paddle alongside and hail them. They quickly lower the launch rig. I paddle into it, grab hold of the chains and they hoist me aboard. "Welcome back!" says the crew member who greets me at deck level. "Did you have a good week?" "Terrific!" I say. "It's an amazing stretch of coast." "It is that," he says, and hurries off to his next task in getting the ship underway.

It is a surreal moment, standing there on the deck. One moment I was a self-sufficient kayaker in the outback and the next I am suddenly back in civilization, with the radio playing, the smell of cheeseburgers drifting out from the galley, and the prospect of hot running water in the washroom. It is an abrupt, jarring change. I am having trouble taking it in and I am glad there is a whole day's journey back to Gold River to ease the transition back to my everyday life.

* * * * *

A few years later and Carla and I find ourselves on the *Uchuck III*, this time with the double kayak, headed for the Brooks Peninsula once more. I am the most fortunate of fathers. Carla has grown up, graduated from university and moved away, yet wants to spend some of her precious vacation time with her dad. The two of us have done previous trips in the Gulf Islands and in the Broken Group. Those were rewarding, but now Carla wants to try something a little more remote. I was fascinated by my first trip to this area years before. I was captivated by the remoteness, the rugged beauty of the open coast, the sea otters and the weather. I am eager to come back, hoping perhaps to repeat some of that original experience but mostly wanting to share it with Carla.

The trip along the outside to Kyuquot is uneventful. Once more the kayak is in the *Uchuck III's* launch rig and we are lowered over the side into the water. We paddle to our night's camp on the big bay of Spring Island. This time I make sure a low tide won't strand us in the morning. The weather for the week ahead is forecast to be a typical summer high pressure system

Evening sun on the Vancouver Island shore from the Brooks

with its sunny skies, overnight calms and predictable afternoon onshore winds. In the morning, we set out for the crossing to the Bunsbys. It is only when we set up camp there that I realize I left my cherished Chaco sandals on the beach on Spring Island, when I changed into my wet-suit this morning. These sandals have protected my feet on rocks and beaches on many kayak trips and are like old friends. It's an oversight I will regret during the heat of the day in the coming week, when all I have is shoes.

* * * * *

We are halfway across the mouth of Ououkinsh Inlet in a calm sea at mid-morning, heading towards Battle Bay, when a puff of spray-laden air spouts ahead and the sound reaches us. "Whale!" I cry. A long, long dark back breaks the surface, followed by a small dorsal fin and the flukes of a huge tail that clears the surface and submerges again. "It's a humpback" I say excitedly. "They must be making a comeback. I've never seen one on our coast before." Immediately we abandon all thoughts of getting across the inlet as we stop and watch the whale. More spouts and long, knobbed pectoral fins appear on the surface. We count at least seven whales feeding in the bay[16]. It is a mesmerizing sight. The size of these huge beasts is overwhelming at close range. Adults can reach forty to fifty feet in length and weigh between twenty-eight and thirty-three tons. I estimate that the whales we see here are at least thirty-five feet long.

I now better understand the danger the First Nations people of the coast faced when hunting these whales from their open dugout canoes. They had to get close enough alongside to drive in the harpoon and then hope to avoid being capsized or smashed by the stricken whale. Whaling is at the core of their culture, their identity. Careful physical, mental and spiritual preparation was required for a whale hunt.

It is a thrill to see with our own eyes the evidence of the recovery of the population. As we paddle away, we hear the long, loud grunts and squeals the whales make as they feed. The sound follows us all day into the evening at camp. It is like being serenaded by a talented bunch of cows with a wide vocal range. Who knew that whales, who live below the water, could make so much noise above it?

*　*　*　*　*

We paddle up the creek at the west end of Battle Bay as far as a little sandy streamside bank, where the water is entirely fresh. We treat ourselves to a freshwater wash and then dry out in the sunshine, hardly having to use our towels. We paddle back to the mouth of the creek and pull the boat up to the inside of the sandbar that nearly blocks the entrance. The sandbar is in the sunshine and there is just enough breeze to keep the bugs at bay while we eat lunch and admire the setting and the view. We are just about finished our lunch of bagels, pungent cheese and sausage. I am sitting on a log with my back to the forest behind and Carla is facing inland when she suddenly sits up straighter and announces, "Bear!" My heart starts to race, and I look around to the direction she is facing, "Where?" I say, not seeing it immediately. "Just behind those elderberry bushes." She says. I look where she is pointing. Sure enough I see a pair of round fuzzy brown ears of a Black Bear[17] periodically showing above the top of the bush. It is disconcertingly close. "It looks like he is seriously focused on feeding on those berries and not interested in us," I say, "but we shouldn't linger in case he changes his mind."

I pick up the dry bag with the food in it and we carefully walk back to the boat. The boat is actually closer to the bear than where we were sitting. The hatch is still open, and I quietly say, "I'll just put the bag in the compartment but we'll try to avoid making any noise by leaving the hatch cover unfastened. You climb in and I'll shove us off. Don't bother with your spray skirt until we're well away."

There are a few tense moments as we get in the boat and, looking nervously over our shoulders, push off. We don't manage to stay completely silent, making the odd clunk and scrape during the process. The bear stops feeding briefly, raises his head and gives us a glance but shows no further interest. We paddle out from behind the sandbar and stop to look at the bear. The bear resumes stripping the berries from the bush. Now that it is safely over, our little encounter is one of the highlights of the trip.

* * * * *

We ground the kayak on the same beach on the Brooks Peninsula that I camped on during my first visit. We left earlier this morning while the wind was still light and the crossing is uneventful. The beach is as I remembered it and the stream is still there at the west end. It will be easy to wash and renew our water supply. When we get to the top of the beach to set up the tent, however, I am shocked by how much the forest edge has changed. Evidently there was a massive storm combined with a high tide the previous winter. Logs, sticks, bits of wood and plastic are layered thickly over the forest understory for at least a hundred feet into the trees. It is hard to imagine the power that must have been in that storm to push that much water that far up the beach. The small tent spots that were previously created by repeated use are nowhere to be found. It takes us half an hour after we set to work to clear a space for the tent.

The day is so fine and the setting so idyllic that we don't do much the rest of the day except wander the beach and rest and eat. We end the evening sitting on lounge chairs that have been cobbled together with driftwood by previous visitors. The sun sinks below the mountains behind us, leaving us in shadow, but the Vancouver Island shore to the south is still in full sun. The colour of the cloud-free sky fades slowly from daytime blue through pale grey to no colour at all as the stars come out.

* * * * *

We are back on Spring Island on the last afternoon and evening of the trip. We are ready for tomorrow's early start to paddle back to Kyuquot and the *Uchuck III*. The morning tide in the big bay will definitely be too low, but we have found a quiet little beach just around the east point where there will be enough water in the morning to launch. After setting up camp, we walk back through the short trail to the big bay and along to our campsite at the beginning of the week, on the off chance that perhaps my sandals have not been carried off by the tide. Miracle of miracles, they are still there, right on the log where I set them!

Back at our camp, we sit leaning against a beach log and rest. We only sit still for about five minutes when a Pacific wren flies out of the undergrowth behind us to the other end of the log. He hops and flits toward us, working his way down the log then detours just a few feet around us back to the log again. He is very industrious, checking into every crack and crevice in the log for insects. He does not seem worried by us as long as we stay still. A flying insect that we have been seeing since we got here, one with four wings and a heavy vertical body, flutters into view. The wren spies it and darts up, flycatcher-like, and nabs the insect. I have never been this close to a Pacific wren before and it is fascinating to watch him as he goes about making his living. His routine seems to be to make a patrol of the driftwood on the beach and then go back to the bushes. He then treat us to a chorus of his wonderful warbling, trilling song[18]. The Wren entertains us for the remainder of the afternoon and into the evening. Our fire seems to attract more of the flying insects, which provides more food for the wren. We feel privileged to witness this small demonstration of the local food chain in action.

As the last of the evening light fades, the high thin clouds turn a most delicate shade of pink and then pale orange before fading to darkness. The only light and the only sound comes from the crackling fire. It is a beautiful and tranquil ending to a magical week. I am glad I was able to show Carla this part of the coast. Seeing the area through Carla's eyes adds another perspective for me, another layer to my experience of this part of the coast, to value it even more for the unequaled gem it is.

Quatsino Sound

I set up my first night's camp on a creek mouth in Quatsino Sound at the end of July. Quatsino Sound does not have a reputation as a prime spot for kayaking. There is some industry on the Sound and a great deal of logging activity. However, a chapter on the Sound in a recently published kayaking guidebook sings the praises of the sound and I am determined to give it a try. As a secondary goal, I want to get to the north side of the Brooks Peninsula. I paddled to the south side last year and I want to see what the north side offers.

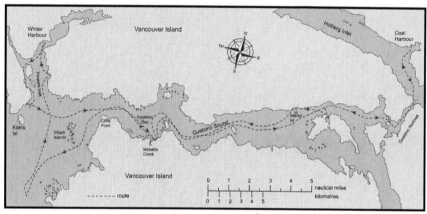

Quatsino Sound

To begin the trip, I launch the kayak at Coal Harbour. I paddle in sunshine and calm across to Quatsino Narrows, timing my arrival to coincide with predicted slack current in the narrows. When I get there, the tide has already turned, likely about twenty minutes earlier. There's a reason they call them predictions. I make it through alright, but the second half is hard paddling against the building flood tide. The wind is still calm on the other side and I paddle on to a cove that looks, on the chart, like it would be a good spot to camp. I stay for lunch but the setting doesn't really attract me and I think I can do better. I carry on for another half hour, when the wind, after a couple of five knot puffs, suddenly rises to about fifteen knots right on the nose. The familiar pattern of afternoon thermal wind has started. Paddling now begins to feel like work and although it is only early afternoon, the wind will only get stronger as the day wears on. Looking at the chart, I can't see many suitable camp spots in the next eight to ten miles. I am alongside the southwest corner of Drake Island and I can see what looks to be a good camp spot just to the north behind Ildstad Island on the outwash of Hawisnakwi creek. I paddle over and when I land I find a nice gravel fan. I set the tent up beneath a young Sitka spruce, just above the high tide line. It has all the attributes of an ideal camp – small clean gravel with no fine sand to get in the tent, a fine breeze blowing across to keep the horseflies at bay, a nice view down the Sound and a creek to top up my water supply.

Later, while I am having supper, I watch the rising tide submerge some low yellow flowers growing at the top of the beach just below the regular high tide line. It is remarkable to me that these small flowering plants can apparently carry on just fine, nodding in the saltwater wavelets just as they nodded in the wind before being inundated. They resemble small daisies but with sticky, thistle-like buds.[19]

When supper is done, I stand drinking the last of some ginseng tea I have brought. I suddenly notice a black bear with two cubs. She is about 200 yards away and ambles down the beach towards me. The food is all still out and my first thought is to grab it, throw it in the boat and get out on the water until the bears pass by. Just as I am stuffing the boat, the mother bear hears, smells or sees me. She stands for a moment on her hind legs, then drops to all fours and scampers into the bush with the cubs close behind. After waiting about five minutes to make sure they won't reappear, I take the food bag and walk down the beach to hang it back up in the tree. I sing loudly in my best three tenors voice to warn the bears I am there. Either they don't like my voice or appreciate my selection of musical numbers, as I don't see them again.

* * * * *

I have a somewhat restive night, startling awake several times at real or imagined bear noises. I am woken again just as the sky is lightening before dawn by a Swainson's Thrush[20]. He alights with a whir of wings in the spruce just above the tent. He commences a defense of his territory with a few low, insistent "whit" calls. He follows these with his song - a nasally, upwardly spiraling series of notes that trail away to nothing. As pleased as I am to know that these secretive birds are flourishing here, at that very early pre-dawn moment I wish he would go flourish somewhere else. I whap the tent roof with my hand and he flies off. I am just drifting off to sleep again when the thrush comes back to repeat his performance. I give the tent a whack and off he flies, and I just about fall asleep again when he is back. I concede him the victory because, clearly, he is winning this game. I get up, have breakfast, pack up and paddle away, to leave him to enjoy his home in peace.

* * * * *

After dawdling along the Sound all morning in the bright sunshine and heat, the start of the blustery afternoon thermals finds me in Koskimo Bay. It has two creeks flowing into it from the south. I pull into the west end of the bay and set up my tent in the shade. I formulate a rule for paddling on the outer coast in these summer high pressure weather patterns. It is a lot like mountaineering, but instead of "summit by noon" it is "be off the water by noon." It proves to be a good rule today as there are big whitecaps out in the centre of the Sound within half an hour of coming ashore.

As the tide rises in late afternoon, I toss my soap, towel and a change of clothes in the kayak and paddle up Mahatta Creek. There is a beautiful low waterfall about half a mile in, just past

Mahatta Creek waterfall

tidewater. I tie up the boat to a handy bollard-shaped rock in a back eddy just below the falls and climb up to a clear pool above the falls. The water is cool and bracing but not cold and I have a wonderful bath and wash out my paddling gear. As I sit on the rocks, drying out in the sun, an immature Bald Eagle swoops out of the trees upstream low, right over me, on his way out to the Sound.

Back at camp, I sit on the beach watching the waves curl up onto the sand at the high tide line. The water is perfectly clear. There is an amazing prism effect with each wave. The stones on the bottom seem to lift up and come forward as the sunlight is lensed onto them from the back of the wave. It is a beautiful and tranquil spot and an ideal end to the day.

* * * * *

I get up early and join the sport fishermen on their morning commute out the Sound to the fishing grounds at its mouth. The forecast calls for a northwest gale later in the day, but I think I might be able to get as far as Restless Bight before it happens. After paddling for half an hour in the calm, the wind begins to come up from behind me, from the east, a land breeze. I make good time to Cliffe Point and around it. I paddle through the fishing flotilla trolling there and on past the Gillam Islands. The swell from offshore increases and I am south of the whistle buoy when the wind rises quickly. It is from the south now and the waves began to build up on top of the swell. I suddenly have that feeling you get when you are sailing, and it occurs to you that maybe you should reef the sails. The rule when reefing is that you should reef when you first think of it, as it will likely get worse if you wait. Although I am only a couple of miles to the next beach south where I might land, I decide that I really shouldn't attempt it. In short, I turn tail and run, although running for it isn't exactly easy, either. The wind is still spilling strongly out of the mouth of the Sound from the east. The combination of wind waves and swell make for tough paddling. I head up Forward Inlet and pull into a pocket beach just north of the reserve at Oyakumla.

I saw a few Sea Otters in Koskimo Bay yesterday and now here they are in my little cove. Sea Otters were once found in great abundance on the coasts that rim the north Pacific. They ranged from northern Japan around down to northern Mexico but were pretty much wiped out more than a hundred years ago[21]. Sea Otters are a keystone species in the kelp forests of the coast. Without them, Sea Urchins tend to eat everything on the bottom, to the point where they create what is known as "urchin barrens." With Sea Otters, the Urchins are kept in check, kelp gets a foothold and becomes a habitat for fish. Between 1969 and 1972, eighty-nine Sea Otters from Alaska were re-introduced to the Bunsby Islands near Kyuquot. Since then, they have steadily expanded into more and more of their original range. It is good to see that they have expanded north from the Bunsbys here in the late nineties.

I retreat to my tent as the mosquitoes come out in force after the sun goes around behind the trees in the evening and the shadows creep out from the forest down the beach to the water's edge. I sit with my back to the zipped-up screen door of the tent totally engrossed in my novel. Suddenly I am pulled from the world of the book back to the present. It is as if someone has tapped my shoulder to get my attention. Compelled by an impulse I don't fully understand, I scramble out of the tent and shove my sandals on, to stand, waiting, for what, I don't know. I stand there uncertainly for about a minute. Then, about a hundred yards along the beach, upwind of me, a huge male black bear steps out of the bush. He starts to amble along the beach, sniffing at the wrack along the high tide line. In a couple of minutes he will be right beside me, as I have pitched my tent just above the high tide line at this end of the beach. I am momentarily frozen with indecision. Several possibilities flash through my mind. Should I just retreat into the trees and hope he doesn't notice me or the tent? Should I grab the paddle and the kayak and try to launch it and sit out in the bay until he passes by? Should I try to scare him off? The moment of indecision passes and I give a mighty shout. The bear looks up and lumbers off into the trees, right under where I have hung my food bag. He doesn't move as quickly as I would like. I go over to the kayak and untie it, ready to drop it in the water should he return.

After about ten minutes, there is no sign of the bear. I get back in the tent, thinking about what has just happened. What is it that interrupted me from my absorption in the book? It isn't anything conscious that I can identify. Perhaps the bear was making some noise that my subconscious mind picked up, although the breeze, which is still blowing through the trees, makes enough noise that this seems unlikely. It is possible that I smelled him, as I am downwind, but my sense of smell is very poor and getting worse, so I discount that as an explanation. What would have happened had I not got out of the tent when I did? It is clear that the bear was working the tideline to see if anything edible had washed up. Had I not noticed the bear until he was alongside the tent, it could have been a very unpleasant encounter. It seems pretty woo-woo but I am convinced that something alerted me to the potential danger in time to do something about it[22].

* * * * *

The marine forecast for the next few days is for gale force northwesterlies, with winds of up to forty knots. This pretty much rules out my plans for getting down to the north side of the Brooks. I decide to look around Winter Harbour in the morning, to avoid the strong morning outflow winds of the last couple of days. I should then be able to ride the afternoon westerly back into the Sound. The community of Winter Harbour turns out to be even smaller than I imagined, and I have no need for supplies, but I paddle up the east side of the harbour and back on the west side just to have a look.

As I come alongside the public wharf, I see a rather beat-up sailboat tied up there. Its mast is broken off and its topside looks very battered. It almost looks abandoned, but it still has a rather salty air about it. As I paddle up for a closer look, two heads pop up out of the companionway. "Hi," I say, "I'm Alex. I don't mean to intrude but I was curious about the state of your boat." "I'm Toni," says the woman, "and I'm Terry," says the man. "We were capsized and dismasted in a terrible storm on our way back from Hawaii last year," said Toni. "Wow," I say. "I think I read about that in our local paper. It sounded awful but the paper didn't give a lot of detail. How did you manage to save the boat and get here?" "It wasn't easy," says Toni, "but we were determined to get it sailing again on our own."

Toni and Terry then tell me the story of the storm, its aftermath and how they saved themselves. The first few days after the capsize were pretty harrowing. They kept the boat afloat by pumping continuously. Terry injured his back and was essentially out of commission. It was six days before they could get the broken mast cut way, and it was battering the topside all that time. They patched the holes in the deck and eventually jury-rigged a short mast which allowed them to slowly get underway again. It took them more than three months to sail back under their shortened rig to Winter Harbour, where they made landfall. The hull of the boat, which Terry built himself out of ferro-concrete, is very tough. It is unlikely that a production fibreglass boat or a wood boat would have stood up to the battering for that long.

Meanwhile, throughout all of this, Toni was pregnant with their first child. The baby is now several months old. Since arriving at this safe haven, they have cleaned up and restored the interior, all while caring for a newborn. They are just about to install a new motor to replace the original that was ruined by seawater. Next on their agenda is getting a new mast and refinishing the exterior of the hull. They anticipate they'll need another year to complete the work. It is a remarkable story of toughness and determination on their part. I congratulate them on their grit and perseverance.

Saying goodbye to Terry and Toni, I head out Forward Inlet and stop at the last sandy cove in the Inlet for lunch. When I leave the beach, the first part goes pretty much as I planned, as the outflow winds die down. However, when I am about a mile off Cliffe Point, the wind suddenly gusts up strongly from the southeast. Southeast! Where is a decent northwest gale when you need one? The wind is at right angles to the prevailing southwest swell and it sets up a cross chop on top of the swell. It is hard, hard work and it slows my progress to a crawl. Thankfully the limited fetch means that the waves never get too high. Even so it takes half an hour to cover the last mile to Cliffe Point. Once around it the wind curves to become a tailwind. It carries me along to Mahatta Creek where I am glad to return to the comforts of that ideal campsite.

* * * * *

The morning of my last day in Quatsino Sound is windless. As I pack up, the resident Kingfisher keeps diving at me, as it did when I camped here a couple of days ago. It must be nesting nearby, although I can't see a bank suitable for their typical burrow nests. I escape the bird and head up inlet in a flat calm and increasing heat under a cloudless sky. I stop for lunch at my previous campsite alongside Ildstad Island. There is no point getting to the narrows before the afternoon slack current. Quatsino Narrows are about two miles long. At paddling speed it takes at least half an hour to get through when the water is slack.

When I round the corner of Ohlsen Point at the south entrance, I find that there is a strong north wind blowing against me. This cuts my speed in half. Fortunately, the period of slack is followed by a flood tide and I have the current with me. If the current was the same direction as the wind, I wouldn't make it.

Once out of the Narrows I find the wind right on the bow, blowing at least twenty knots. It creates three to four-foot waves that are particularly steep and close together. I am dismayed as I anticipated that the wind would be in my favour. I thought it would blow in to Holberg Inlet on the other side of the narrows and help me on my way back to Coal Harbour. I didn't look closely enough at the chart, though. A careful study now shows me that the head of Holberg Inlet far to the north is not separated from the open ocean by much land, and that land is low. Consequently, when the northwest wind blows on the outer coast, it skips right over the low divide and blows right down the Inlet to the Narrows. I learn another lesson about how the interaction of land and sea changes as the coast indents to become a long inlet. It is a vital lesson for successful travel in human-powered boats on this coast.

It is another hour of very hard work to reach the dock. I can't complain too much, as it is a glorious day. The sun is high in the sky, the whitecaps crest white and the spray throws sparkles into the air as the bow of the kayak buries itself in green water every second wave.

Clayoquot Sound

I arrive in Tofino in a bit of a state. The summer traffic, not helped by a forty-five-minute construction delay, is heavy on the long drive up here. As a result, by the time I launch from the beach alongside the town dock it is later than I planned. I am worried about encountering strong afternoon winds once I get around Wickaninnish Island and into the open ocean south of Vargas Island. In Duffin Passage in front of the dock I encounter whale-watching boats, crew boats, sport fishing boats, float planes and helicopters. There is also a strong current that sweeps by the dock. Once clear of all that I find that I worried for no reason as the afternoon winds are still moderate, surprisingly.

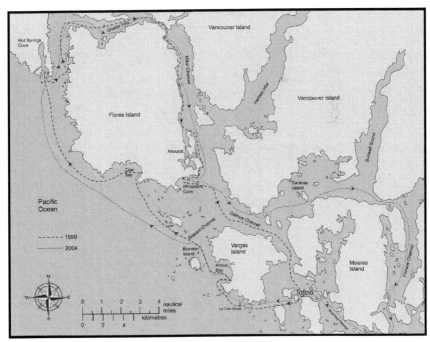

Clayoquot Sound

I paddle around to the south end of Ahous Bay on Vargas Island and set up camp there. I am only a few miles from Tofino but I seem to have the area to myself, as there is no one else camped on the bay. The lack of wind and the declining sun in the evening makes my beach camp hot. Eventually the sun drops low enough that it begins to cool and I am able to go to bed.

In the morning the fog is thick and there is no need to hurry. While I wait for it to thin I plot some waypoints from the chart into my non-mapping GPS. After a couple of hours, the fog begins to dissipate a little. I pack up and get underway. The fog is not deep and the sun can be felt through it, but the visibility is not more than a mile.

This is a chance to practise my low visibility compass paddling skills. I take a bearing from each waypoint to the next ahead and paddle toward it using the resulting compass bearing. It would be very challenging without the GPS. I am being set off course due to the swell offshore and the flooding tide. The visibility gets gradually better. As I weave my way through the kelp beds and rocks of the Garrard Group just before Cow Bay on Flores Island, seabirds are scattered about on the swells. There is a representative sample of some of the usual suspects on the coast. I see Surf Scoters with their orange and white bill tips, Rhinoceros Auklets with the protuberance on the upper bill that gives them their name and Heerman's Gulls, unmistakable with their black-tipped red bills. On one of the larger rocks I see a juvenile gull of some sort. He is impossible to identify in his grey fuzzy feathers and feet nearly the size of an adult. He is untroubled by my close proximity as I paddle past. I keep an eye out for Tufted Puffins, which are rumoured to nest in this area, but none appear. The swell and surf waves in Cow Bay diminish to almost nothing as they refract around the rocks at the south end of the bay and I have no trouble with the landing.

* * * * *

Lighting and thunder wake me just before dawn and it starts to rain as I get up. I hurry to rig the tarp as a shelter while I cook breakfast. The tide is just starting to flood as I get ready to launch. On this wide shallow beach that means a long carry down to the water. I am getting better at judging just how far above the incoming water to place the empty kayak so that it will be just at the waters' edge by the time I have brought the rest of the gear down and loaded it. Get it right and you can just climb into your boat, give a little shove with your paddle, and off you go, with dry feet and no water in the cockpit.

It is a little over nine miles from Cow Bay to Hotspring Cove, but it is exposed to the open ocean all the way. Again, today the wind is moderate, and as a bonus it is a tailwind. The wind boosts the flooding tide and I make the crossing in two and half hours.

I paddle up to the government dock, get my swimsuit and towel out and set out along the boardwalk to the hot spring. It has long been a tradition for visiting boaters to carve the names of their boats into one of the planks on the boardwalk. While reading the many names I come across a couple of people carving the name of their boat on a blank board. At the springs themselves, it is fairly crowded with people both from the boats anchored in the Cove and with others who have flown in by floatplane from Tofino.

The hot spring water bubbles out of the rocks and cascades in a series of pools down to the sea a hundred feet away. The water is hot, hotter-than-hot-tub hot, and it takes a while to ease into it. It is not advisable to stay long. Suddenly, there is a commotion above me. "Quick, get him out of the water!" I hear someone say. "Help me, he's fainted," says someone else. I look and see several people hauling a portly, comatose young man out of the water on to the rocks. "I'm a paramedic," says another young man, climbing out of a different pool. "Lay him down and get some cold water," he says. Someone else brings cold seawater up in a water bottle and the paramedic douses the young man with it. After a couple of minutes, the man revives and is able to sit up. He seems to be OK. It's a good thing that the paramedic was there, as it would have taken quite a while to get the man to any more complicated medical intervention.

After a good wash and a soak, I return to my kayak, I paddle out of the Cove and around the point in a rising wind and lumpy sea to a beach on Flores Island a couple of miles away. It is a good, healthy beach, as evidenced by the abundance of beach hoppers and bloodworms. These provide lots of feed for small flocks of shorebirds. I can identify Semi-Palmated Plovers and Dunlins for sure, with perhaps some other smaller sandpipers[23]. They keep me company as they scurry up and down the beach while I sit by the fire in the evening as the wind slowly drops and the light fades from the sky.

* * * * *

The ebb tide is with me as I come through Hayden Passage at the north end of Flores Island in mid-afternoon. The wind, at the south entrance to the Passage, is blowing briskly up Millar Channel from offshore, in my face. It sets up quite an ugly chop where it meets the tide, and it will only get worse as the afternoon progresses. Spying a gravel beach marked on the chart just to the west, I decide to call it a day. Calling the beach gravel is rather generous – it is actually small rocks. But it is out of the wind and it looks like there is enough space for a tent against the forest. I empty the kayak of gear and carry it up over the rocks. There is a very small stream there and I find a little cleared tent spot back in the forest above the stream bank. After the open water and sunshine, it feels oppressive to me under the trees. I go back to the forest edge and flatten a spot just big enough for the tent at the top of the beach. Not only is there a nicer view, enough of the breeze reaches in to keep the mosquitoes away. After supper, when I check the tide tables for overnight and the next day, I am not completely sure that my tent is far enough up to avoid being flooded at high tide. I build a fire as it gets dark and I sit to watch the water creep slowly higher as the night deepens.

About an hour and a half before the predicted high, when it is totally dark and the water has covered most of the rocky beach, I began to hear small splashing, coming from all along the beach. I think at first it is crabs, but when I get up and step beyond the firelight with my flashlight, it is clear that it is something moving quite quickly in the water. I can see pairs of red eyes darting along in the shallows, and the merest suggestion of a vertical tail fin. The light isn't powerful enough to illuminate the whole beast. Perhaps they are small dogfish, feeding on the hermit crabs that I saw earlier under the rocks.

I go back to the fire and my tide vigil. As the water rises closer to the fire and my tent, I see that the fire will soon be extinguished. I begin raking the coals up the gravel and adding new firewood at the top. In the end I move the fire up about five feet. I place sticks in the gravel to mark whether the water is still rising or falling. Finally, about midnight, it starts to retreat from the last stick, about ten feet from the tent and I know I can turn in until morning.

* * * *

I make my camp behind a monstrous beach log, half buried in the fine, soft sand in the middle of Whitesands Cove on Flores. I quit early in the day as the onshore afternoon wind is strong as I come around out of Millar Channel and it brings fog with it. The Cove is well protected from the swell by an arm that forms Kutcous Point at the west end. I just get camp set up when another solo kayaker comes in. It is Andrew, also from Victoria. While we talk, a man comes out of the bush on a trail I haven't noticed and puts up a sign that reads "Warm Springs – 25 minutes, Hostel, Store and Café – 90 minutes." I have read about the warm springs but have forgotten that this is where they are. Feeling in need of a bath, I set off in search of the springs. It turns out to be more than twenty-five minutes and the trail is very sketchy. Nonetheless it goes through some interesting habitat including a bog that has Sundew plants[24]. The springs, when I get there, can better be described as tepid instead of warm, but the water is fresh, and it is warmer than seawater. I come back slower than I went, not wanting to get sweaty again after being clean. As I loiter in the bog examining the plants, I get stung in the calf by a wasp. I don't feel particularly grateful for the natural world just now.

The fog clears off by evening and it is still clear at two in the morning when I get up to pee. The fog is back when I get up in the morning, thicker than ever. It is so thick I can't see the waters' edge from my campsite. I have just fetched the food bag and have everything spread out on the log ready for breakfast. Suddenly, out of the fog, three wolves appear on the other side of the log, not more than ten feet away. One starts to circle around the end of the log behind me. I grab my paddle (I'm not sure what I think I am going to do with it) and brandish it at the wolves and yell at them, "Bugger off!" They look at me, the smallest one gives a yip, and they trot off, none too quickly. The whole encounter didn't last more than ten seconds and the fog closes in like they were never there. I wonder if I have just seen what I thought I have seen. Maybe, I rationalize, it is dogs from the village of Ahoushat which is ninety minutes away by trail. No, I think, as I go over the details from the scene just enacted, although the animals themselves weren't that big, their feet were huge, their eyes were yellow and their coats were very long and thick. Definitely wolves[25]. In retrospect, they weren't terribly menacing, although I was a little nervous when one went around behind me. I definitely had the feeling that this is their beach, and that they have a proprietorial curiosity about anything new on it. The more I think about it the more remarkable it seems. I feel privileged to have such a rare encounter.

* * * * *

Five years have passed and I return to Clayoquot Sound with Carla and the double kayak. We launch from the town dock beach again on a sunny, windless afternoon. We paddle slowly through the La Croix Group of rocks and islets at the south end of Vargas Island, enjoying ourselves. We are in no hurry to get to the campsite on Ahous Bay. Approaching the beach, the swell from offshore, which is not high, suddenly begins to break before I realize it. Although we dig in with the paddles, we are too late and the kayak slews sideways, the breaking wave capsizes us and dumps us out. The water is only a couple of feet deep by this point and we regain our feet quickly. The kayak, together with a few dry bags that have been bungied to the deck or stowed in the cockpits, washes ashore ahead of us. We right the boat, I pump the water out of the cockpits, and we get the gear and the kayak up to the top of the beach and set up camp. The dry bags that have floated ashore have gotten some water in, even though they were rolled up tightly and fastened. We empty them and set out all the gear to dry on logs in the sun.

We are lucky. Since we were nearly ashore and it is a warm sunny day, all we get is an unplanned swim. It could have been much worse if we had been caught in a breaking wave offshore. It is entirely my fault. Even though I took a kayak surfing course years before, to learn how to handle just this kind of landing situation, I was far too complacent. I was lulled into letting my guard down by the mild day and lack of wind. It is a good lesson that I need to be constantly vigilant.

While sitting in the sun and drying the gear, we are treated to some entertainment. "Look at that, Dad!" Carla says, "It's a hummingbird sitting on the log." "So it is," I say, "it's an Anna's Hummingbird. What's it doing?" Carla says, "It's crawling under the red dry bag. Now it's licking it!" "Jeez, I've never seen anything like that before," I say. "What does it think it's getting? The bag is all salty from being dumped in the water." We sit, marveling at this diminutive creature, trying to divine the reason for its strange behaviour. The bird keeps it up for a couple of minutes and finally flies off.

* * * * *

Carla and I leave Whitesands Cove the second last day of the trip and head towards the north end of Meares Island. We want to see what the inner waters of Clayoquot Sound hold. We paddle through Calmus Passage and approach Saranac Island. The charts are usually pretty good at showing places where strong currents occur, and we are a little surprised when the flood current takes us in its grip and speeds us up. There is nothing showing on the chart, but the tide is flooding, and we are moving over the ground considerably faster than we can paddle. I turn on the GPS to see just how fast we are going and am amazed to see that we are doing eight to nine knots without paddling. When we dig in and paddle, the speed over ground increases to eleven knots! This is heady stuff for a kayaker, nearly four times our usual speed. We rocket through the channel south of Saranac, close by the Meares Island shore. As we round the corner we sweep by a black bear, who is foraging on the beach, not twenty yards away. Neither we nor the bear have time to do anything more than look up at each other before we are past.

We hope to find a campsite somewhere on the north shore of Meares Island but nothing attractive turns up and we carry on to the east, down Fortune Channel. The day turns from sun to partly cloudy and there are dramatic clouds that threaten showers ahead of us. No rain materialises however, and we arrive at the beach at Heelboom Bay. This bay is known as C'is-a-qis by the local Tla-o-qui-aht First Nation. In 1984 it was the site of a protest over planned logging[26]. The hills and western slopes of Meares Island tower over and dominate the town of Tofino. The clearcut logging of the island's ancient rainforest that were planned would have devastated the views and harmed the town's main industry, tourism. It would also have caused destruction to salmon habitat, to Tla-o-qui-aht medicine plant gathering areas, to spiritually significant sites, and to the Tofino drinking water watershed. The protesters built a cabin that still stands and we pitch the tent on the cleared area in front of it. Just upstream we find an old sauna that was built right over the creek. As the day draws to a close, it is easy to imagine the people occupying this place and the historic stand-off that occurred. It is a fine way to end the trip.

Hakai Pass

It occurs to me as I go through my usual pre-launch routine on the second-last morning of the trip, that preparation for paddling the outer coast is very much like a matador preparing for a bullfight. There is the same admiration, apprehension, respect and fear of what I am about to face, in my case the sea and wind, rather than the bull. The preparation is a ritual. I ensure that everything is done that can be done, including all the gear closed up, safely stowed, weight balanced and lashed down. There is the final dressing in the suit of lights (pardon me, paddling gear). It is all there, the tight-fitting wet-suit, the sprayskirt, the glittering vest (life jacket), the hat and finally the sword/paddle. There is the moment of truth – is my preparation adequate? Will my planning, judgment and skills be up to the task? This time, when I step into the ring, will the bull gore me or will I live to enter the ring another day?

Arrival at Grief Bay

I think it is at this point that my decision crystallizes, uncharacteristically, to pack in the trip early and head back to Bella Bella and the ferry home. I had planned to carry on to even more exposed islands and beaches. It takes time to become accustomed to the mental challenges posed by solo backcountry trips. Despite my previous solo trips, I have not yet become entirely comfortable with my judgment of potential risks that come with travelling off the beaten track.

* * * * *

The trip begins auspiciously enough. The skies clear about an hour south of Port Hardy during the drive up-Island. This seems to herald a mid-June start to the summer weather patterns that I am counting on. Since building the kayak five years ago, I served an apprenticeship of increasingly demanding trips, most of them solo on Vancouver Island. I made trips to the Broken Group several times, to Clayoquot Sound, to Quatsino Sound and to the Brooks Peninsula. I think it is time for a more challenging trip. I look forward to the two weeks I have set aside for exploring the islands, passes and lagoons of the Hakai Recreation Area on British Columbia's mid-coast.

Loading the boat and gear onto the mid-coast ferry the next morning, I am the only kayaker. I am the first of the season, a crew member informs me. I request a wet launch somewhere near the south end of Fitz Hugh Sound. I intend to work my way north on the outside of Calvert Island, weather permitting. As the day progresses, I begin to get a little nervous. The system that brought the clear skies also builds the wind to twenty-five knots plus gusts in Queen Charlotte Sound. The seas look uncomfortably large as we pass Egg Island north of Cape Caution. The skies remain clear, though, and it is hard to be pessimistic in bright sunshine.

The Captain calls me up to the bridge as we near Cape Calvert at the south end of Fitz Hugh Sound. "The seas are too high for me to safely stop and drop you off at Cape Calvert," the captain says, "It's too exposed." "That's what I was thinking, too." I say. "What do you suggest?" There's a reasonably large cove about

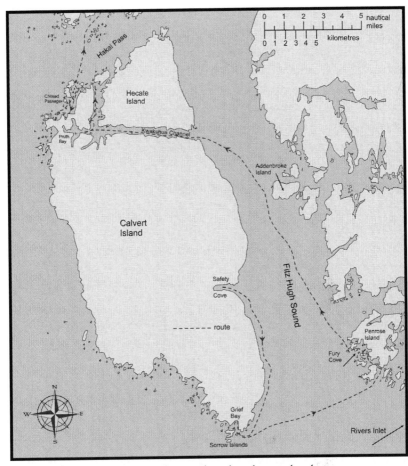

Fitz Hugh Sound and Calvert Island

seven miles north, on the Calvert Island shore, called Safety Cove," the captain says, pointing to it on the chart. "It's protected from the wind and I could drop you there." I study the chart for a minute, gauging distances and looking for alternatives, but don't see any. "All right," I say, "That looks like the best option for me. The wind will be behind me if I head south like I planned and if it's too strong I can stay in the Cove overnight."

I sit in my kayak, bobbing on the waves that refract into the bay, as the *Queen of Chilliwack* moves out to resume its journey north, while I judge the wind and contemplate for a moment just what I am about to do. I'm committed now. I paddle out into the Sound and find that the wind is not quite as strong as further south. The eight mile paddle south to Grief Bay is more exhilarating than scary. The tailwind pushes me along, surrounded by the white horses of the breaking wave tops on the blue seas. The last half-mile into the bay against the wind that spins around the Cape is a struggle, but the water in the bay is flat. It is a lonely but starkly beautiful scene. There is not another boat in sight. The beach is a beautiful south-facing wide crescent of fine white sand enclosed by rocky headlands and off-lying islands, treed with cedar and Sitka spruce.

It is an idyllic scene as I empty the kayak and set up camp. It is not quite so idyllic after the sun goes behind the trees in the evening. As soon as it does, the sand flies come out in hordes along with the shadows and furiously attack me before I have the sense to get out the repellent. That night as I roll out of the sleeping bag at two in the morning for a pee, the full moon is bright enough that I don't need a flashlight, even inside the tent. The light from the moon makes a bright white path across the water and continues, glistening, up the wet sand of the beach. I don't regret the break in sleep at all.

* * * * *

The evening before, in planning for the days ahead, I realized that I failed to bring a chart for the outside of Calvert Island. It is nearly thirty miles to a sheltered beach at the north end of the island, which will be a very long day, even if the wind is with me. While it is likely that there will be a suitable beach to stop somewhere along the outer coast, there is no guarantee. Even if there is, it will at best be an exposed surf landing and launch. I decide I can't afford to take the chance. I change my plan and decide to paddle up Fitz Hugh Sound instead.

My morning routine is rusty as usual, and it is nearly three hours before I get going. The wind is light at the start and goes calm soon after. Facing into the morning sun the light glitters and sparkles off every glassy wavelet as I paddle over to the east side of the sound. The forests and snowy tops of the mainland mountains behind Rivers Inlet make a magnificent backdrop. Fury Cove in Schooner Anchorage has been recommended to me as a good camping place. When I arrive, I find that it is a snug little place with a snowy white shell beach. It looks so inviting that I decide to stay, even though it is early, and to explore the anchorage for the day rather than press on further north. I find a small creek to top up the water bags with water stained dark by the cedar and hemlock forest that it flows through. There is a family of Mergansers[27] in the anchorage. The young ones look incongruously like zebras, with their black and white striped plumage, not at all like the more conservatively dressed adults.

Late in the day as high cloud moves in, the forecast is for more big northwest winds the next afternoon but there should be southerlies ahead of the front that is coming. Examining the chart and my options, I hope that if I leave early I can reach Pruth Bay at the north end of Calvert. I treat the exercise like a training run for a marathon. I get up at quarter past five, swallow a power bar and some juice, and am packed up and on the water by quarter to seven. The day is cloudy, but the wind is light from the south, just as predicted, and the forecast hasn't changed. I push hard, wanting to make the shelter of Kwakshua Channel before the wind shift. I am moving quickly, doing more than four knots over ground according to my GPS.

The cloud lowers and thickens as the morning passes and alongside Addenbroke Island lighthouse the visibility drops to less than a mile in drizzle and fog. The boundary between sea and sky disappears. A large tug pulling an even larger barge looms up close behind me and passes to the east. I keep pushing and arrive at the entrance to Kwakshua at twenty past ten. I've beaten the wind shift and I've covered twelve and half miles in about three and half hours. It isn't the end of the effort for the day, though. Kwakshua Inlet's shore, although bordered with little indents and coves, is mostly rocky and has nary a landing-place for a kayak.

I push the remaining five and half miles to the west end. There I encounter westerly winds sweeping in over the low land separating Pruth Bay from the outer beach to the west.

It is raining steadily by then, and I am getting cold and wet. I study the chart and realize that what at first looks like inviting beaches in the bay are in fact extensive tidal drying mud flats. These may be productive marine environments, but they are less than ideal camping spots. I find a small bit of inter-tidal beach just to the north of the bay, where I can land in order to have lunch and figure out my next move. Climbing out, I am stiff and hardly able to move. I look at my watch and see that I have been in the cockpit for over five hours. Lunch over, I have to find a place to camp. I decide that I can reach the beaches of Choked Passage to the north, and reluctantly I climb back into the boat for another five miles of paddling. Choked Passage is sheltered from the wind when it is still in the southwest, as it is now. I paddle to the westernmost of the beaches, finding a landing that is sheltered from the swell by an off-lying rocky point. I have come twenty-three miles by mid-afternoon, which, for me, is a significant accomplishment.

* * * * *

I set up camp and rig the tarp over the tent entrance, as it continues to drizzle. Warm and dry at last, I find that I do not have much appetite for supper. I eat it anyway, without enthusiasm, knowing that I will need the energy. I turn in early in the rain but I wake just before two o'clock by a great flapping clatter of the tarp – the wind shift has finally arrived. I drift back to sleep but an hour later the whole tarp comes adrift with a bang in the strengthening wind. I crawl out and see that the sky has cleared, with no further threat of rain. I coil the lines, roll up the tarp and rig guy lines on the windward side of the tent. It feels just like shortening sail in the middle watch of an offshore passage.

In the morning the wind is still blowing at least thirty knots and the forecast is for it to continue. I can't paddle in this and decide that it will be a good rest day. The wind coming in the bay across the beach creates an invisible standing wave of air over the trees behind it. Half a dozen Bald Eagles and several Ravens find it irresistible for hang-gliding. They put on a show all day, soaring along above the beach, peeling off at the end and swooping back to repeat the manoeuvre in the other direction. The bay is beautiful in the morning sunshine, with a long shallow sloping beach of light brown sand lapped by aquamarine water. The wind begins to dry out the sand and I begin to be blasted as the wind picks it up and throws it at the tent. I re-rig the tarp at a different angle for more protection from the wind and sand. It helps some, but the fine sand filters into everything - the sleeping bag, the dry bags, my pockets. These open beaches are very beautiful to look at, but are only hospitable in nice weather or when you have someplace to retreat from them in bad weather. They are actually pretty hostile environments for humans when the weather turns nasty. The size and position of logs driven high up by past winter storms show just how nasty it can be.

Back in the camp on the beach after an afternoon walk, I feel very lethargic and somewhat down. I wonder if I might be suffering from dehydration depression[28]. I probably didn't drink enough during and after yesterday's push, as it was cold and rainy and I didn't feel very thirsty. I drink about a litre of water and begin to feel a little better, but am still off my feed, so to speak, at supper.

* * * * *

It is still blowing in the evening, but the forecast for the next day is for another front to move in, after a period of light winds in the morning. I reckon I have the morning to get across Hakai Passage before the weather closes down again. Much of the water from the inlets on the mainland to the east flows out throughout this pass, making for some significant tidal currents. The guidebook warns of the dangers of west winds against these ebb tides, which is exactly what I will be facing in the morning if the wind doesn't drop. I go to sleep fretting about winds and tides.

The wind is still blowing at three o'clock but by the time I get up at five it drops, spurring me to pack quickly and launch. It is an easy paddle through Choked Passage and I pause in the

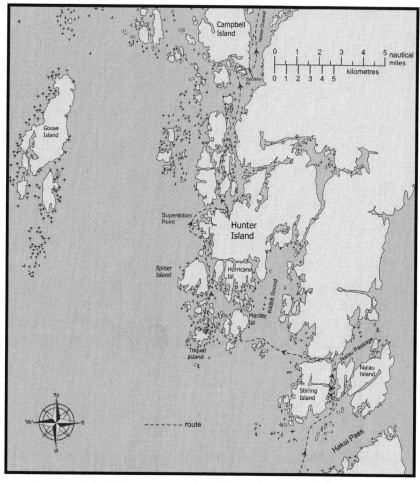

Hakai Pass, Hunter Island and Goose Group

shelter of the last island, judging the conditions for the crossing. The wind is calm here in the lee of the islands and each island sits atop its wavering reflection in the water. Out in the channel there are swells, but no wind or wind waves to speak of. I start across. As I get out from behind the protection of the islands, the swells left over from last night's wind are bigger than they appeared to be before I set out. I estimate their height at seven to ten feet. I am a long way from seeing over the crests of them as I drop into the troughs. In the middle of the channel, the swell kicks up against the outgoing tide to produce some unpredictable and scary wave shapes, but I keep paddling hard and it doesn't last too long. The sun is shining brightly through it all, lessening the fear.

It calms right down behind the outlying islands on the other side of the passage. I poke into Lewall Channel on Stirling Island, as there are reputed to be pictographs there, but I can't find them. I do find a trickle of water sufficient to refill the water bags, and as I do, the west wind begins to funnel down the channel. It is enough to convince me to look for a campsite for the night. Paddling out of the channel I find a small island with just enough room for my small tent above the high tide line on a beautiful shell micro-beach. The lee side of this island has a charming collection of spring wildflowers including Indian Paintbrush, Columbines, Shore Blue-eyed Grass, Yellow Monkey-flowers, and Black Lilies[29]. This island also has just one bird, a warbler that I can't identify. Whatever it is, its calls and busy search for insects among the bushes and trees are present the rest of the day. Towards evening, as I sit on the beach in front of my tent, a harbour seal swims across the low shelly spit that is covered by the tide. It startles me when it slaps its tail fins on the surface, like a beaver giving the alarm.

* * * * *

Next morning has the potential to be another nail-biter. The tide will be ebbing out of Nalau Passage and there is the possibility of southwest swell and west wind opposing it both there and across Kildidt Sound. I start at five o'clock again. In in the narrowest part of the Passage the incoming swell kicks up two-foot standing waves against the ebb current. I worry about conditions further out, but it becomes calmer where the constriction eases. The weather thickens once again and I lose visibility halfway across the Sound as the rain and fog descends. I am forced to navigate by compass. By the time I reach Manley Island, it is raining steadily and the southwest wind feels much colder than the day before. On the crossing I see Marbled Murrelets[30] and my first Rhinoceros Auklets of the trip. They are just bobbing on the swell, and in the mood of the day, it seems to me they are too dispirited by the rain to either dive or fly.

The myriad small islands of Spider Anchorage all begin to look the same in the rain and fog and I find it hard to stay focused to keep my bearings. Approaching Triquet Island[31], it bears no resemblance at all to the tropical scene described in the guidebook. The only thing I recognize is the quicksand-like low tide mud and slippery eel grass. I have to drag the kayak through this, step by sucking step, to reach the beach. I find a camp spot well away from the shore under the trees, rig the tarp and set up the tent in a steady downpour. A change to dry clothes and some hot soup improves the situation, but I feel all damp around the edges. The positive side to it is that I am able to collect enough water off the tarp to fill all my water bags without having to do more than reach out. After lunch, a short snooze is in order while the rain drums down on the tarp and tent. I pass the rest of the day slowly, reading and listening to the resident Pacific Wren proclaiming his territory above the sound of the rain.

* * * * *

Tomorrow's forecast is again for twenty-five to thirty knot northwesterlies by afternoon. If the wind arrives early it will pose a problem for the next leg - getting around Superstition Point into Cultus Sound. Listening to the forecast, I find myself not looking forward at all to the last week I have planned and I am surprised by the feeling. The conditions haven't really been that bad, but I am physically tired. The thought of the planned long crossing out to the exposed Goose Group islands, under the continuing threat of high winds, fills me with unease. I know that I don't have the same recovery rate as I did twenty-five years ago. But I also know that I am still capable of putting up with a tough physical challenge - I don't really understand what my problem is. Last year's rough weather offshore sail to San Francisco with friends was something I took in stride, when the daily effort was much greater. I think the difference between that experience and this is in mental preparation. This time, I just haven't been as prepared.

As a result, I haven't attained that sense of connectedness that I found on my previous solo trips. Having come to this realization doesn't magically change my outlook, though, and I think about heading in early to my take-out point in Bella Bella. It is a little humbling and there is an inner voice that accuses me of being a "quitter." Against that I figure it is better and safer to return some day, when I have managed to adjust my attitude, than to press on.

* * * * *

After on and off rain overnight, it is still drizzling in the morning. I set out early once again to make the rounding before the wind comes up. I paddle through the channel separating Hurricane Island and Spitfire Island from Spider Island and reflect on their names. In World War Two, there was a radar station base on Spider Island. Hurricane, Spitfire and Typhoon Islands commemorated the fighter planes of that era. Off Superstition Point, the rounding I have been dreading what little wind there is, as it is in the same direction as the swell. The paddling is easy and I glide through into the bay just past the entrance to Cultus Sound. I land on the beach for a rest and to stretch my legs. By mid-morning the clouds begin to thin and break and this little pocket cove is so pleasant in the bright light I decide to spend the day here.

As the sun comes out in the afternoon with the wind shift, I feel slow and lethargic. I don't do much of anything except dry out my gear and read. A female Rufous Hummingbird checks out my red beach seat at close range while I read. It's as if she can't quite believe that anything that red in this setting is not a flower. There is another bird in the trees on the cliff face to the west that sings relentlessly all day long. It is probably the usual suspect, a Swainson's Thrush, but it isn't the familiar song that I am used to hearing from them.

* * * * *

Today's destination is just a few miles away through sheltered waters to a spot near Soulsby Point at the south end of Hunter Channel. I sleep in, get up late, have a full breakfast and don't get underway until mid-morning. The last mile or so just before the point is exposed to the twenty-plus knot southwest wind coming in off the open ocean. It is choppy and wet with the spray coming off the wave tops. The campsite is described in the guidebook as being on a shell beach on an island off the point. There are in fact three islands shown on the chart, and no obvious indication as to where the beach is or on which island.

I have been reading biochemist Rupert Sheldrake's *"Seven Experiments That Can Change the World."* One of the subjects is a discussion about how our modern paradigm, which views the mind as an artifact of the physical brain, is really a doctrine arising from the thinking of Descartes, and is actually unproven by empirical science. Pre-Cartesian western thought, and much of the rest of the world to this day, instead conceives of the mind as something that inhabits the whole body and indeed extends beyond it to connect with the natural and physical world.

I think of this as I approach the islands from windward. I have a gut feeling that the campsite is in a particular place at the downwind end of one particular island. But my rational mind still drives me to circle the other islands to rule out the other possibilities in order to avoid having to paddle upwind if I am wrong about my feeling. Sure enough, the beach is right where I first thought it would be. At that moment I am sure that Descartes is wrong and all it takes is a week of solitude to discover how to tap into my extended mind.

* * * * *

Next morning, the last of the trip, comes early. I noticed yesterday that this island is Crow Central. They start up their ruckus at quarter to five in the ancient cedars and hemlocks above the tent. I lie there for a few minutes listening to their disputes, but the first rays of the rising sun flood the tent, immediately driving the temperature up to the point of discomfort, forcing me out of bed. It is calm, and quiet and the high tide has reduced the width of the shell beach to a couple of boat lengths. I slip the boat into the water and head north. It remains calm as I paddle up Hunter Channel, but the sun doesn't last. The first high cloud drifts in and the low sun underneath it produces beautiful mauve colours in both the sky and the water mirroring it below. The high cloud is soon followed by lower cloud and finally a south wind and rain, which blows me right into Lama Passage. This is a major intersection on the Inside Passage, and for the first time in days, there is steady marine traffic. The wind and rain persist along to McLoughlin Bay.

McLoughlin Bay is the site of the BC Ferries Bella Bella terminal, where I plan to load the kayak on the ferry when it comes in later tonight, to return to Port Hardy. It is early in the

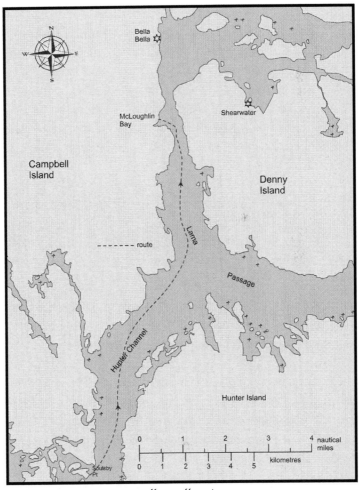

Bella Bella Area

day yet as I paddle past the terminal, looking for a landing place, when I spot a small dock just beyond the terminal. I paddle in and see a couple of young guys on the dock. "Hi," I say, "Can you tell me where the Heiltsuk Cultural Centre is?" One of the guys gives a little grin and points to the head of the dock. "Right there," he says. Feeling foolish, as I hadn't looked that far, I say "Thanks. Can you tell me when it opens?" "We'd take you up there but we're just finishing our break from working on the Centre," the other guy says. "Frank will be down soon and he can show you around. You can tie your kayak up to the dock, if you want." I tie up the boat and climb out and as I do Frank arrives and invites me to have a look at the Cultural Centre. Coming out of it, I admire the walkway around it, which seem to be made of small white and purple shells. "Where did you get the shells for this beautiful pathway?" I ask. "Come down to the beach and I'll show you." Frank says. On the beach Frank's arm sweeps up and down the beach and points to a depression in it. "Sea Urchin spines and shell fragments." he says. "At least twelve feet deep." I am gobsmacked. "How long does it take to accumulate that many spines and shell pieces?" I ask. "Thousands of years." Frank says. "This was the site of the main village before the Europeans came and sea urchins were a mainstay of the diet. They discarded the shells you see and built up the beach." Seeing that, I can hardly fathom how long it must have taken for that amount of shell to accumulate. I dimly begin to grasp the sense of deep time and connection that the Heiltsuk have with their land.

We sit in the dock shed and talk as it begins to rain. I have been introducing a new sustainability framework to my company and I explain to Frank that it is based on four fundamental principles, derived from basic laws of physics. Frank says that four is a very important number in Heiltsuk culture and that it is related to all sorts of significant concepts. We talk about the need for a more environmentally sustainable way of life and Frank tells me that the Heiltsuk language has no word for environment or nature because for them, there is no division between humans and the natural world, it is all one. This starts, in a small way, to get at what they mean when they say it is all sacred.

I think this is a way of being and thinking that the world needs to heed. We often talk, in modern Western culture, about "wilderness" and the word generally is taken to have positive connotations. It usually describes the natural world without humans, untouched by or degraded by humans. The unspoken, deeply rooted assumption in this way of thinking is that humans are somehow separate from nature, from the natural world. In reality, it is a form of alienation, where nature is seen as *"other."* It is a modern concept not shared by indigenous peoples anywhere that I am aware of. The truth is that humans have been modifying their environment and have been an integral part of that environment for a very long time. While not all pre-industrial indigenous relationships were positive, most had economies that interacted with the natural world to make the surroundings more productive, for both humans and other plants and animals. Many First Nations peoples actually see the term "wilderness" as a negative one, connoting neglect and waste. James Rust, a Southern Sierra Miwok man from California, was quoted as saying *". . . the white man sure ruined this country. It's returned back to wilderness.[32]"* For our own long-term survival, we need to find a way of being where we regenerate the capacity of humans and the natural world to support life in all its forms, for both humans and for all the other species on the planet.

* * * * *

Later I walk along the beach towards the Bella Bella town site. As I climb up from the beach to the road a small woman comes out of the bush on the other side of the road, carrying a couple of bags that look very full. "Hi, my name is Alex." I say. "Can I help you carry those bags, they look heavy?" "Sure" she says. "My name is Adele. These bags are heavy." She says. "What's in them" I ask? "Salmonberries" says Adele. "I pick them when they are ripe like this and sell them. $10 a bucket." We chat about the village as we walk along. As we get further into town we come alongside a small house by the water where an old woman sits outside the front door on a chair. She waves to us. "Adele, come on in and have some coffee. Bring your friend." I am glad to accept as I skipped coffee that morning. I am also interested to hear what a local elder might have to say. "I'm Alex," I say. "My name is Josie," she says, "Pleased to meet you." Inside, the house is nearly devoid of furniture and both the front and back door stand wide open, in spite of the very cool wind blowing through off the water. The coffee is good and Josie tells us many stories of her life growing up in the community and the changes she has seen. She tells each story twice, with a few minutes pause between, in exactly the same words. Eventually we say our goodbyes and carry the berries home to Adele's house.

As I walk back along the inland road to the ferry terminal, it turns into a construction zone. I come across a man measuring and marking the old road with a can of spray paint. "Hi, what's up? What are you measuring?" I ask. "The plans don't match the reality on the ground," he says. He introduces himself, "I'm Mike. I'm the foreman/clerk of the works/general contractor for the road widening and alignment project." "Do you live here, or do you fly in from outside to supervise the project?" I ask, never imagining that there is enough full time work for a position like his. Mike says, "I have worked in civil construction all over Ontario and BC but came up to Bella Bella fifteen years ago for a project and I never left." I ask, "Has there has been work here all that time? What do you do in slack periods?" "It is the damnedest thing," Mike says, "I have lived all this time with my suitcase by the door, ready to move away when the last project finishes, but another project always comes along, and here I still am. I guess it's not easy for governments and construction companies to find experienced construction supervisors on this area of the coast, so I have always been in demand. It's a good life but it certainly isn't what I planned on."

* * * * *

As the ferry pulls in at quarter past ten that night, and I load the boat and gear, I reflect that BC Ferries promotional name for this service, the Discovery Coast Passage, is apt. As with all worthwhile journeys, it is a journey of inner, as well as geographical, discovery for me. I discovered, or perhaps re-discovered, that mental preparedness is just as important to success as physical. I assumed that the weather conditions would be much the same as on previous trips on Vancouver Island's outer coast, with calm mornings and predictable afternoon winds. I was not mentally prepared for the succession of weather systems and the strenuous dashes needed to make progress between them. I never really encountered conditions I couldn't handle but the constant threat of them wore me down. I also discovered that life and the people in a small, isolated island community are not what I expected. It is a different way of being. There clearly is not a lot of money in Bella Bella, but that doesn't make the people any less vital or interesting than in more cosmopolitan places on the coast.

Gwaii Haanas

Iwalk into the arrivals area of Sandspit airport on Haida
Gwaii[33] at the end of July. My old friend Ren is waiting
there to greet me. "How are you, man?" he says. "It's good to see

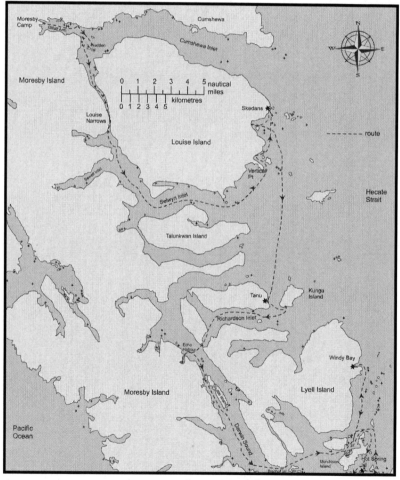

Gwaii Haanas North

you. How long has it been?" "Must be ten years at least," I say. "Since then I've moved from Edmonton to Victoria and you've moved from Prince George to Masset." "And now I'm about to move away," Ren says, "but I'm glad you could make it up here before I do." I reply, "I'm glad, too. It always seemed like such a remote place to me. But I've always wanted to kayak here and seeing you before you left was the just the spur I needed to get here." Gear loaded in the car, we drive back to Ren's place. The next day it takes me the whole day to put the boat together. I am not moving fast because Ren and I have a lot of catching up to do. It takes me nearly eight hours to assemble the kayak.

I just recently completed building a folding skin-on-frame baidarka kayak after being given George Dyson's book, "Baidarka." I was so enthused after reading the book I felt I just had to build one for myself. I wanted to see if it performed as well as baidarka proponents say. I sent for the plans and started in, but I made two modifications. First, I made the frame out of wood rather than the specified aluminum tubing. Second, I designed the frame so that it can be disassembled and the skin folded up for easier transport. It took some head-scratching, and I had to dust off some structural-engineering neurons that hadn't been disturbed in a long time, in order to calculate sizes for the wood frame to have equivalent strengths. Eventually it came together in time (just) for this trip. It is a bit of a leap of faith to set out on a multi-week trip with a kayak that has only been in the water once before, and not loaded down at that, but this kind of trip is exactly what I had in mind when I made my modifications.

Yesterday morning dawned cool, windy and rainy and I had a migraine that got worse as the day progressed. I felt quite ill for much of the day and only started to improve once I went for a long walk before supper. I am really quite down about the whole venture, feeling bad as I do, and consider calling it all off. I am not looking forward to setting off feeling ill. However, I continue to take my Excedrin at regular intervals and am a little improved this morning, but still off my feed. When we finally get packed up and underway, I am on the mend. This beginning-of-the-trip migraine has happened before, too often to be coincidence. I think it must be due to either stress at the start of the trip or coming off the constant stress at work. I will have to make a conscious effort to slow down this trip and not feel pressured by weather or distance deadlines. I have certainly allowed myself enough time to cover the distance at a leisurely pace.

This morning's departure from Ren's place seemed to take forever – not because of me but because of Ren's preparations for his trip to Vancouver Island. He will be gone for a month and seems quite scattered in trying to ensure that he has remembered everything. As a consequence, we leave a little late and just barely make the eleven o'clock ferry from Skidegate to Alliford Bay. Once on it, though, the weather actually warms up and is quite pleasant. The road to Moresby Camp is in relatively good shape – certainly better than the gravel road to Barkley Sound on Vancouver Island. We arrive at about twenty past twelve, but with all the re-sorting and first time packing, plus the absence of hatches on this boat, I don't get away until just after two. Two big Zodiacs from Moresby Explorers come in just as I am leaving. I am pleased to see what their boats look like, as I have arranged a ride back with them at the end of the trip.

By this time, it is a little drizzly, but fine for paddling. I stop within half an hour to check out some old pilings and a meadow connected with the abandoned logging camp of "Aero." It is the site of the only logging railway ever built on Haida Gwaii. There is not much left except pilings, which make convenient Kingfisher perches, and flat spots on land that the trees are reclaiming. I leave Aero and come around Barge Point, looking for suitable beaches. There is a light chop coming into Gillatt Arm and I can feel the boat flexing. It is very much more stable fully loaded than empty but is riding lower in the water than I expected. It behaves well so far.

I decide to stop on Nedden Island at four o'clock as I can't see anything better on either shore, and Carmichael Passage, which is next, looks very steep-sided. A tiny gravel cove no more than fifty yards wide opens up and it looks like a perfect one-kayak camping spot. I take about an hour to get the boat unloaded, level the tent spot, set up the tent and tarp and rig the camp. There are a pair of resident Oystercatchers[34] making noise on the rocks at the east end of the cove. As I cook supper, two Pigeon Guillemots[35] paddle tentatively into the west end of the little cove, each holding a small Sculpin[36] in its beak. After a bit, it dawns on me that they are trying to come ashore. Sure enough, after ten minutes of hesitating, one waddles into the bushes and comes out a minute later, sans fish. They have a burrow in there, just underneath a couple of large rocks, as I discover, and are feeding chicks. They seem to be used to me after about half an hour and fly back and forth regularly. As I go to find a place to hang the food bags in the trees the next cove over, I surprise another pair there and spot another burrow.

At the end of the first day of my Gwaii Haanas[37] odyssey, the wind is almost calm, the clouds are showing some blue sky in gaps and I feel good.

* * * * *

The end of a long day in the boat finds me at Vertical Point on the southeast corner of Louise Island. I see the evidence of a lot of logging all the way around Louise Island, hearing trucks and seeing dust from them rising above the trees. I can also see activity up Sewell Inlet, which is where the work boat I saw yesterday and today is going. I can also see the ruins at the head of Pacofi Bay, but the wind and tide behind me are too good to pass up and I don't go in. I do not see a lot of wildlife, except of course the ever-present Bald Eagles. I see many. I do get a glimpse of a couple of Harbour Porpoises[38] in Selwyn Inlet. They are hard to spot, as they are small have small fins and don't spend much time on the surface – two or three breaths and then they are gone.

Vertical Point has a very small cabin perched on the bluff. It was apparently once the home of an artist from New York, Benita Sanders, who lived here for a while in the 1970s. It must have been summer only – I can't imagine living in the place in the winter, exposed to the southeast gales. There is quite a

Vertical Point camp

meadow under the trees – perhaps once cleared for a garden, but now given over to grass. The grass attracts the deer. A two-point buck wanders through as I am making supper. It is not collared as some of them are, according to a note in the cabin from the Research Group on Introduced Species (RGIS) - deer are not native to Haida Gwaii.

There is a very light breeze from the west, but it doesn't penetrate under the trees in the meadow, which is a shame, because it would keep the mosquitoes at bay. There are a lot of them and I finally have to retreat to the tent, in spite of having put on repellent. On reading the guide, I find that this was originally the site of an old Haida village and then later a home for hand-loggers in the 1930s. The latter explains the apple tree, which looks older than the thirty years since the artist lived here.

* * * * *

I have been unforgivably stupid. Last night, when hauling the kayak up the beach, I disconnected the paddle from the tether and left it lying there in two halves on the beach beside the boat and forgot to go back to fetch it. I woke up at quarter past five and suddenly remembered what I had done. I leaped out of bed and spent a fruitless three quarters of an hour searching the beach in the pre-dawn dimness in the vain hope that, one hour after low tide, they might have been deposited there with the other low tide junk. No such luck. I will have to make a thorough search of the bay when I launch – the paddle halves might still be afloat. I see a log out there that was there when I came in yesterday, it's just possible the paddle might be afloat out there, too. I know I was tired, but that was very stupid. Luckily I have a spare paddle so my stupidity isn't fatal.

* * * * *

It is said that the gods look out for children and idiots. I am not a child; therefore I must be an idiot. Within two minutes of launching in the morning, there, right in the middle of the bay, not fifty feet apart, are both halves of the paddle. As it was a calm night, the tide must have just carried them out and then carried them right back in. I realize I definitely have to be more careful, with everything. Not every critical piece of gear has a backup.

I paddle straight to Skedans Village and raise the Haida Watchman[39] on the VHF for permission to land. This may actually be the first time I've used the transmitter part of the radio – glad it works! I'll have to see what it does to battery life. The Watchmen at Skedans are a young couple, James and his wife (whose name I don't catch), with a two-year old. James offers me a coffee and shows me around the village. The poles that are still standing are mostly mortuary poles, plus a few memorial poles. Everything else has fallen. Still, the scale and setting are impressive. There were 500 people in Skedans at its height - twenty Raven crest families and six Eagle crest. The house pits are impressive, too. One, is especially impressive and was said to be able to hold the entire village. Although the village has bays to the south and north, all the houses faces south, right into the winter storms. James thinks there may be some geographical alignment with other important sites, such as Tanu and Reef Island. James also picks some licorice fern root for me to try, out of the moss growing on the bark of an ancient alder. It has a strong licorice flavour but it is not sweet and has a bitter aftertaste.

* * * * *

Well, it is a rare day in Gwaii Haanas, actually sunny. After a cloudy start to the day, it became gradually more and more open and now, in late afternoon, there are only a few puffy clouds. I don't know whether it will last because I haven't yet heard the latest forecast. The wind has come up now from the southeast, a little ahead of what was predicted, I think. I almost always have music playing in my head and I often find myself humming some snatch of song. When I pay attention, it often has some subconscious connection to what is going on in the moment. Today it is *"I can see clearly now the rain has gone"* by Johnny Nash. This is a song that is to recur in the weeks ahead many times as the rain comes and goes.

The thought of making breakfast this morning with all those bugs is too much to bear. I hurriedly eat a power bar and launch shortly before nine. It is one or two miles to Tanu, by GPS. I make good time across the mouth of Selwyn Inlet into a breeze coming out from the west. The breeze dies after a bit and I paddle in still air, and the sea only has a long glassy swell from the north. I am well out from the land with no markers immediately beside me to measure progress and the time seems to pass very slowly. In the calm air the intermittent sun makes it very hot. Finally a bit of variable breeze shows up the last mile or so, offering cooling relief.

Coming into Tanu, a power boat is just leaving and the Haida Watchmen take off in their skiff. As I am drying out on a log, a group of twelve kayakers come in. They are two teachers and a group of high school students from the Isle of Man, of all places. They have been out two weeks and were in Windy Bay last night. The woman is the organizer. She talks to me about a next trip they want to do, with the kids, by kayak, from Port Hardy to Cape Scott. I try to tell her that it is a lot riskier than this sheltered east side of Haida Gwaii, with more wind, big waves and stronger currents, but she is not altogether convinced. I walk around the village at Tanu, without a guide this time as the woman in the Watchman's cabin doesn't come out and I don't like to disturb her. The village is beautifully situated and southeast landing beach is very pleasant. The whole village site has the right combination of rocks, views, sun, breezes and adjacent stream that resonates with some deeply felt sense of pattern. No poles remain standing, just house pits. I get a better sense here of how deep they were and of the multiple layers of seating they have than I did at the pits in Skedans. One of the house pits is huge. It must have been able to hold hundreds of people, perhaps the entire village.

* * * * *

It's nine o'clock in the evening and I am halted from further progress south by southeast winds that came up mid-day, ahead of a frontal system and I'm serenaded by flapping nylon. The day starts beautifully, dead calm, although cloudy. A very light breeze wafts me west from Kunga Island, where I stopped for lunch. At some rocks part way up Richardson Inlet, there are two otters, one Oystercatcher and one Wood Duck – quite an inventory for just three small tidal rocks. Yesterday's party of kayakers are on Kunga Point, where it looks like they are taking a rest day. I am tempted to stop and say hi again, but don't for some reason. As I go south through Richardson Passage, it breezes up a little and rains a bit. A Bald Eagle swoops low after a fish, changes its mind and flaps up away from the water. As it does, it drops a white feather on the water just ahead of me. I paddle over and pick it up. How often do you get white Eagle feathers dropped from the sky for you? I take it to be a good omen[40].

I poke the bow of the kayak into Echo Harbour in search of fresh water, as I only have a day's supply left. Inside, it is beautifully calm and there is a picturesque little waterfall tumbling in at the end. I head straight for it when suddenly a Peregrine Falcon stoops on a small flock of Crows and hits one. The Crow struggles, its flock mates make a huge racket and the

Crow escapes, although he is wounded – I can see the blood. Just then, a Bald Eagle darts in to try to pick off the Crow. The Eagle isn't able to catch the Crow either and the whole flock gets away to the shelter of the trees. This incredible performance is all over inside of six seconds. The amazing thing is that the Peregrine was able to get the Crow in the first place as the Crow is nearly his equal in size.

The waterfall is a delight of clear water pouring over the smooth rock. I passed over two shallow rock ledges on the way in and the tide is dropping, only leaving me time to pump five litres and have a quick wash of my upper body, head and paddling shirt. As brief as it is, it feels very good. Coming out of Echo Harbour, I retreat downwind back north a short distance to a small spit at Gil Island. I find just enough room for my tent and a fine view up and down Darwin Sound. I rig the tarp over the tent entrance and listen to the forecast. It is not encouraging for the next few days, with one front after another due to move through. The wind blows all night up the Sound and is still strong next morning. I'm not going anywhere in this wind, but at least the rain solves my water shortage. I spend forty-five minutes patiently holding down one edge of the tarp and filling up the rest of my water bags.

At noon, it is still rainy and I take a little nap. I get up for some lunch and the rain quits. The wind is not as strong now and it looks like I might get a calm-ish break before the wind shifts to the southwest. I decide to go. By the time I strike camp and get on the water just before two, it is dead calm with sunny patches. I make good time down the channel beside Shuttle Island, as the tide is with me. I cover the five miles in an hour and a half. Past the end of Shuttle it is decision time – should I go for it?

Once past Shuttle, there does not look to be a good place to stop on Darwin Sound except perhaps on an emergency gravel beach just at the southeast entrance. I leave and of course the wind comes up. Although it has shifted to the southwest, the Sound funnels it around and the effect here is just the same as a southeast wind. It never amounts to more than fifteen knots, usually ten to twelve. It is enough to make the paddling hard and wet work as the spray from the bow continuously splashes back over me. The boat handles the cross swells I am encountering very well, except for a tendency to weathercock, as do all rudderless boats. Around the end of Darwin Sound, the chop gets very uneven, all the way to the Bischof Islands. Just before the last push to Bischof Islet, a big Zodiac slows to a tops alongside me. It is Steve from Moresby Explorers, who I met at Moresby Camp. "How's it going?" Shouts Steve. "Fine," I say, even though I'm kind of tired. "Do you need anything?" Steve asks. "No, I'm pretty well fixed," I reply. "Got enough food and I'm not having any trouble finding fresh water." 'OK, see you in a few weeks then," says Steve, and he throttles up the Zodiac and speeds away. Once alongside the Bischofs, I am tired and am prepared to camp, but can't spot any obvious site. The ones that I do see don't look all that inviting – rather stony and exposed to the southwest wind.

I decide to press on to Murchison Island as it is more downwind than any nearby alternatives. Although it is about the same distance to Ramsay Point or Hotspring Island, the track to them would be decidedly more across the wind, making for more difficult paddling. This wind rises again shortly after I set out. It is another hard, wet slog, trying to keep the boat from broaching. I begin to think I inhabit some sort of kayak purgatory - never-ending waves, a cold wind, wet through and no friendly beaches in sight. Although it seems to take forever, it is really only an hour 'til I reach the flatter waters of the bay at Murchison. After ranging back and forth in the bay in search of a good camping spot, I end up under the trees at the west end, where the beach is the least rocky. Still in my wet-suit, fearing heavier rains, I quickly throw up the tent and the tarp and bring the boat up. I finally change into warmer, mostly dry, clothes. I make do with a cup-o-soup and some munchies, as I don't feel much like supper.

* * * * *

In the immortal words of Zsa Zsa Gabor – "I feel like a new man, darling!" I having spent a pleasant hour and a half at the hot spring. With sheltered waters between Murchison and Hotspring

Island, the wind doesn't really hinder the paddling. What bliss to climb under the hot water and shower and then sit in a natural hot pool! After being wet and cold for a couple of days, plus being grimy from paddling, repellent and campfire smoke, it is sheer heaven. I have a nice visit with a group of people of a Moresby Explorers three-day tour by Zodiac. One fellow, Ian, his wife and kids are on an extended holiday before heading back to England after being posted abroad for five years. He invites me to share their lunch, which I accept.

* * * * *

I locate a small north-facing sandy beach on Ramsay Island that was recommended to me. I set up camp in the late afternoon. It begins to rain at supper-time and as the evening wears on the rain gets heavier. The wind backs into the northeast, which has not been forecast. Suddenly, that snug little beach, protected from the southeast, is totally exposed to the northeast. The 9:30 pm forecast scares the hell out of me as it calls for an unseasonably strong southeast gale three days away. The next two days are not supposed to be too windy, though.

It blows and rains hard all night. The tent is dry, just, as it is tucked totally under the tarp, but everything else gets wet, even under the tarp, as the wind blows the rain in. The stream beside the camp, which was a nice little rill that didn't make it all the way down the beach last night, has increased ten-fold. The surf has added about two feet of sand on top of the old level at that end of the beach. I decide I have to move camp, because if last night's front, which wasn't noteworthy in the forecast, is as bad as it was from the northeast, then what will the *"unseasonably strong southeast gale"* be like? This beach will clearly be untenable. I had an earlier notion of scooting over to the hot spring while waiting out the gale, but the beach there is just too exposed.

While I have breakfast I consider my options. I still want to see Windy Bay village and the camping is supposed to be good there. If I get stuck with the weather, there will be company at the Watchman's cabin and perhaps other kayakers to talk to. I can also just go to Murchison Island again and sit tight for two or three days. I don't really want to cross Juan Perez Sound just yet and there will likely still be a big swell from the storm. I decide to paddle to the east end of Murchison, which will expose me to the open swells in Hecate Strait for a little. I can judge from there whether to carry on to Windy Bay.

Outside Murchison Island the swells get rougher and the wind picks up just enough that I don't think I can face the thought of slogging through that for another five and half miles. I turn the kayak, come into the bay on Murchison and set up camp where I was two nights ago. I am now set to strike out for Windy Bay, weather permitting, or I can sit it out here. The afternoon is mostly cloudy with a few patches of blue sky showing occasionally. It is surprisingly pleasant, given what is forecast. On a short stroll down the beach, I startle an Eagle who is bathing in a little rill that appeared bigger with last night's rain. That rill may also be the source of the mosquitoes. I find another rill further on, then a nice dry rock in a bug-free zone, to sit on. While sitting there and scanning out into the channel at the north of the bay, I see what I think is a black sail of a small boat. I look with the binoculars and see that it is in fact a tall dorsal fin for a male orca[41]. I see a female, together with the male, a couple more times on the surface before they swim out of sight. These are the first whales I have seen on this trip.

There are deer everywhere. Every beach I've been on has deer walking up and down morning and night. I've also seen quite a few of them from the kayak. With no wolves or cougars to keep them in check they have multiplied like crazy. They have reduced the forest understory to a mossy mat, according to RGIS. This bay is also full of Pigeon Guillemots, diving and catching small fish. They are definitely the most numerous sea bird so far. I occasionally also see Murrelets and Auklets, and yesterday I saw a Western Grebe[42].

The rain has just started again. This is getting to be a nightly occurrence. Can the wind be far behind? I dig out the harmonica. This seems to be as good a time as any to learn some new tunes, although one crucial note on the G side of my double-scaled harp seems to be jammed. It was working fine at home – must be the damp.

* * * * *

I get up early this morning and listen to the lighthouse reports on the coast. Winds are calm at Cumshewa, not too far north of here. I think it's a go for Windy Bay. It is the right decision. I start at quarter to eight and the winds are calm or light all the way to Windy Bay. The only real swells are in the gap between Murchison and the Agglomerate Islands, and then again the last mile into Windy Bay. The islands do a good job of protecting the rest of the way. I arrive just past low tide and most of the bay is dry, or at least has no water. The rocks are covered with seaweed of all description. I walk the boat up the creek part way, carry up the crucial gear and leave the boat and the rest until the tide comes in. I think I have sprung a leak in the boat's skin covering, but it is just the spout on the freshwater Dromedary bag that opened and leaked about three of the bag's four litres into the boat. Not good to lose the fresh water, but better than a leak in the boat.

When I get here, there are no other kayakers, only the two Watchmen. Gary, the older man, has been a commercial fisherman and logger all his life and seems like a very nice guy. Buck, the younger man, is not of my generation and I don't relate as well. Gary is a well-known local artist, a carver with some of his work on display at the museum. I ask Buck if he carves. He says he tried once but came to the conclusion that had "no effing talent" and gave it up.

Hlk'yah GawGa is the Haida name for what Europeans called Windy Bay. There is a long house here[43], with a wood stove and bunks, that kayakers can stay in. In heavy rain it is pure luxury compared to a tent. I get a fire going and dry everything out. If the predicted gale arrives tomorrow morning, this is about the best place I can be. I already asked Gary if I can stay over one more night if the weather deteriorates and he agrees. Gary offers to share their supper with me, and I gratefully accept.

Gary says, "If you're looking for something to do between now and then, there's some firewood that needs chopping." "Sure," I say, "I can chop firewood."

Gary shows me a pile of lengths that he has bucked out of a three foot diameter cedar drift log and hands me an axe. I take the axe and start wailing on one of the lengths, trying to split off a piece, while Gary looks on. I am not making any progress.

Gary says, "You haven't done that much before, have you?" I say "I've chopped a lot of wood but I grew up on the Prairies and the biggest trees we had were only about a foot in diameter. I don't have any experience with anything this big." "Well, there's a trick to it. It's not so hard once you know how," Gary says. "Here," he says, "Take a close look at the log. See where it has started to split radially as it dries? Find the biggest split and use the axe to enlarge the crack so it runs from the edge to the centre. Then chop on that crack with the axe and it should split."

He demonstrates and the length falls in half with one well-aimed blow. He silently hands me the axe. I set up another length and carefully enlarge the biggest split. I take a first swing and miss, but on the second I hit the split and the length splits open. "What do you know, it works," I say. "You've got to work with the wood, not try to overpower it," Gary says, "I'll leave you to it." I work away and manage to get a respectable amount of wood chopped before supper. I have a whole new level of respect for loggers.

There is quite a running VHF chat show going on between all the Watchmen camps. Everyone knows everyone else and there appears to be a lively trade in visits, gossip and seafood. I go for a walk in the afternoon on the trail alongside the creek. It is original old growth and very spectacular. Rather different from Pacific Rim Park, but there are no Douglas Fir this far north, just huge Western Red Cedar[44], Hemlock and Sitka Spruce. Having a fire in the stove means that I can heat water and have a much needed sponge bath. It feels good to be clean again. The only thing that might get in the way of a good night's sleep is bugs.

The long house is not bug-tight. However, warm and dry more than compensates for a few bugs.

The predicted gale[45] arrives sometime after two o'clock in the morning. The wind builds all morning and the rain is mostly heavy, although it slacks off at times. It would be very unpleasant to be in a tent, even in a sheltered cove. Apparently a well-known guide with a tour group, currently camped on Ramsay, is intending to come here today. I think there is not a chance they will come, at least not if they have any sense. It is blowing at least thirty knots out there and maybe more. The forecast is for the front to pass through late today and for the winds to go from gale to merely moderate-to-strong. It will build again overnight as the low that is driving the front tracks to the northeast across Haida Gwaii. If that happens, the seas and wind won't subside at all tomorrow and I'll be here another day.

I get the fire going again next morning and it keeps the place warm and dry but not hot like yesterday, as the breeze through the cracks in the plank walls steals some of the heat. I am very grateful to be inside on a day like this. The rain, which is heavy and steady all day, lets up just a little in late afternoon, but the wind seems strong as ever. I play the harmonica a little but get tired of that and go and borrow a book from the Watchmen, along with a couple of Reader's Digests. There is no point in getting antsy. The weather will do what it does and I can't leave until it calms down.

I have supper again with Gary and Buck. I contribute Thai noodles and do a shake and bake on some chicken they have. I wash the dishes afterwards – it's the least I can do in return for their hospitality. The wind in the bay goes down significantly in the evening. The automated reports at the evening roundup still report twenty to thirty knots at the South Hecate buoy, although it is only twelve knots at Sandspit and fifteen at Cumshewa. There is still a significant swell running, judging from the surf that I can see with binoculars on Tuft Island offshore. The forecast is not terribly encouraging, though, with the winds still expected to be moderate-to-strong for Hecate Straight overnight and tomorrow.

However, if the actual winds alongshore are no worse than right now, I might be able to go in the morning. If I absolutely have to, I can spend another night here, but I don't want to impose.

Something making noises (raccoon probably) in the woodshed and fuel shed wakes me at five in the morning. Since I am awake now, I switch on the VHF to listen to the four o'clock forecast and weather station reports. It is still blowing eighteen to twenty-three knots at South Hecate buoy. The seas at the buoy are still eight feet high, which is too much for me. Winds are twelve to fifteen knots at both Sandspit and Cumshewa, which, on top of eight foot seas, is still too much. Perhaps there will be a window this afternoon, as the forecast is for the weather to moderate then. If not, tomorrow is definitely supposed to be light and variable winds. When it gets light enough, I walk out of the long house to the edge of the forest and look out over the bay to Hecate Strait beyond. The wind feels strong, even here under the trees. The breaking waves march relentlessly by, rank on rank, as far as I can see to the east. I am glad I am not out there.

About two o'clock, a group of ten kayakers arrive from the south. It is a tour group led by tour guide Colin from Vancouver, together with his assistant Tara, from Victoria. Colin does several of these trips every summer and he says this is the wettest trip he has ever experienced. They are a lively bunch but in talking to them they admit that they don't have a lot of kayaking experience. Given that, I am surprised that Colin led them up in this weather, although they did have the wind and tide behind them. They encountered a few breaking crests and one paddler had a wave break completely over him from behind. Colin says one of the doubles almost capsized. It sounds like a near disaster, but it reinforces my own decision to stay put. I might have made it south, paddling the opposite direction into that, but it would not have been comfortable and possibly even dangerous. Besides, I am only halfway through my trip, not the last night like it is for them. I am reluctant to get thoroughly wet and cold again, without a warm dry place to end up in, if I don't have to.

We have a great sushi supper in the Watchman's cabin, courtesy of Colin. Sushi the last night in Windy Bay has been a tradition with him for the eleven years that he has been coming here. Not too long before supper, another solo kayaker comes in - Jerry, from Washington state. He's into marathon sessions, having paddled here today all the way from Wanderer Island, with a stop at Hotspring Island. Tonight is a good time with good food and good conversation.

* * * * *

I wake in the morning to a very light, steady drizzle and thick fog, but almost calm winds and much reduced swell. I have breakfast and try to make as little noise as possible, even though only two others are sleeping in the long house. We had a little re-arranging to do at one in the morning, as a rat was investigating the food left out by the tour group. I get the boat packed, say goodbye to Gary and Colin and line the boat down the creek, finally getting underway just before ten. I still have about an hour of ebb and I make good time to Murchison Island. After that the flood slows me a little, but I stop at hot spring again, just before noon. Paddling in the fog today, I am a little rusty at keeping to a compass course. I am glad to have the GPS to keep me on track, although it is calm enough to paddle just to the sound of the surf on Lyell Island to my right. Visibility is only about a quarter mile until I get to House Island.

I have another great soak and wash at the hot spring. I meet and have a pleasant chat with a couple from Hamburg, who have brought their folding double kayak with them. They are travelling with friends, a younger couple with a young teenage son, who paddle into the back beach just as I arrive. The man paddling the other double comes over to me. "May I have a look at your boat?" he asks, "We don't see such boats in Germany, where we live." "Certainly. It's a baidarka, a traditional Alaskan Inuit style of kayak," I reply. "Are your boats all Kleppers[46]?" I ask?" "No, ours are boats that are not well known outside of Germany. They were made before the war in the part of Germany that later become East Germany. One boat was built in the late 1930s and the other was built in 1921. They are both in original condition except that the oldest boat had its canvas deck replaced once, at the factory" he says. "I would never have guessed that they are that old. They are in remarkable shape" I say. "Where is your boat built?" the man asks. "I built it myself," I explain, "It is a design by George Dyson but I converted it to wood frame and made it folding." "It is not so common in Germany that we build such things ourselves," he says, "May I take pictures to show my friends back in Hamburg?" "Of course. Enjoy the Hot springs. Maybe we'll see you again as we paddle the islands," I say.

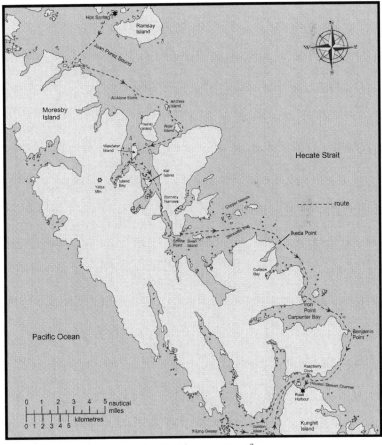

Gwaii Haanas South

I have a look at the wind and the fog, which, although lifting, is still pushing in from Hecate Straight with the northeast wind. I listen to the updated forecast. I decide to change my plans and to take advantage of the northeast wind to cross Juan Perez Sound, as the building high pressure system is supposed to bring northwest winds tomorrow. Northwest wind will be perfect for pushing south to see All Alone Stone and go on to Arichika or Wanderer Island, but it wouldn't be so good for crossing Juan Perez from here.

Crossing the Sound under a hazy sky, I find a campsite behind Marco Island that is sheltered and has a great view north to Darwin Sound. While I make supper, an immature eagle flies in and perches on a tree almost above my kayak. The eagles are beginning to feel like old friends.

* * * * *

I crawl out of the tent at one o'clock to pee and am completely astonished to see clear sky. There is a fringe of low fog across Juan Perez Sound, but the sky above and around is clear and full of stars. In the morning everything is damp from condensation, not rain, for the first time on the trip. I guess this means there really is a high pressure ridge. I hope it will stay. I am on the water shortly after nine, catching the last hour of the ebb going south. I hope to see Arichika Island and All Alone Stone. Within twenty minutes of leaving, the two orcas, that everyone I talked to has been seeing for the last few days, make an appearance. They are also moving south, but are a mile east of me. I paddle hard to try to catch them, but can't, even though they are in slow travelling mode. It is thrilling to see their effortless, fluid, rhythmical motion.

The wind stays relatively light from the north, occasionally northeast, until I get to Arichika Island. I intended to stay here, but can't see the beach recommended by Steve of Moresby Explorers. I pass it by and push on to Alder Island. I am just sizing up a nice looking spot above the beach at the south end when I notice a big male bear nosing along the high tide line.

All of a sudden, the beach doesn't look so attractive. I paddle across to Burnaby for a bite of lunch and decide to continue on to Huxley or Wanderer Island. The breeze is picking up from the east now. I figure that it is a sea breeze due to the heating of the mountains to the west. I don't see anything I like the look of on Huxley but I do recognize the beach and cliff from the dramatic picture in John Ince's sea kayaking guidebook.

I push on to the south end of Wanderer Island. I find a flat place to camp behind a narrow east-facing beach that is covered with sea cabbage seaweed. There is a moderate breeze to keep the bugs off all afternoon. There are so many sand flies and mosquitoes you wonder what they eat when there are no kayakers to feast on. About supper-time another solo kayaker go by, but he must be seeking solitude, as he doesn't stop here but pushes on a couple of small bays to the south.

I am sitting on a rocky point, trying to catch the last of the breeze, in order to keep the bugs at bay, but also to keep cool from the sun. Sun! Who would have believed it after all the steady rain and gloom? When I was getting all the gear out of the boat and laid out on the beach, I noticed the GPS had a tiny bit of condensation inside the screen. I took the battery cover off and set the unit in the sun and breeze for a couple of hours, which seems to get rid of the moisture. I hope no more will get in. This is the first time it has happened. Mind you, I haven't used it in ten straight days of rain before either.

There seems to be the usual Guillemots and Oystercatchers here, along with Ravens and Eagles. I am getting quite blasé about Eagles, there are so many of them. I am not as excited to see them and seem to be taking for granted that they are around and keeping me company. There are a lot of salmon streams entering Juan Perez Sound and many of the salmon are just gathering in these waters now. That may be part of the reason for the increase in Eagles.

I originally entertained the notion of hiking up Yatza Mountain from Island Bay and tomorrow would be the day to do it. However, looking at the ruggedness of these mountains, the fact that there are no trails and that I am here alone, I think it will be too risky. If anything were to happen, I really would be in trouble. Likely the only way up there will be up the creek beds and they are all full of downed trees, the undergrowth is wet and slippery and the mountains are steep. Sour grapes? Maybe, but all in all, I think it will be too risky, solo.

I hear the most extraordinary noises in the night, starting at about two o'clock. It sounds like something large doing a belly flop off the rocks on the point. At first, of course, I imagine it is a bear turning over beach rocks and flipping them into the water. I get up to check. The visibility is good because the moon is up but I can't see any bears. The noise recurs again and again through the night until dawn. It must have been seals hunting fish and making a lot of noise about it.

Wanderer Island sunrise

* * * * *

I get up about twenty past six as I am awake anyway, to the most beautiful sunrise. The sun is well up over Burnaby Island but there is haze on the horizon turning the sun into a big orange ball hanging in the middle of it. I snap a picture, quickly, to see if I can capture it. I leave about eight thirty, not because I'm pressed for time, but to escape the mosquitoes, which are relentless in the morning calm. Paddling slowly south I find a good clear stream to top up my water – not even tea-coloured. I can see that the other solo kayaker has spent the night on a little spit between the northwest tip of Kat Island and an unnamed islet. It actually looks like a better site than where I was on Wanderer Island.

I poke into Island Bay, while waiting for the slack at Burnaby Narrows, and study Yatza Mountain carefully through the binoculars. The upper slopes are more open than most of the other mountains here, but there is very thick forest lower down. Getting through that to get to the slopes above would be a major challenge. Also, I want to get around Ikeda and Benjamin Points in the next couple of days. I'll have favourable ebb tides in the mornings, when the winds are likely to be lightest, and while this stable high pressure system keeps the winds settled in the northwest. I don't change my mind about not climbing the mountain.

I drift into the Narrows and chat with the skipper of a sailboat who was anchored there overnight. He charters here regularly and says he is just as nervous about Ikeda Point as Benjamin Point (which is the one all the guidebooks warn of). Jerry, the kayaker I met at Windy Bay, also talked about Ikeda Point being hairy, and he seems to relish the big weather. I take these lessons about the Point seriously.

Burnaby Narrows doesn't quite live up to its billing as a biological hot spot. It is an interesting passage, with the old cabins in the meadows to the east. Without going ashore, which the park authorities don't want you to do, you only get a kind of drive-by experience. In addition, the wind is ruffling the surface of the water by now. I can't see the bottom very clearly to view the intertidal life reputed to be there. I am interested in the large number of very large orange jellyfish[47] on both sides of the narrows. I've never seen so many in one place.

I paddle into the bay just around Smithe Point. The cove has a very nice pebble beach that is ideal for my camp. Bugs are already a problem by mid-afternoon because the breeze doesn't reach into the cove consistently. I bring my chair out on the point to the east to try to catch the breeze to cool down. I never thought I'd be complaining about the heat this trip, but it is surprisingly hot without the breeze. As I sit here I can see across to Harriet Harbour, the site of a brief-lived copper[48] mine that operated in the 1960s. The slope of overburden piles from the open pit are clearly visible. Apparently all the buildings and infrastructure are removed, but remains of roads and wharves are still there. The town is called Jedway, which is odd, because Jedway Bay is the next one to the west.

The Sitka spruce in this cove are incredible. They are not the tall straight giants of Windy Bay or like the Carmannah Giant on Vancouver Island. Rather they are multi-trunked and branched patriarchs of great character and antiquity. The tree I am camped under is a prime example. The main trunk rises for perhaps twenty feet, then a huge branch, some six to eight feet deep vertically, juts out almost horizontally from the trunk. Above that the main trunk splits in two, then higher up into three, topping out with several crowns at, what, a hundred and fifty feet? Each branch has a whole community of mosses, lichens and salal growing from it. Some branches look like gardens elevated well above the ground. Who knows what communities of life each of these micro eco-systems harbour? What do these hanging garden communities do for the spruce? I have to believe there is a mutually beneficial relationship even though I can't imagine what it is.

It seems that every cove has a designated deer[49] or two. The two for this cove just came down to munch on the new kelp brought in by the high tide. The afternoon sea breeze dies away but there is still a faint breeze coming from the back of the cove, through the trees. It must be from the other side of the island, down the narrows. This breeze is better at keeping the bugs down as it carries my scent and carbon dioxide out over the water, not back into the trees where the bugs are. A Kingfisher flies raucously over. It's one of a pair here that has been working the bay all day. I've noticed a higher density of them in Gwaii Haanas than further south on the coast. I presume that it is due to the plenitude of small fish, the same ones that support the Guillemots.

* * * * *

It's mid-afternoon the next day and I am warm, clean and dry, sitting on a nice pebble beach north of Iron Point by Carpenter Bay. I am up at five thirty in the morning to be away by quarter to seven at the latest. I want to cover the six miles of Skincuttle Inlet from the campsite out to Hecate Strait with the assistance of the ebb tide. I want to get around Ikeda Point while the winds are still calm or light from the overnight lull. The first part goes as planned, the ebb tide and calm winds part, but I haven't anticipated the ebb tide flowing contrary to the northeast swell. The swell originates out in Hecate Strait and is running three to five feet high. Off Ikeda Point, it is ugly. With the swell both coming into and rebounding off of the point and opposing the ebb current, the waves are absolutely chaotic. There is no way to predict which direction the next wave will come from. Waves lump up out of nowhere, leaving half the boat suspended over nothing, to crash down on the other side. Some of the wave shapes are nothing short of fantastic, with square sides and tops. On top of all the big waves are zillions of tiny little wavelets, as if from a light wind, except that there is no wind. I have never encountered conditions like this before. It is deeply scary, but the worst part is not knowing if it will get worse. Fortunately it doesn't and I just keep paddling (not like I have a choice) and get through the worst of it in about half an hour.

Once past the point, the swell becomes much more regular going southwest into Collison Bay. I make pretty good time, getting past the point by twenty to nine or so. After that the wind starts up from the northeast. It is not strong enough to be a problem at first, but by the time I get past Goodwin Point, I am surfing a little bit on the bigger waves generated by the wind. By that time, the option of going into Collison Bay is gone. I can see ahead that there is a cove with a pebble beach that will make a good landing place. The last couple of miles to the point at the entrance of the cove are very tiring. I brace with the paddle alternately on both sides of the boat to keep the boat from broaching[50] as the following waves try to slew the stern around. I take a few waves right over the back deck and forward across the spray skirt onto the foredeck. One of those waves washes my binoculars out from under the shock cord on the deck where they drag over the side, retained by the strap. I dare not stop paddling long enough to haul them in and tuck them under the cord again, but just have to trust to their waterproofing. I finally make it to the beach and gratefully haul myself ashore just before ten. For a while I had my doubts whether I'd make it. I decide to call it a day, having taken three hours to cover eleven and half nautical miles, for an average speed of three point eight knots. I feel that is good progress given the circumstances.

I am very dehydrated when I get in, not to mention hungry. After setting up the tent and bringing the gear up, I make a full breakfast and finish it off with a big mug of coffee. I am just finishing the Red River cereal when two kayakers come around the point of the cove from the south. They head into the beach to land in the surf. They are Jacques and Brent from Nelson and Kamloops. It turns out that we know some of the same people through our work connections. They have been stuck at Benjamin Point for two days, and before that Koya Bay another day, pinned down by northeast winds. Even though they have only come about two miles this morning, they both find the conditions pretty bad, with breaking waves on top of the swells. They are going to try early tomorrow to get around Ikeda point at slack water.

The wind picks up after they come in. By mid-afternoon the wind and waves look like a maelstrom out in the Strait. By late afternoon the wind begins to drop. I am amazed to see a double and a single kayak go by the cove then, heading north into the wind. They are presumably making for Collison Bay at least.

They will have very heavy going to get around Goodwin Point, but will probably make it if the wind keeps dropping. The boats appear to be overloaded, with a lot of gear strapped onto their decks. I think, quite frankly, that they are nuts or foolhardy to attempt it. It is still gorgeously sunny, which may give them a false sense of the danger they are in. I have noticed that the same water and wind conditions will seem much more benign to me when it is sunny than they will if it is cloudy or raining.

I take advantage of a small stream behind the beach to fill my water bags, rinse the salt out of my paddling shorts and shirt and have a complete soapy wash and rinse. I feel great. The bugs are ferocious when the breeze finally dies after supper and I sit with Jacques and Brent in the smudge they make to keep the bugs away. The wind becomes nearly dead calm in our bay at sunset, and even the water flattens. If the calm holds overnight, it should be good for paddling tomorrow. There is still some swell out there, judging from the surf on the beach, but if the wind dies in Hecate Straight, that should diminish by morning too.

* * * * *

After scaring myself yesterday by coming round Ikeda Point at full ebb, I don't want to make the same mistake with Benjamin Point. Benjamin Point is five miles from the cove at Iron Point, and in order to be there at slack, which is about quarter to seven, I will have to get a very early start. The alarm rings at four-thirty, in thick, black darkness. I am extra careful breaking camp in the dark with only the aid of my headlamp, to avoid inadvertently leaving something behind. I am on the water and paddling at twenty to six. The air is initially calm, but soon a light wind rises from the northwest, across the land, out of Carpenter Bay. A bonus to getting an early start is heading into the sunrise. It is beautiful this morning, with the darkness giving way to assorted shades of orange and red then turning to pink before the colour morphs into the blue sky of full daylight. I paddle hard and arrive at the point at twenty to seven. Judging from the direction the kelp is streaming, the current has turned already, but it isn't strong.

As a result, the swells are low and the wave tops oily smooth. This morning, thankfully, the swell direction and ebb tide are more nearly the same direction. Once past the point, I back off the effort as it is still nearly calm and the tide is now boosting me. The paddling is easy for the next four miles until I am into the entrance to Houston Stewart Channel. The entrance isn't showing any of the nasty behaviour it is famous for, probably due to the moderate difference in height for these two tides.

In looking at the chart, I surmised that I might meet with wind coming out of the Channel. I suspect that part of the northwesterly from wind the outer coast might reach this far and that's what happens. Not a lot of wind, but just enough that I can't loaf and have to work again for the last couple of miles. As I paddle past the shore, I see a bear browsing the high tide line in the next bay to the east of Raspberry Cove. The Cove has the campsite I headed am for. A Harbour porpoise surfaces briefly in greeting in the Cove as I turn into it.

A tour group that is led by Steve of Moresby Explorers is on the beach. It is just past eight when I arrive and they are just packing up go out to SGang Gwaay. I inherit their fire and keep it going as a smudge, as there are biting flies and the breeze is variable. Another solo kayaker is camped at Raspberry Cove - Robert from Jasper. He is here for a month or more. He originally was heading for two months in Glacier Bay, Alaska, but had his wallet, passport and money stolen in Prince George. Not wanting to abandon his vacation altogether, he regrouped and came here as an alternative. He tells me he has taken a number of extended trips with his folding kayak in the past, including one from Mexico to Honduras. He clearly has a lot of experience. He says that his rounding of Ikeda Point is as scary a thing as he has ever done. I feel vindicated by my fear - it wasn't just me being wimpy.

After early cloud, and with the exception of a few cumulus clouds over the islands, it is now clear and sunny. The low cumulus must mean that there is more moisture in the air than there was the last couple of days. It feels good to just sit and rest after the morning's work. There is nothing quite as satisfying as being warm, dry and safe after a much anticipated and fretted-about channel crossing or rounding of a point. The worst of the exposed conditions are now behind me, depending of course on weather getting across to SGang Gwaay, but I don't actually have to go out there if the weather turns bad or the winds are too high.

I only covered about nine or ten miles today, but it seems like more. It must have been the big push the first hour. I laze away the rest of the day, content to sit in the sun and recover after the morning's paddle. Robert is planning to go to the beaches of southeast Kunghit Island. This is the weather for it, if it holds. He dithers all morning but finally leaves at two o'clock or so. I expect him back as it looks as if the swell is still running high out there, but he hasn't returned yet. It mustn't be as bad as it looks.

* * * * *

The bear that was seen the previous night at Raspberry Cove didn't materialise last night, thankfully, or if he did, he was very quiet about it and nobody heard him. I leave at about quarter to eight in order to catch the ebb going out to SGang Gwaay[51]. The paddling goes quickly, in beautiful sunshine, until I reach Cape Fanny, when the fog rolls in, reducing visibility to less than a quarter mile. I have to get out the GPS and focus on the compass to maintain my course. The fog is not deep and the sun above it filters through right down to the water surrounding me with a kind of diffuse glow. The sea is glassy smooth, with no discernible swell. With the fog, there is no horizon to be seen. It is the strangest feeling, a little like a sensory deprivation tank, with nothing to indicate that I am moving or even to indicate which way is up. Without ordinary visual cues I have to concentrate hard on the compass to maintain the course and it is surprisingly difficult. I paddle in this limbo for a time that seems disconnected from time. In reality, these conditions don't last long and the fog soon dissipates. When the island shows up ahead I feel like I have gone through some sort of dimensional warp and have arrived in another, more primeval world.

The kayak landing beach is around to the northwest of the island and, approaching it, I paddle by some rocks guarding the cove. The sun is very high now and shines directly into the clear water. I can see down perhaps thirty feet along the vertical rock wall below me. The wall is almost completely covered by sea urchins, with no other living thing attached. I suddenly realize that what I am looking at is probably an urchin barren. I land in the sunshine amidst other kayaks and boats and join the next group to tour the island. The totem poles here are the best preserved of all the Haida villages. They are wonderful works of art but I do not get the same emotional feeling as I did years before on the west side of Vancouver Island. The village site is well protected, which is good because the island itself is very exposed. The village was never as big as Skedans or Tanu but it would have been easy to defend by virtue of its location. The burial cave is quite dramatic. It is an old sea cave that was raised when the island rose out of the sea and it has a cleft in the sixty-foot high rocks, leading to the cave. Entrance is forbidden but you can imagine the conditions inside.

When I remove the food bag at lunch time I discover that the top deck stringer behind the cockpit is broken. I suddenly remember that when I got in the boat to launch this morning, I inadvertently sat with my whole weight on the stringer behind – it must have broken then. The stringer isn't completely broken through, it is more like a serious greenstick fracture. I lash it together temporarily and plan make a more complete repair at my evening campsite. The fog begins to roll back in, but not as thick, as I leave. I paddle out past the rocks to the north and west of the island and am rewarded with the sight of Puffins going by. I believe they are Tufted Puffins, although Horned Puffins apparently nest around Cape St. James. I paddle east past Flat Rock Island south of Cape Fanny but see no unusual sea birds beyond Gulls, Cormorant and Guillemots. I am startled to see one Guillemot shoot into a cleft in the side of the cliff, which doesn't look big enough, but obviously is.

Gordon Islets black sand beaches

I find a camp spot above the high tide line on black sand on the east side of the Gordon Islets. In a big tide, this spot will be under water, but I will be safe tonight. I have been told about a good campsite on these islets, but this doesn't quite fit the description. I set to work to make a better repair to the deck stringer. I unlash the tension lacings to get at it. I dig out the repair kit and find some fine braided nylon to tightly bind the greenstick fracture more tightly than my earlier temporary repair. To back that up, I find a piece of Sitka spruce on the beach about two inches in diameter (but seventeen years old – I count the rings) and carve a piece to the right length. I oval it, split it and hollow it somewhat. I then splint the break with this, lashing it tightly with more braided line. It should be fine, as the main function of the deck stringer is to prevent the boat from sagging in the middle. The stringer is mainly in compression, not tension or bending. That whole effort takes a couple of hours, but now it is done.

When looking for wood for the repair, I find the most amazing thing – a seven foot piece of bamboo cane, with branch stubs still attached. You can't buy commercial bamboo like that.

Any bamboo grown further south on this coast would never have made it here if tossed into the ocean, as the currents flow the other direction. I can only conclude that it drifted here from Japan or China. It certainly has enough barnacle glue marks on it. Also, when you consider the glass ball floats from Japan found on these shores, it's not so far-fetched an idea. It also bolsters Tim Severin's contention, in his book "The China Voyage," that bamboo rafts from China could have made it to this coast without disintegrating. I resolve to write to him and let him know.

The low cloud that came in with the fog lifted in Houston Stewart Channel some time ago. It may be a clear night after all as the clearing seems to be have worked its way south. I sit outside as I write up my log, as the bugs aren't bad here. Just a few flies that don't seem to bite, but just crawl annoyingly. The rocks behind me provide shelter from the wind. Speaking of which, the winds must be fierce here in winter as the trees are all like bonsai or like krummholz[52] trees at treeline in the mountains. It gives the islets a very different feel than everywhere else with the big trees.

* * * * *

Today starts well enough. I pass a very quiet night on the Gordon Islets and don't hurry in the morning, for a change, as the tide is against me in the morning and the winds are light. I finally leave at about ten thirty. I paddle south a couple of miles to look at the north cove inside Bowles Point and walk over to the south cove. The south cove is extremely exposed to the south and so, as a consequence of the winter southerly storms, it has very fine sand and a lot of junk on the beach. Not a place to be stuck during a southeaster. The north cove looks as if it may have been a village site once, but there is nothing here now except maybe a midden, even that is hard to tell. The rocks to the west at sea level are all fissured, and you can imagine caves suitable for burial further in, which is why the rocks are off-limits. I stay in the cove for a while, have lunch and wait a little while until it is close to the time the tide will turn. I push off in sunshine, which has made an appearance, and light winds, and laze slowly up the shore to take advantage of any back eddies in the last of the ebbing tide. The whole of this coast of Kunghit Island is quite rugged, with only one or two tiny potential landing spots. Several Eagles are riding an invisible wave of air above a higher ridge, just south of the west entrance to Houston Stewart Channel. That should have been a clue had I been paying closer attention. As I enter the Channel, the wind starts to build behind me and blow right up it. The waves from the open ocean are somewhat at an angle to the direction of the Channel. Soon I am fighting to keep from broaching, riding three, and occasional four-foot waves. The wind follows me right in to the beach at Raspberry Cove although the waves decrease somewhat as the Channel turns east.

It is sunny here at the campground and a stiff southwest wind is blowing. How I am heartily sick of fighting strong tailwinds that generate quartering seas from behind. Give me a good headwind on the nose any time, I am sure it is less work, even if slower. I figure the wind is fifteen to twenty knots with a few gusts higher than that. I think it is the offshore high pressure system northwest wind which funnels and bends up the channel, and which is strengthened by the daytime heating effect of the sun on the land. You wouldn't think the islands are wide enough to generate these sea breezes, but I've seen them several times now. The forecast this morning was, and still is in the afternoon, for light to moderate variables, not the steady kind of wind that has developed.

I am tired from weeks of paddling, my right shoulder is strained from the sweep strokes needed, my left hand has a slightly pinched nerve and, in spite of the welcome sunshine, the paddling and camping now begins to seem like work. I've seen everything that I really came to see. I think I'll just park myself here tomorrow as a rest day and perhaps head over to Rose Harbour the day after, a couple of nights early. It will be good to eat somebody else's cooking and make some human contact.

I think I've had enough introversion this trip and am ready to engage society again.

As I come in I notice the local bear on the beach about a mile to the west and I find fresh scat on this beach at the last high tide line. I suspect he patrols the whole channel and comes by here every second day at least, since we didn't see him yesterday. I must be scrupulous with my food, as usual, and hope I don't see him. As soon as the sun angle begins to decline, the wind becomes surprisingly cool and when the sun goes behind the trees, it is actually cold. The wind starts to drop in fits and puffs around supper-time, and is much less strong on average now than it was in late afternoon, but it has not gone calm. I retreat to the tent, not because of the bugs, but to stay warm, even though it is still light out. A fire will just be a waste of time in this breeze.

* * * * *

On my self-declared rest day, I sleep in until almost eight o'clock, which is almost unheard of for me. I get up and have a very leisurely breakfast and linger over a second mug of coffee. It is not sunny and it was almost drizzling earlier, but it lets up to just be overcast with light variable winds. I think I heard a bear last night down at the west end of the beach, overturning rocks about one o'clock, but I didn't go down to see. Alternately, it may have been a hunting seal, now that I think about it.

Rose Harbour and this channel are by far the busiest area of the South Moresby, with the exception of the Hot Spring Island. In addition to a couple of float planes a day, there are skiffs going to SGang Gwaay, as well as Moresby Explorers Zodiacs every few days or so. In the evening a converted fish trawler drops anchor over at Rose Harbour and the people just go ashore, perhaps for supper. A big ketch motors towards the Channel from the southeast and turns in towards Heater Harbour, where there is apparently a mooring buoy, although it looks somewhat exposed, especially to the east. I had Raspberry Cove to myself last night and again this morning. I half expected one or the other tour groups that are around to be back, or perhaps Robert will be back from Kunghit Island's east side. I was half-tempted to go with him the other day but I had been up very early that day and had already put in a day's paddling. To set off for another ten-twelve miles, in mid-afternoon, as Robert did, didn't seem to be a good idea. I questioned his judgment, in spite of his experience, in setting off when the winds are likely to be at their highest. By his own admission, he tends to hang about on shore when the weather is nice and ends up paddling when it deteriorates. Exactly the opposite of my philosophy. If I'd gone with him, I could foresee paddling even more in big winds and waves. I don't want any more of that on this trip.

Around eleven o'clock, the four kayakers that were dropped off here Saturday come in to have lunch while waiting for the tide to turn and take them north. They are Karen, JP, Pauline and Ian, from Vancouver and Toronto. Ian is the fisherman of the group and he has caught a greenling and a rockfish. They graciously share them with me after baking them on the fire I have going. I keep the fire going to keep the bugs at bay, as they are bad when the wind drops. The four kayakers have been having difficulty hanging their food in the trees at night. I show them my messenger-line and pulley system, which they think they can copy using a carabiner and lines that they have. They get away at the start of the flood with the intention of getting at least as far as Benjamin Point, maybe even around it at the evening slack. They will probably make it without difficulty as the winds seem relatively light. The wind has dropped a lot now, by later afternoon, although it hasn't quite gone calm. The sky suddenly clears after supper and it is very pleasant to sit with a small fire, read and watch the passing scene. That scene includes the doe and fawn that were here this morning. At one point this morning there were this pair plus a three-point buck all munching the same patch of kelp. I haven't listened to the forecast since first thing in the morning. There is still some cloud in the west, but it appears as if the high pressure ridge is rebuilding somewhat.

* * * * *

I wake next morning and I haven't slept at all well. I have been waking up more sore and stiff every day. I am still tired. I will head over to Rose Harbour Resort, where I have a reservation starting a couple of days from now. If they will have me, I'll spend the extra couple of days doing not much of anything, maybe a day paddle but not far. I hope they can find room for me. I am slow to get going but finally leave at about ten thirty and paddle across to Rose Harbour in less than twenty minutes, in spite of the current. I am grateful that they can take me in, although tonight I will be in my tent again. I will take my meals here, and there will be interesting people to talk to. I am feeling really tired, still, and my right shoulder is really bothering me.

I have a shower and put on clean clothes – what luxury! Also, Susan put on a great, albeit late, lunch for a group of Japanese tourists who have been out at SGang Gwaay. They were late because they diverted to see four humpback whales. I also do a hand wash of all my paddling and camp clothes, which are incredibly filthy. I don't suppose they are really clean even after that, but they are an improvement at least.

Rose Harbour itself is the site of an old whaling station where they cut up and rendered the whales for their oil. There is a lot of old industrial junk around; vats, old fire-tube boilers, valve assemblies, pistons - all rusted almost beyond recognition. You can tell that the operation must have become uneconomic before it shut down by the way maintenance was neglected. The evidence is in the number of burnt out tubes in the boilers that have not been replaced but simply plugged. Normally that would only be a temporary fix and the tubes would be replaced during an off season. What is worse than all the junk is that the landing beach is covered with huge cinders and clinkers from burning the coal. The clinkers are very sharp and hard on the boats. However, the vegetation is slowly reclaiming it all and it actually has a kind of beauty now.

I set my tent up on the old helicopter pad, no longer used, and it is open to the breeze and the afternoon and evening sun. A group is coming in tonight and filling up the guest house but they leave tomorrow. After that I will apparently have the place to myself. The converted fish boat I saw the other night just came in. They will, no doubt, be staying for supper.

* * * * *

This is certainly a funky place. Rather rustic, in its lack of mod cons, but comfortable nonetheless. Outhouses and solar composting toilets, not much electricity, and what's there is from solar, blessedly avoiding generator noise most of the time. Susan, the co-owner with Goetz, is self-admittedly an original hippy. She came out in the late 60's or early 70's and originally lived in cabins on Burnaby Narrows with a bunch of others. I gather most of the others drifted away but Susan never left Haida Gwaii. She did whatever it took to stay. One of her sons works for Moresby Explorers. I never do hear Goetz's story and how he came to be here. Goetz takes me for a walk in the forest behind the lodge and shows me a partially hewn cedar canoe. The log had been cut and the outside of the hull shaped but the work was then abandoned for some reason. It is impossible to know when this happened or how old it is.

Susan is the cook and does wonders with a wood cook stove and a propane three burner stove top when the cook stove is not fired up. She also has a huge organic garden, which, together with the fresh seafood, means no need for refrigeration. I am sitting talking to Susan in the afternoon when she says, "I've got a big crowd coming for supper tonight." "Yeah? How many are you expecting?" I ask. "Let's see. There's a Moresby Explorers tour group. There's a group off a converted fish trawler. There's you. There's Gord and Suzanne of Butterfly Tours. There's me, Goetz and visiting friends with their kids – probably twenty people in all," Susan says. "Wow, I say. That's lot of people. What are you going to feed them?" I say. "I don't know yet," Susan says.

Seeing as it's already three o'clock, this strikes me as being a little casual, but at about four o'clock, Patrick, one of the neighbours, walks up from the beach with a four-foot ling cod for Susan. The cod, together with a halibut caught earlier, is the mainstay of supper. Susan gets out her sheet of plywood that serves as a fish-cleaning and cutting board and in no time at all has the fish gutted and cut up. Fresh garden greens for salad, couscous, bread baked with flour that I milled from grain on a bicycle-powered grinder, and some sort of sweet square, fresh-baked for dessert, make up the rest. The food is wonderful but the shock of switching from re-hydrated dried food to all this fresh organic stuff is hard on my system. After supper Goetz plays his guitar for the assembled crowd. He writes his own stuff – rather improvisational in the nature of, say, Jesse Winchester. He has put out one CD and is doing another. It is very congenial with only the kerosene lamp for light and the lingering heat from the wood stove.

The night is brilliantly clear but the cloud starts to move in intermittently in the morning. It soon becomes solid overcast, with the promise of showers later. I am glad to be out of the tent and into the guest house, which I am now sharing with a Japanese couple who paddled in just before lunch. Nori and Misa have their four-year old with them and have done some epic trips in the past, including two months in Patagonia and two months in Baja. Nori paddled solo from Alaska to Vancouver in twenty-two days in 1990. This trip for them is a mere short jaunt by comparison – six days in rented Feathercrafts (a double and a single) from Moresby Camp to Rose Harbour.

I haven't done much of anything today except rest, talk with the various people and slowly overhaul my gear. My shoulder is significantly improved, but my back is still sore. Maybe a night in a real bed will help. Tomorrow afternoon I will take my boat apart and pack it for the return trip by Zodiac to Moresby Camp. Dinner tonight is a much more subdued affair socially, because of fewer people, but from a culinary view it was every bit as good as last night. Burritos and more of the ling cod done Cajun style in a wok, with salad and dessert.

I am glad to be under a roof again as it is raining a steady fine drizzle that will be very drenching after a while, and it is considerably cooler. Goetz asks me to light a fire in the guest house, to take the chill out, as the Japanese couple have no experience of it, surprisingly. I set the fire and light it, watch it until is going well then turn down the dampers. There is wood enough in the stove for an hour's burn, after which we will be asleep.

* * * * *

The day starts off pretty slack, with a lot of socializing after breakfast and a phone/VHF call to Moresby Explorers to confirm pickup time tomorrow. I also hope that the morning's rain will give way to clearing in the afternoon, for disassembling and packing the boat. It doesn't, but I find a dry spot under a huge Sitka Spruce on the beach to do the take-apart.

The first part goes without problem, but, when it comes time to slide the sleeves back on the keel and gunwales, it is, to put it mildly, a bastard. The constant moisture has swollen the wood and made all the joints stick. I have to borrow a chisel and hammer to drive the sleeves back. I attract a small crowd of onlookers at first but fortunately they mostly drift away by the time I have to resort to the heavy tools. Equally fortunately, Nori comes by to help and take pictures. He sticks with me and loans his not inconsiderable strength to pulling the frame halves out of the skin, which is especially difficult for the bow half. I end up breaking two stringers and have to chisel off one of the carbon fibre sleeves from the keel centrepiece. I can easily make another when I get home, but I despaired of getting it apart at all at first. The whole job takes over three hours, almost an hour longer than I planned. Perhaps, once I get it repaired and re-assembled, I won't ever take it apart again. I will definitely have to think of a way to deal with the damp and the swelling if I ever want to do another long trip like this.

I learn more about Nori while talking to him. He is a professional adventurer of the solo Japanese endurance warrior type. He has done all sorts of long solo trips, including a solo climb of Mt McKinley, a solo climb and bicycle descent of Aconcagua, a year paddling the Amazon and other mountaineering feats. He has written ten books about his expeditions, all in Japanese. Quite the guy, and quite out of my league. I fire up the hot water heater wood stove after that for a shower and it feels well deserved. Robert comes in after making it round Kunghit Island. He ran into some weather and rotten camp sites the first two nights and some hard paddling. I think I did the right thing by not going with him.

* * * * *

I have the usual great breakfast with Susan and Shannon the morning of the last day and the sun starts to come out. I am the only guest for breakfast, as the Japanese couple prefer to eat their own Japanese breakfast. I finish organizing my gear and moving it down from the guest house, ready for the Zodiac. I walk over to the other tourist operation, Gwaii Haanas Guest House, to talk to Patrick and Mary and see how their operation is run. They run a tidier ship, with fewer guests, and don't have any deals with outfitters. It seems to me that Patrick is not so extroverted and likely can't deal with as much chaos. He is just as much an iconoclast though, and as committed an environmentalist. His operation is also solar powered. He tells me he went outside to take a course on how to set up a satellite internet connection. That will be his next project.

Doug, owner of Moresby Explorers, shows up himself at one thirty. I dress with three layers on my legs, three layers plus my Gore-tex jacket, plus their floater coat on top. I am just comfortable in the wind created by the boat as I sit up front talking to Doug. The boat is their big Zodiac, twenty-four feet long with twin 155 HP OMC outboards, and it does thirty knots even when fully loaded. It is a fine day for the run, not too much wind. We blast quickly by Benjamin and Ikeda Points, where the tide rips are almost non-existent today, to stop and pick up a kayak at the Swan Islands. Then we're back on the water for a longer run to the float camp at Crescent Inlet to pick up two more people and another boat. By this time, it is starting to cloud over and become cooler. The last leg to Moresby Camp is through a few rain showers, which, at that speed, feel like heavy squalls. There is a bear feeding alongside Louise Narrows and he doesn't even look up as we roar by. He must be used to it by now. Back on the west side of Huxley Island, we slice a small shark in half as we go over it. It was just below the surface and neither Doug nor I saw it until after we hit it. Very unfortunate, but nothing to be done after the fact.

By the time we get the boat out of the water, the gear in the van and drive back to the Moresby Explorers office, it is past seven. I settle into the B and B and then walk down to the pub, as it is "Wing Night," which is an event. This is not a big town. I have a couple of glasses of draft beer with the wings and conversation with the crew but the spicy wings come back to haunt me at four o'clock in the morning. I wake up and can't really get back to sleep. I get up at seven, have breakfast and a good yak with a couple of guys who are going to Raspberry Cove tomorrow, weather permitting, which it likely will not. The impending gale warning has been upgraded to a storm warning, making it even less likely that they will go.

On my walk towards the ferry terminal in the morning, I come across cabins being built across from the marina and remember that Shannon says that Lou Kelly is helping build them. Lou is one of the people who helped George Dyson build the original six triple baidarkas and paddle them from Alaska, the trip talked about in Dyson's Baidarka book. Lou is there at the site and we have a good chat about baidarkas. He is very interested in my folding one and says he might stop in Victoria in September to see mine. I take the ferry over to Queen Charlotte City to have a look at the six new totems and the museum. There is a lot of good material in the museum, but the gift shop has less than I thought it would. I end up walking from Skidegate to Queen Charlotte City as nobody gives me a ride when I hang my thumb out. Three quarters of the gift shops there are closed. Rainbow's is open and I end up getting a few souvenirs there. I have fish and chips in Charlotte, and can't get either taxi on the phone, but have better luck hitching back to the ferry and then cadging a ride from there back to the motel.

* * * * *

I escape Haida Gwaii just in time, weatherwise. I wake up this morning to patches of blue to the east out in Hecate Strait and nearly calm winds. This gives no hint of a 980 millibar low that is developing in the Gulf of Alaska, moving southeast and pushing a front ahead of it. The front is expected to produce forty to fifty knot storm force winds this afternoon and tonight across Haida Gwaii. By the time the plane throttles up for its takeoff run, the wind is blowing thirty knots from the southeast and we climb so steeply away from the runway it is like going up an elevator. I look down at the churning, white-capped sea below and pity any kayakers just starting out.

Further south, as the plane passes over Desolation Sound, I can see that it is a beautiful sunny day down on the north Strait of Georgia. There are a lot of boats of all kinds out on the water. I can count twenty in Squirrel Cove alone. It will be hard to convince anyone who has been enjoying a typical warm sunny summer in Victoria about the weather I've experienced. It doesn't matter, I know how it was, I know what I did and that is what counts.

The Broughtons by Kayak

The low August morning sun is directly in my eyes. The ebb current in northern Johnstone Strait slows my progress over the ground as I paddle south on the first morning of my kayak trip to the Johnstone Strait and the Broughton Archipelago of islands, off the northeast corner of Vancouver Island. I launched at Alder Bay Resort, avoiding the circus of Telegraph Bay, the more popular but highly commercialized jumping-off point to this region for kayakers. It adds about five miles to the journey, but as I have never paddled here before, I don't mind. Within half an hour of setting out, two Dall's porpoises[53] surface a few boat lengths away from me, their dorsal fins leaving a tell-tale wake. I'm delighted to see wildlife this early on the trip. Fishing boats are abundant, both trawlers and gill-

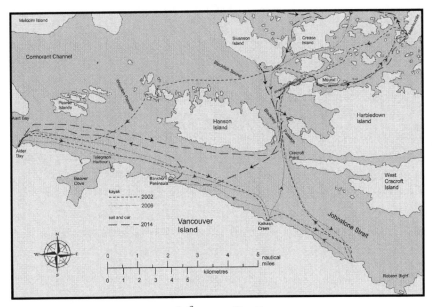

Johnstone Strait

netters, travelling to the fishing spots. The openings are usually so short that they are entirely focused on fishing, to the exclusion of all else. One large gill-netter steams by me at full speed within a hundred yards, trailing a large curling wake that I have to brace into. The wave breaks and dumps all over my deck and spray skirt. I am convinced yet again that skippers of most large power boats have no idea how large and how steep the wakes of their boats are, and have no idea of their effect on kayakers and other small boats. As I pass the Blinkhorn Peninsula close to shore, another gill-netter drops its skiff and pulls the net to the beach just ahead of me. The parent boat then begins to circle around to close the net. All well and good, except that I am in the middle of the patch of water that it is circling around. I have to turn around and paddle quickly to avoid getting caught in the net. They get very focused on fishing.

The wind stays calm, the sun leaches most of the blue out of the perfectly clear sky and the day warms up quickly. I am hot and thirsty by the time I reach Kaikash Creek, a popular kayak camp spot. I eat lunch in the shade of the trees while watching the passing parade of boats in Johnstone Strait. Although it is only early afternoon, I decide to stay put. I have only come about ten miles but I figure that is enough for the first day, and it really is a pleasant spot. One of the advantages of getting off the water early is that you get the pick of tent sites. It is a beautiful afternoon and I am content to laze it away. I have no particular agenda for the week ahead, only to paddle a little every day, see what is to be seen and be open to whatever experiences present themselves. Towards the end of the afternoon, three more groups of kayakers come in and set up camp. It does not feel crowded, though, as there is a lot of room under the trees and along the beach. I talk after supper to two families from the BC Interior and I sit up with them around their fire, watching meteors, as it is mid-August and the time of the Perseid meteor shower again.

* * * * *

It is a restless night, with the rumbling engines of passing tugs and fish boats going by at irregular intervals. After being awoken for the fourth or fifth time, I dig earplugs out of my kit and sleep better the rest of the night. In the morning, low fog is drifting across the Strait, concealing boats and ships, which we can hear but not see as they pass. It is bright above the fog, with no clouds in the sky, meaning the fog will likely burn off soon, but there is no hurry to get going until it does. After a leisurely breakfast I am just getting coffee ready when an excited cry comes from the kayakers on the beach; "Orcas!" I drop my gear, grab my camera and go out to the beach. The fog has largely lifted and there, just outside the line of kelp, are eight to ten orcas swimming slowly along. One is a male with his incredibly tall dorsal fin. In the calm, the clear water, defying gravity, clings to the backs and fins of the whales as they surface slowly, giving each whale a shimmering coat before it slides off to show shining black backs. The scene has an air of unreality about it, as if we are looking at near-mythical creatures, not just animals. In these waters, the ancestral home of the Kwakwaka'wakw people, whose relationship with the killer whales was rich and complex, this seems entirely appropriate.

I get going late and paddle slowly south along the shore towards Robson Bight Ecological Reserve. The Reserve restricts entrance of boats in order to provide sanctuary for the killer whales. Just before the reserve, I am just about to cross the Strait to the eastern shore, but I decide to first stop for lunch at an attractive pebble beach. I no sooner get out of the kayak and pull it up, when suddenly it goes from calm to a stiff wind from the north. There are two other kayakers already on the beach. Nobi is there in his single. Larry, a guide from a touring company, has paddled a double kayak down from the group campsite with several jugs to fetch water from the stream at the end of the beach. Against the ebbing tide, the rising wind soon kicks up a nasty chop. We sit there after lunch watching the wind and waves. I think that there is no point in trying to move further that day but Larry, who has no camping or sleeping gear with him, is anxious to get back to his group and bring them the water. About three o'clock, Larry says "I think the wind is easing off a little. I'm going to try to get back." "Are you sure?" I say, "It doesn't seem to me like it has dropped." "Yeah, I'm sure," Larry says, "If I pile the water jugs in the bow compartment, it will keep the bow from being blown off-course. Besides, it's mostly straight upwind." "OK, if you're determined, I guess. But be careful," I say, "I don't want to have to try to come get you if you capsize." I think it is a little foolhardy but we help Larry load the boat and hold it steady for him as he climbs in, then give him a good shove to start him on his way. He is barely moving, but he is moving (he is clearly a strong paddler) and he only has a little more than a mile to go. He eventually gets there but it must have been very hard work.

* * * * *

The best laid plans and all that. I intended to get up early and get across the Strait in the early morning calm. I set my alarm for half past five but when I get up there is no early morning calm, it is still blowing fifteen to twenty knots. The forecast, when I listen to it, calls for stronger gales than yesterday. I decide it will be another stay-put day and I turn over and go back to sleep. When I get up again a couple of hours later the wind has picked up to at least twenty-five knots.

I go along to the stream at the end of the beach and find a lovely little waterfall. I pump some water to fill my water bags and then have a very bracing shower under the waterfall. Although it is sunny, it isn't as warm as the day before. I check my thermometer and wish I hadn't – I see that the air temperature is only 13 degrees Celsius! The rest of the day I read, watch the boat traffic and talk to Nobi, who is also still wind-bound here. We are entertained by the many Steller's Jays[54] along the beach, squabbling, squawking and searching for food. After supper, a group of orcas show up off the point separating us from Robson Bight. They don't get very close but they are very active, spy-hopping, breaching and tail-slapping. It is difficult to tell whether this is social or hunting behaviour. It is probably the latter as earlier we saw a lot of salmon jumping.

We turn in not too long after sunset but are awoken at about eleven o'clock by the return of the orcas. It is too dark to see them but they are clearly much closer in, as we can hear them blowing. They keep it up sporadically through the night. I eventually have to resort to earplugs to get some sleep as their exhalations are quite explosive and startling when you are asleep. Who would have thought you can sleep ashore and be kept awake by whales?

* * * * *

Paddling in to Village Island, to see the village the island is named for, I see what looks to be an inviting beach in front of the village. The wind-ruffled water of the rising tide is just covering a number of barnacle-covered rocks on the mudflats in front of it. I manage to hit a few of the rocks on the way in. When I get to the beach, I find it full of broken glass and the bank behind the beach is very steep. I get back in the kayak and paddle around to a float just north of the village. Walking in to the village, I find Tom, a member of the local Kwakwaka'wakw first nation, who is about to give a tour of the village to a group of boaters that have stopped. Among the groups is a crew off a passing fish boat, and one of the crew is Buck, who I met last summer at Windy Bay in Gwaii Haanas where he was a Watchman.

Tom tells us that the village is called Memkumlis (also referred to as Mamalilikulla) and that it had been a fortified winter village. He explains that this village had long been a target for raiders from other First Nations and that there are defenses that are not obvious at first glance. These start with the boulders that have been placed randomly on the mudflats at various depths. The boulders are designed specifically to intercept war canoes which would have been paddling at full speed as they come in to raid. The canoes would have hit the boulders and capsized. The boulders are still doing their job, as I ran into them! The next line of defense is the high bank. The bank above the beach is a mixture of charcoal and broken bits of shell. Tom says that the charcoal is from generations of fires and that radiocarbon dating of the charcoal shows that the village dates to at least 4,000 years ago. It has been continuously occupied over all that time and the bank has been building up throughout. The bank edge, by the beach, was deliberately kept steep so as to be hard to climb. The only method of direct access was via log ladders, which could be pulled up when the village was attacked, denying the attackers easy access to the village. Defenders could then rain down logs, rocks and arrows on the attackers. The final defense feature of the village is a kind of back door – a hidden cove around the back where, if attackers were to get into the village, the villagers can escape on boats kept there. Tom says the village was never successfully attacked.

Tom tells us about the history and tradition of the Potlach to coastal people and how, among other things, it reinforced kinship and raised status for the chiefs who hosted them. Along with acquiring material goods, chiefs would sometimes acquire slaves through trade or by raiding to be given away at Potlaches. "Tom," I ask, "You talk about chiefs, commoners and slaves in First Nations society. Was there any upward mobility in that society? Could a slave ever become freed or could a commoner ever become a chief?" Tom says, "You ask hard questions. Generally, the answer is no. The Potlaches were very competitive, though, and slaves were very high value property. Giving them away really enhanced the status of the giver."

The village was occupied into the late 1960s but was abandoned then. The vegetation is slowly reclaiming the site, growing over the few frame houses that were built in the Twentieth century. Still evident, however, are some impressively large posts and beams that formed the front and back of a large long house. The roof and walls are long gone, but the three foot diameter posts and beams, with their fine adze work, lets you imagine what a large structure it was and how much coordinated work it required to build. Further along, in tangles of berry bushes, are a couple of fallen totems at the top edge of the bank. An exquisitely proportioned bear is evident on one and a very

Totem fragment at Memkumlis

fine wolf head at the end of the other. A few more years and these too will be gone, but that is the intention, to let them return to the earth from which the trees grew.

* * * * *

I have a small beach to myself just off the northeast side of Weynton Passage on the afternoon of the last night of the trip. I arrived at the Passage in good time but at full ebb. I don't risk the crossing as it looks dangerously turbulent out in the middle. I set up camp in the bright sunshine at the top of the beach just under the shade of a big tree. I spy a hammock slung between two trees up the hill on the opposite side of the bay. I walk over and climb in for a nap in the sunshine and breeze. On the way back, stumbling through the bush in my sandals, I stub my toe on a sharp branch end. I clean it off in the seawater back at the beach and think no more about it. I should have paid more attention to it as it develops into an infection when I return home, one that requires a course of antibiotics. I go out to the point to find some relief in the breeze from the heat. I pass the afternoon sitting with my binoculars birdwatching and boat-watching and, between spottings, learning a new harmonica tune.

Weynton Passage is an active place. On the way to the camp that morning, I saw rafts of Rhinoceros Auklets and Marbled Murrelets in Blackfish Sound north of Hanson Island. Here at the cove there is a pair of Oystercatchers that appear to own a rock just off the point, winkling out shells from the cracks. A Bald Eagle, perched in old growth tree on an offshore islet, surveys the pass all afternoon. Gulls, Cormorants and Murres[55] work the currents and eddies in the pass and a pair of Chickadees patrol the bush behind me. Three porpoises show themselves briefly just off the kelp. Out in the pass one of the world's ugliest vessels, a blocky container ship looking like a milk carton tipped on its side, heads north. As the afternoon turns to evening, sport fishermen and water taxis returning to Telegraph Cove and Alder Bay buzz by at full throttle, while transiting yachts take advantage of the last of the ebb. The day ends with the breeze dying away as the last of the light fades from the sky over the Vancouver Island shore. I haven't covered much territory on this trip, but as I didn't have any goals in mind, it doesn't matter. This is one trip where the journey really is more important than the destination.

*　*　*　*　*

Five years later, but a week earlier in the season, Carla and I return to Johnstone Strait with the double kayak. We make our first night's camp at Kaikash Creek again. Carla rinses out her paddling clothes, which took a dose of salt water as we nosed into the breaking wake of a huge inconsiderate mega-yacht that passed at speed too close to us this morning. The creek mouth is also popular with hundreds of California Gulls that are busy bathing and preening in the fresh water. They rise into the air in a noisy, wheeling cloud as we near the creek but soon settle back down as we crouch down to rinse out the clothes. On the paddle south this morning, we saw at least a dozen Harbour porpoises just past Telegraph Cove. This is more Harbour porpoises than I have ever seen in one place before. The campground is, as usual, very popular with kayak tour groups.

In the morning, as I sit after breakfast grinding our coffee beans with my portable grinder, a young man from the tour group next to us on the beach hears the noise and comes over to investigate.

"Are you grinding your own fresh coffee beans?" the young man asks. "Yes," I reply, "I am willing to put up with a lot of hardships while kayaking, but bad coffee is not one of them." "Oh man," he says, "we only have horrible instant coffee. Would you consider selling me your grinder and some beans?" "I feel your pain," I say, "But no, I'm afraid not. We're just starting out and we have a whole week to get through. Can't do it without fresh-ground coffee. It's a mission-critical thing."

The young man wanders disconsolately away.

* * * * *

As we paddle through Blackney Passage at slack, along with dozens of other kayaks and small boats, we are treated to a close-up viewing of a humpback whale and calf. They surface a number of times and, suddenly, the calf launches itself completely free of the water in a full breach. The sound of its landing is a loud as a cannon shot. It is a spectacular sight.

Climbing out of the kayak at the campground on Owl Island, Carla says, "My butt is really wet. There is a lot of water in my cockpit." I say, "It's probably leakage through the spray skirt from your paddle." "No," she says, "It's a lot more water than that, I'm really soaked." I look in the cockpit and sure enough, there really is a lot more than can be accounted for by splashing. When we have unloaded the boat and set up camp, we bring the boat up above the high tide line. I empty the water out of the forward cockpit and examine it. I can see very fine cracks in the epoxy coating of the hull plywood below the seat. The wood under the epoxy is looking a little wet. Turning over the boat, I can see that the oil-canning of that wide section of the bottom of the hull, which isn't really supported by much structure, has produced these cracks. I don't think the boat is about to fail structurally, but I have to do something about the leaks. I wash the outside of the hull where the cracks are and dry it. I dig out some heavy duty Lee Valley Tools duct tape that I have and lay down a series of strips over the whole area. I use my pocket torch to lightly heat it in order to partially vulcanize the glue and duct tape. At least, that is the idea. As long as we carry the boat and don't scrape the bottom over gravel or rocks, it should hold to the end of the week.

* * * * *

The light morning fog that greets us on rising in the morning thickens as we leave Owl Island and head north into Spring Passage. We can't see across to Bonwick Island or the cluster of Sedge Islands to the east. We debate whether to stay and wait for it to clear or to push on. After listening carefully, we decide there isn't that much boat traffic, and that we will be OK if we are careful. We take a compass bearing from the tip of tiny Wolf Island and head for the gap at the southwest corner of Bonwick. It is only a little more than a mile across, but a slightly tense twenty minutes later the shore of Bonwick appears to the right and High Island to the left. We feel somewhat safer creeping through the small islets around into Arrow Passage and across to Spiller Passage. The fog varies in density but clearly is not very deep as it begins to get lighter when the sun climbs higher in the sky. As we move past Mars Island and Tracey Island, the fog lifts altogether and shows us our destination, a beautiful little shell beach on Insect Island. Shell beaches of course don't happen by accident here and this is no exception. It is the site of the First Nations village of xoxop'a and a sign on the beach proclaims "This is Musgamagw Dzawada – Enuxw Territory Respect Our Land[56]" We are happy to do so with no-impact camping and we set up our tent on an area with no vegetation above the midden.

We have the island campsite to ourselves until dusk, when a trawler chugs into the bay in front of the beach, stops and lowers three kayaks into the water. On talking to them, we learn that they started from Seattle and drove up island but were delayed by a cancelled ferry. The late arrival means they have to set up in the dark, but they don't seem put off by that, which is not too surprising, as they are just about to embark on a great vacation. Getting a ride to the middle of the kayaking area instead of paddling there under your own power seems to me to be a little like cheating, but really, it is no more cheating than me driving my boat north on to a launch point on the other side of Johnstone Strait. If I was going to be a purist, every trip would start from my home in Victoria.

* * * * *

Travelling through Blackney Passage on the way to our next camp, we come on a large flock of Phalaropes[57] working the tide line. They are a shorebird, but have an unusual feeding strategy. They swim quickly in tight circles, which causes a small whirlpool to bring up small organisms to the surface, where the birds pick them off. A flock of hundreds of birds, like this is, looks quite frenetic when they are all feeding. They are so intent on feeding they ignore us as we drift through them without paddling, only lifting up and fluttering away a little if we get to within ten feet of them.

In need of fresh water, we ground the kayak on the fine pebbles of "lunch beach," as the beach north of Robson Bight is known by the kayak touring companies. I remember the fine stream and waterfall from my previous visit. The day is quite cool and cloudy, a good day for soup to warm up and re-hydrate. Although the wind doesn't rise, this is such a nice spot, with a fine view of the Strait, we decide to camp for the night. The cloud of earlier has thinned to the point where there is watery sunlight in late afternoon, but it stays cool as the sun goes behind the mountains and leaves the beach in deep shade. On the pebble shelf above the high tide line I start a fire to ward off the chill.

The evening clears right off and we sit by the fire and watch the busy traffic in the Strait - three cruise ships, several tugs towing large barges and innumerable commercial fish boats, yachts and sport fishing boats. Orcas also swim by offshore, twice, once heading south and later heading north. As the rising tide brings the small waves closer to our fire, an occasional larger wave sluices up through the porous beach stones and touches the hot pebbles and bottom layer of the fire, causing a great hissing and small cloud of steam, but not quite extinguishing the fire.

After one of these episodes, Carla says "Do you hear that?" "Hear what?" I say. "At the end of the beach, in the bush, I hear something crashing around," Carla says. "I don't hear anything," I say. A few minutes later Carla says, "There it is again." "Well," I say, "your hearing is definitely better than mine, what does it sound like?" "Something large, moving erratically," Carla says. "OK, it's likely a bear," I say, "I'll dig out the bear bangers and fire one off. You wanted to know what they are like anyway." I get out the bear bangers, screw one into the pen launcher, aim it down the beach, pull back the spring and flick the launch button. Bang! goes the launch cartridge and BANG! goes the banger at the end of its arc. There is more crashing, that even I can hear this time, which quickly dies away. We keep a sharp ear open, but there are no more noises for the rest of the night.

* * * * *

On the last evening of the trip, we find ourselves on the south side of the Blinkhorn Peninsula. We set up the stove down the beach in the open in order to catch the remains of the afternoon breeze and avoid the bugs. Black Swifts[58] dance in the clear air above the peninsula, feeding on unseen insects. We only wish they would come lower and reduce the population around us a little. Carla is watching the pot on the stove. The meal was a gift to me but it is something I have never tried before, a prepackaged meal with its own liquid. It is vegetables with some kind of cheese sauce. I step away from stove and am returning when Carla says "Dad! The sauce has gone all funny!"

"What do you mean?" I say. "What did you do to it?" I ask, unhelpfully. "Nothing, I was just stirring it when it suddenly thickened right up and wouldn't stir anymore!" Carla says. "Let's have a look," I say. Sure enough, the sauce has gone to a condition beyond congealed, to almost a rubber-like consistency. "Well, so much for that," I say, "We'll just have to have something else." We take the pot to the water's edge and pry the viscous mass out of the pot into the water. It sinks like a stone right to the bottom and some sculpins immediately rush over to experimentally nibble at it. It is too hideous even for them and they all take off again. Good thing we hadn't tried to eat it.

I build a fire and mix up a stiff batch of bannock. Winding the bannock around a couple of pealed alder sticks, we hold the sticks over the coals until the bannock is baked. As the sun declines, the light pales and the first stars begin to glimmer, we pull off the chunks of steaming hot baked bannock with our fingers while the swifts dance overhead.

View south from the Blinkhorn Peninsula

Vancouver Island
East - Shipyard Raid

As I accumulate more kayaking trips, I don't get any younger. By the early years of the Twenty-first century, I am having increasing problems with my shoulders, especially on the longer trips. Before I was a kayaker I was a sailor. While kayaking gave me access to amazing adventures, I began to think seriously about whether I could have it all. That is, find a small boat that I can sail when the wind serves and row when it does not, figuring that rowing will place less stress on my shoulders. I cast about for a couple of years, not finding what I was looking for. I went so far as to write up a little scenario that described how I might use such a boat, which I thought would serve as a design brief. I thought I might have to go to a naval architect and get a boat designed specifically for what I had in mind. Eventually, though, I discovered a class of boats known as "beach cruisers" or "sail and oar" boats that seemed suited for just what I intended. I focused my search on this type of boat. In 2003, I found plans for a boat designed by Don Kurylko of Nelson, British Columbia, based on just the kind of cruising that I had in mind. He designed the boat after making a 500 mile cruise on the east side of Vancouver Island. The design incorporated the lessons he learned from that cruise. He named the design Alaska, with the inference that the completed boat would be capable of making the journey up the coast that far.

The design is an adaptation of a type of traditional ship's boat called a Whitehall. It is essentially a long, transom-sterned (square stern) rowboat widened a little for increased sail-carrying stability. The cross sections have a classic wineglass shape at the back and it has sweet curving lines forward. It has a ketch rig that has a lot of sail area for the size of boat, about 130 square feet. I thought it looked ideal for my purposes and I sent away to Don for the plans. They arrived and I set about starting to build it in early 2003. I didn't have a hard deadline for completing the build, but what with starting a new career that summer that demanded much more of my time and learning the new building skills required, it took me more than 1,700 hours to build her. Five years after starting the build, I launched her for the first time

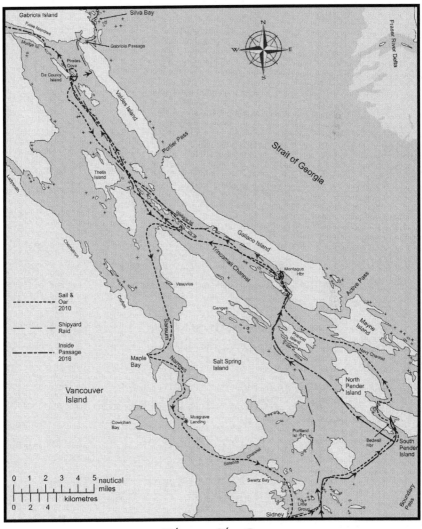

Sidney to Silva Bay

in August 2008. I named her *"Hornpipe,"* which means, according to the dictionary, *"a lively jig-like dance, performed usually by one person, and traditionally a favourite of sailors."*

* * * * *

I'd only had *Hornpipe* out on day sails in protected waters near home when I launched last year. This summer will be the first chance to go farther afield, to learn more about the boat and what it is capable of, and to use it more in the way in which I intended when I built it. I decide to enter myself and my new boat in the annual Silva Bay Shipyard Raid. It will be a chance to sail the boat in diverse conditions, to experience parts of the coast that I haven't seen before (at least by boat) and to hang out with like-minded people. The idea for this kind of event originated in Europe. A Raid is a multi-day, multi-stage race for rowing and sailing boats. It was brought to British Columbia by Tad Roberts of Silva Bay. Tad is a talented naval architect with an interest in small traditional boats and an encyclopedic knowledge of the traditional boats of the region. This Raid starts in Silva Bay at the south end of Gabriola Island in British Columbia and ends in Heriot Bay on Quadra Island, some 103 nautical miles (as the crow flies, not as the boat tacks) later. I also decide I will launch the boat three days earlier near home and row and sail it up to Silva Bay. I hope to get a little more familiar with the boat before the raid starts.

I launch *Hornpipe* at Sidney, British Columbia, on a Wednesday morning before the Saturday start of the raid. I set off in a steady rain and flat calm but at least it is not cold. The horizon is low and familiar landmarks, like our local volcano, Mt. Baker, are invisible today. What I can see is the layered effect of a typical rainy west coast day – the nearer landmarks clear, each island or object farther away a little more indistinct in the rain and mist until all is lost in the grey. It doesn't feel like an auspicious start but I can't afford to delay to nicer weather as I have to get to Silva Bay. My objective for the first day is Montague Harbour on Galiano Island, sixteen miles away. There are not too many other boaters out this morning except those who have to be because of their work – ferries, tugs with barges, crew boats. The first test I face is to stem the ebb tidal current in the "Little Group" Islands just north of Sidney. I am stymied, rowing against the current in the first opening I try and have to find a smaller opening and work the back-eddies. I finally do squeak through but painfully slowly. The next milestone is getting past Portland Island, which is a marine park. There are lots of boats in the favoured anchorage on the southeast corner as I row past but no one is venturing out in the rain. By this time it is getting on for lunch. I can't afford to stop for long, as the tide is still driving me back, so between strokes I grab bites of the sandwich I brought with me. I see some Harbour porpoises while I am eating lunch, and they are close enough for me to hear the soft sound of their blow when they surface.

The rain finally quits as I come abreast of Salt Spring Island and the tide is beginning to turn in my favour. I am making better progress but it is nearly half past three by the time I get to Captain Passage alongside Prevost Island – only ten miles of the required sixteen for the day. Fortune is in my favour as a light southerly breeze begins to rise and within twenty minutes I have all sail set and am broad reaching across the top of Prevost Island and into Trincomali Channel as the cloud begins to clear. The wind holds across the Channel and blows right up to the dinghy dock at the marine park. I tie up at the dock for the night as it turns out to be just as cheap as picking up a mooring and cheaper than camping ashore. I rig my tarp-and-batten tent over the boat for the first time and, once the dinghy traffic from the moored and anchored boats abates, settle in for the night.

* * * * *

I wake the next morning at dawn to the prehistoric squawk of a Heron[59] as he comes gliding in to the dock for his breakfast of small fish which he spears from the dock. Last night's wind has gone. The tarp worked well enough to keep the dew off but it moves around more in the wind puffs than I anticipated. I make my usual breakfast (Red River Cereal – a stick-to-your-ribs kind of Canadian porridge) and grind the beans for my coffee and think about the distance I have to cover today. It is eight o'clock by the time I pack up and row away from the dock. Contrary ebb tide and calm conditions are the story for the morning. I know at some point that I want to cross over to the opposite side of Trincomali Channel in order to avoid being drawn in to the tidal flow and turbulence of Porlier Pass. This happened to Spanish explorer Dionisio Galiano in the summer of 1792 when he explored the area. Like him I don't have a motor and I am subject to the same forces. I begin to cross too soon, however, and I'm caught in a strong current that begins to sweep me backwards. I have to cross back to the shore close under the cliffs of Galiano Island and work the back eddies, the same way I have always done when kayaking. I make much better progress and I'm pleased to find a quiet micro-bay under a cliff to stop for lunch. I carry on after lunch and cross the channel towards Wallace Island. By this time the clouds have largely broken up and the day is turning hot.

Progress along Wallace Island seems painfully slow but at length a breeze blowing in through Porlier Pass makes itself felt and I am able to raise sail. I am soon belting along at five knots on a beam reach, hiked out on the rail. The breeze grows stronger and gustier as I get opposite the Pass and I have to reef the main sail. Once past the pass the breeze gradually weakens and my speed drops to that of a slow saunter. Although I have found that *Hornpipe* ghosts along, with barely a ripple, on so little wind you can barely feel it on your cheek, eventually there is not even that much wind and I drift to a stop. Down comes the sail rig and I take up the oars on a glassy sea that reflects the high sun, baking me from both above and below as I row. My preferred destination of Pirates Cove on De Courcy Island is still five miles away. As I slowly sweat my way past a beautiful becalmed Atkin sloop from Gig Harbour, they offer me a tow, as they are going that direction on their way to the afternoon slack at Gabriola Passage. I'd been rowing on and off for seven hours by that point and a new set of blisters is forming. In a moment of weakness, I accept the tow. After a pleasant hour of motoring in the breeze created by the boat's motion and chatting with my hosts, they cast me adrift outside the cove on the south side of De Courcy. I row into the beach of the Marine Park, unload my gear and set up the boat on the clothesline mooring system[60] I have worked out, based on Don Kurylko's design. I am a little nervous about it, being the first time I have used it. After a little fiddling about I have it set up. It takes longer than I think and while I am absorbed in setting it up, the rising tide engulfs a few of my dry bags that I didn't set far enough up on the beach. Cursing myself at my inattention, I discover that the dry bag, an old one, that holds my charts, isn't as a watertight as I think it is. As I open it up, I find that there is not that much water in it. There is no real harm done as the affected charts soon dry in the sunshine. I set up camp ashore and, aside from raccoons investigating my dry bags at dusk, I pass a quiet night.

* * * * *

It is Friday morning and the critical timing for the day is to arrive at Gabriola Passage at slack tide at half past twelve. The tide can run more than six knots at full flood or ebb, far too strong to row against. I am in no particular rush as the Passage is only four miles away. I pack up the camp, haul the boat in and unrig the mooring. I row across Pylades Channel to investigate the sandstone formations on Valdes Island. The formations occur all along here and are the result of differing hardness in the various sections of rock reacting to rain, wind and sea. This results in the most fantastic shapes, scoops and hollows and trellises. As I get closer, I can see swallows swooping around and into and out of nests they have built in the stone pockets. By this time a north wind starts to fill in, enough to sail. I rig the mizzen sail only, in the centre mast position as I don't want to sail too quickly and arrive before the tide goes slack. This proves to be a better move than I anticipated as the wind coming over the south end of Gabriola Island from the Strait of Georgia builds and becomes quite gusty. In the gusts, the mizzen is just the right sail. Soon, a steady parade of powerboats starts to head for the passage. They are the bane of my existence the rest of the way to the pass. I swear some of these boats are dragging tsunamis behind them, their wakes are so steep. However, aside from a little water shipped over the gunwales, no real harm is done.

Getting close to the pass and close to slack water time, I tuck in behind a log boom moored to the shore, to escape the wind and wakes and eat my lunch. Then I'm out and into the last of the ebb to get through the pass at slack water. The wind is blowing stiffly straight across the pass. At this point I discover that the boat wants to weathercock[61] into this much wind. I am at a loss to explain why, as the bow ahead of the rowing station presents more windage, if anything, than the stern. I get through it first by rowing more on one side and then by dropping and lashing the rudder a little to one side to give me a counteracting force.

Silva Bay is about a mile past the pass, in protected channels, and I soon arrive in the bay. It has been decades since I was last there by boat and it has gotten a lot more crowded, with anchored boats nearly filling the bay. After a couple of false tries, I find the marina where the Raid is to start from and the designated float for the Raid boats.

I get *Hornpipe* tied up and her gear sorted away. I look around at the other boats on the dock. Next to me is a Wayfarer dinghy and a woman is standing next to it. "Hi," I say, "I'm Alex. Are you taking part in the Raid?" "That's right," the woman says, "I'm Jan. We've done the Raid several times." "Pleased to meet you," I say. Just then I notice a great roiling of bubbles under the Wayfarer's stern, and a diver's head surfaces. Jan says, "Meet Scotty, the other half of our crew." Scotty pulls his mask and regulator off, looks up and says, "Hi, welcome to the Raid!" "Glad to be here," I say, "Were you waxing the dinghy's hull to get more speed?" Scotty laughs, saying, "I wish. No, I was just having a scrub to get the weed and slime off. We keep the boat in the water and the growth builds up pretty quickly." "Well," I say, "I'd like to talk to you more about the Raid and what to expect." "No problem," Jan says. "Where are you staying tonight?" "I was planning on sleeping on the boat," I say. "Why don't you stay with us?" Scotty says, "We've got a small guest house and we live just across the road." That would be awesome," I say, "I look forward to it."

As the afternoon wears on, the other raiders begin to arrive. Cameron and Nigel drove down from Whitehorse in another Wayfarer. There are both Mower Dories belonging to the Shipyard School. The Port Townsend sea scouts are there with the longboat "Bear" as are the Kent, Washington seas scouts in the skin-on-frame Umiak, "Tuvaaq." Adding to the sail fleet is "Ratty," a gaff ketch designed for raiding by Tad Roberts and crewed by Trevor and his three very young sons. "Greyling," a Drascombe Longboat are crewed by Damien from Bowen Island and his buddy Jack from the UK. There is also "Tart," a heavier Brewer cat boat, built at the Shipyard School, in the cruising class. Finally, the most remarkable boat and crew has to be the only other single-hander, Colin, in his 1930s handliner, "Bus Bailey" (named after the original owner). There were once hundreds of these handliner boats in the Strait of Georgia in the 1920s and 30's, fishing salmon from these small boats using hand lines and selling their catch to buyer boats at the end of each day. Bus Bailey is a double ender about fourteen feet long, about four feet wide and weighing about 200 pounds. Colin normally rows it to work and back in Nanaimo about an hour each way. What Colin can do with that boat is remarkable. He puts everything he has into it and moves it at nearly four knots. Downwind, he puts up a little lug sail behind him and keeps rowing and moves it even faster. He can keep this up all day. All this I am to discover later, though.

The day ends with supper on the dock for all the raiders. It is a chance to get to know the other crews and talk about the upcoming Raid. Many crew are repeat offenders from previous editions of the Raid, and the stories of past Raids and weather and incidents abound. It turns out that I am the oldest participant, by a couple of years. For my part, my main motivation is to finish and finish safely. I am under no illusions that I will be competitive in an untried boat and a single-handed crew.

* * * * *

Saturday, day one of the Raid. The day's destination is a relatively short eleven miles along the outside of Gabriola Island to Pilot Bay at the north end. The wind is still from the northwest, but it has dropped in strength a little from last night. I am still a little apprehensive, never having raced the boat before. I am not at all sure how the boat will perform sailing upwind into the chop that is sure to be running outside the bay. The start line is inside the bay, between the many anchored boats. With the long straight keel on my boat hampering the ability to tack quickly, I am not likely to win any tacking duels in confined waters. Rather than a sailing start, I row out of the bay into open water before raising sail. I am still nervous about the wind and am way too cautious about sail area to start with – not putting up enough. Eventually I realize that I can, in fact, carry all sail if I hike out on the rail. I shake out the reefs I initially put in and I start making good progress to windward but I have likely lost nearly an hour compared to the rest of the fleet.

The day wears on with successive tacks on and off shore in the brilliant sunshine and the dancing blue summer water. Closing the shore, I can see beachcombers, sitting and generally just enjoying the weather at the seaside. Late in the afternoon, I reach the passage between Entrance Island, with its iconic lighthouse, and Gabriola Island where the shore turns to the northwest, for the run into Pilot Bay. At that point, the wind kicks up a little more, the sea gets very lumpy and this time I really do have to reef down. I find that with the reefed sails and the confused, lumpy sea in the pass, I simply cannot sail to windward. The pitching motion from the sea scrubs off the speed from sailing. I might have been OK if I had been able to drop the main mast and shift the mizzen to the centre mast position, but I am unwilling to lie broadside, without drive from the sails, in that sea state for long enough to make it happen. It seems to me there is not enough luff length with the reefed sails to produce the forward drive necessary in those conditions. After four ineffectual tacks I drop the sails and try rowing, but don't make much progress that way either. Tad comes along in the clean-up boat, and, once more I accept a tow, this time through the mess into Pilot Bay. With hindsight I should have anticipated the conditions in the passage, and changed the sail down to the mizzen before I got there. Live and learn, which is partly my motivation for the journey. I find out later that others also had difficulty weathering the pass and a couple of people who have outboards started them up and motored through.

Supper is provided on the mothership for the raid, "Temujin," a steel Colvin schooner. The boat crews swap stories about the day and talk about the day to come. That night at anchor in Pilot Bay, I rig the tarp over the boat again and turn in to sleep. The night is unsettled with the wind sending small wavelets into the bay, making for a jerky rocking motion. It doesn't keep me awake for long though. All goes well until about two thirty in the morning when a few gusts come up, They start pushing the boat around on its anchor line and flapping the tarp enough that I can't sleep in the snapping and banging noise it makes. I get up and take it down, spending the rest of night with it draped over me as a cover to keep the dew off. While I am unrigging the tarp, there is an amazing show of bioluminescence in the water, as the waves disturb the luminous small sea creatures. If I wasn't so tired, it would have been worth a swim just to see the light show.

* * * * *

Sunday morning dawns clear, and the wind has shifted overnight to a light southeast breeze, with a forecast of more wind to come later in the day. This is welcome news, as we face the longest leg of the raid. It is twenty-two miles north-northwest across the Strait of Georgia to our destination on Jedediah Island, between Texada Island and Lasqueti Island. This suits me fine, as it means we will be on a broad reach most of the day, which seems so far to be *Hornpipe's* best point of sail. After breakfast and the skippers' meeting, we organize ourselves for the start. This time, as the boats glide back and forth across the bay under easy sail in the bright morning sun, I am among them.

The start horn goes off and we sheet in our sails for the short beat out of the bay. Once out of the bay, we settle in to getting the best performance out of our boats in the light air downwind. Those boats with spinnakers fly them and the rest of us pay close attention to our steering and sail trim. I actually pass one of the Wayfarer dinghies, feeling good about it, only to find out later that they have neglected to raise their centreboard and which causes extra drag and slows them down.

The breeze begins to turn into a real wind sometime around about half past eleven. It occurs to me that if this is the start of the predicted stronger wind later in the afternoon, now will be good time to eat my lunch before I get too busy. It's a good strategy, as soon after that the wind gets stronger and I keep busy reefing the sails to reduce the area. Reefing the standing lug sails that comprise *Hornpipe's* rig involves dropping the whole sail into the boat, shifting the tack pennant, tying in the reef points as you come aft, then shifting the sheet to the reef clew. After that, you hoist everything back up again, haul down on the tack pennant

Hornpipe near Entrance Island

to tighten the luff and then sheet in. It doesn't take long, as I have the main halyard and tack pennant lead aft – perhaps two minutes. When the mizzen is up, the boat behaves very well with the main down, sitting there quietly hove to while the mizzen and tiller look after themselves.

As the wind increases, I first reef the mizzen and the immediately the boat's motion is more comfortable. Within twenty minutes the wind increases again to the point where I have to take the first reef in the main sail. The boat is again more manageable but within another twenty minutes the wind rises again to the point where I need the second reef in the main. The wind keeps rising until finally I drop the mizzen sail altogether. By the time I am down to just the double reefed main, in early afternoon, we have made a lot of progress across the Strait, and don't have far to go. The wind, however, is really strong, and more to the point, the sea state is beginning to catch up to it. I estimate the wind to be twenty knots with gusts higher than that. We find out later that this is wrong, that the wind is in fact a steady thirty knots, gusting to at least thirty-four, on the edge of being a gale. That is a huge amount of wind for a small open boat. Waves by now are routinely four to six feet high, with occasional waves to eight feet. At the bottom of the wave troughs I can't see over the tops. The day remains clear and sunny though, and with the sea sparkling blue in the sunshine, the foam showing bright white from the breaking waves and the snow-capped peaks on the mainland shore shining in the distance, it is irrepressibly beautiful. It is hard to feel properly apprehensive about the high wind.

I find out something about my boat then. *Hornpipe* is essentially a rowboat hull, and with its tucked up transom, it is a displacement hull[62]. I find out that the boat will in fact surf, which is a capability that displacement hulls are not thought to possess. At the top of those bigger waves, the wind strains the doubled-reefed main sail, the rudder starts to vibrate and hum and the boat takes off, surfing on the centre part of the hull. The experience is like the scene of the parting of the Red Sea in the Cecil B. DeMille movie "The Ten Commandments," with a foaming wave thrown out either side, high above the gunwales. After a few seconds of this, the peak of the wave gradually slides past under the boat and the boat subsides down off the surf into the following trough. On the milder surfs, when I have time to look, the GPS routinely records peak speeds of eight knots, and once more than nine.

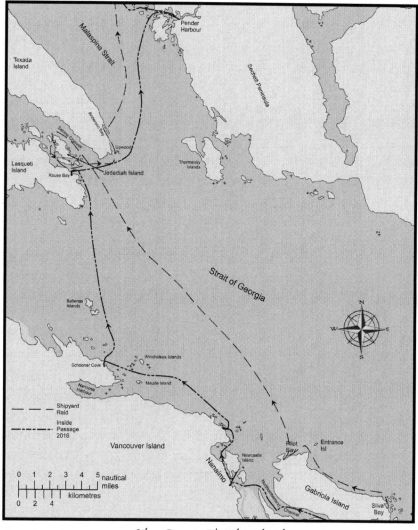

Silva Bay to Texada Island

I realize that I really have too much sail up and will be much better served by having only the mizzen sail up or the even the mizzen with the reef in it. But I have left it too late and am afraid to let the boat lie to while I shift masts to put up the mizzen in the centre mast position. I am afraid of rolling too far and maybe capsizing. Even without dropping the sails, I am worried about either broaching or having one of those breaking seas break on top of me from behind. This is not just a theoretical problem, as on the top of one wave in a bigger than usual gust, the boat starts to turn and the wave top begins to drive it further. I haul with all my strength on the rudder and hoist myself to the high side while I watch the gunwale get closer and closer to the water as a rush of fear spikes my adrenalin. Somewhat shakily, I manage to get the boat back under control. Time loses its meaning as I focus on my steering to avoid a repeat. My world has narrowed to only water, wind, breaking waves and sunshine. Slowly, slowly the islands ahead grow larger, until finally I can distinguish the opening to Sabine Channel, between Jedediah and Texada Islands.

About then I catch sight of a small blue lug sail showing above the waves just ahead. It is Colin in Bus Bailey, the fourteen foot handliner. Earlier as the wind and sea state increased I was convinced that, in those seas, Colin would be a goner. Not so. There he is, rowing like a mad thing to maintain direction (the boat has no rudder), with the sail behind him straining at its reef points. It nearly brings tears to my eyes to see that he is still afloat. I am amazed that he has come so far so quickly. I pass him, but not nearly as fast as I thought I would, given my bigger boat. It is a revelation to me to see what such a small boat can accomplish in the hands of a strong and skilled operator.

Codfish Bay on Jedediah Island, the days' intended destination, is completely exposed to the south. In this south wind it is a mass of white breaking wave crests and surf as I approach. Landing or anchoring there is clearly out of the question and I don't see anyone else attempting to enter. I carry on north up Sabine Channel following the Jedediah shore and finally the waves begin to lessen a little as the curve of the island begins to dissipate them. At the northern point of the Island I put the tiller over, and round up in the lee of the point. I drop the sail and just sit there in the williwaws that swirl around the point, drinking water and eating a power bar, recovering from all the tension, fear and excitement. A few minutes later, Colin shoots around the point and stops alongside me.

"Well, that was exciting!" Colin says, as he takes a swig of water. "Exciting?" I say, "I thought for sure we'd never see you again."

Colin laughs, "I had some tense moments, for sure, but this old boat can handle a lot." "That's clear," I say. "Where do we go now? The original landing place is obviously out." "Deep Bay," Colin says, "It's just down the west side of the island a ways. It faces west and there is plenty of anchoring room. Follow me."

I get out my oars and follow Colin into the narrow bay and up to its head, grounding on the rocky beach. Colin climbs out, reaches under the thwart into the bag he has there, pulls out a couple of beers and hands one to me. Right then it is the best beer I have ever tasted! We sit on a mossy rock above the bay and raise some of the others on the VHF. Some of the boats have gone to another bay while some have yet to come in. After talking to various boats and the mothership, we determine that where we are is the best place to stay for the night.

Supper that evening is a good thick stew served up by the Raid chef Trevor and his assistants. It is exactly the right thing after such a day. The talk flows freely as we hear the tale of the day *Tuvaaq's* tiller broke and she had to be towed in. One of the Mower dories, *Swordfish*, broke its mast at the base. They lashed it up to reduce its movement, reduced sail to just the jib and limped in. Everyone had an exciting time, a little too exciting for some of us. The more we talk, the stronger the wind was, and the bigger the seas. Generally, the bigger, heavier boats thrived and arrived in fine shape. After supper *Swordfish's* crew borrow some five-minute epoxy, scrounge some large pipe clamps, manufacture some splints from a beach log, repair their mast and re-install it just as darkness and high tide catches them. The wind is still blowing in the treetops above the cove as we turn in, but down at water level all is calm at anchor. I fancy the wind begins to ease as we go to sleep wondering what the next day will bring.

* * * * *

The following morning the strong south wind of the previous day has dropped but it hasn't completely died away. Today there

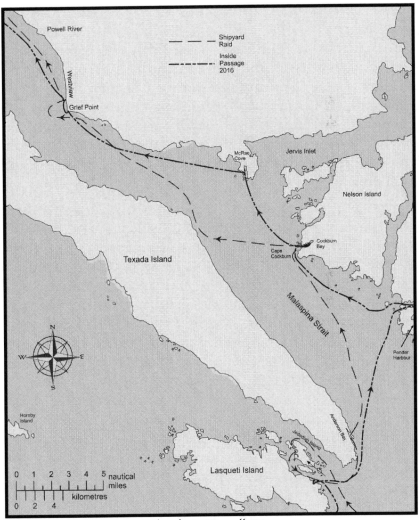

Texada to Powell River

is to be two legs. The first leg is to be around the south ends of Jedediah Island and Texada Island and into Anderson Bay on the east side of Texada, with a stop there for lunch,. This will be followed by a longer leg in the afternoon to Cockburn Bay around Cape Cockburn on Nelson Island, near the mainland.

The start is upwind south around Jedediah and then, theoretically, is a reach across to get around Upwood Point at the south end of Texada Island. The water is mercifully flat beating out past Jedediah and the Wayfarers and the Mowers soon take the lead. The rest of us are scattered at various distances behind. Part way across Sabine Channel the wind shifts a little to the southeast and what had been a reach turns into almost a beat. None of us can fetch[63] the point on one tack, so, one after the other, we all tack out into the Strait to gain enough offing. At the point itself, the tide and wind are at cross-purposes, making for a lumpy confused sea. The confused patch doesn't extend very far and we are soon around and gliding downwind into Anderson Bay. As we collect for a very late lunch at the mothership, the last boats straggle in.

By the time we re-start for the afternoon leg it is after three o'clock and the winds are beginning to build in Malaspina Strait between Texada Island and the Sechelt Peninsula. I find at the start that I can carry all sail on a broad reach, but in less than an hour, I have to drop the mizzen again. It is another afternoon of sparkling water, sunshine and rising wind. This time the wind really is about twenty knots, and pretty much a dead downwind run to Cape Cockburn. This also turns out to be a good point of sail for *Hornpipe*. Once again I am smoking along, surfing on the bigger seas, although they aren't nearly as big or scary as yesterday. The sailing is exhilarating and although there isn't quite the same edge of fear as the day before, there are mishaps in the fleet from carrying spinnakers too long. One boat muffs its spinnaker take down, sails over the spinnaker and loses a lot of time sorting it out. Another decides to cut the spinnaker sheet and let all fly as the wind suddenly gusts dramatically.

Running dead downwind and making good speed, I catch up with all the boats but one before Cape Cockburn. I know I will have to gybe the main sail just past the Cape for the right turn into Cockburn Bay. I contemplate just how to do this safely (I really have too much sail up again) when all of a sudden the boat rolls to windward on top of a wave. The wind catches the back of the sail and it gybes over by itself with an awful slam, shaking the mast in its step and vibrating the whole boat. Nothing breaks or carries away and there I am, gybe accomplished. I ease the sheet, change course and run in behind the protection of the Cape, towards the Bay.

The Bay turns out to be relatively sheltered from the wind but Cape Cockburn is low and narrow. It doesn't offer much resistance to the south wind which reaches across the top of the Cape into the bay and which blows out of the bay erratically in gusts. The gusts are strong and in one of them *Hornpipe* heels so much that her gunwale is nearly driven under the water. At this point, I figure discretion is the better part of valour and drop the sail to row in the rest of the way. I hear later that one of the Wayfarers actually rolled over far enough in one of the gusts to ship twenty gallons of water into the cockpit. The Bay is the site of an old logging dump and marshaling yard, now overgrown. It makes a relatively flat area for tenting, though, and several of the boats crews elect to set up their tents ashore. After a quiet evening, we all turn in for an even quieter night.

* * * * *

Hornpipe was rafted up overnight to Greyling, which was moored offshore. I wake to find that both Damien and I have misjudged the state of the tide, and both boats are sitting with their forward halves on the shore. The tide is rising, though, and we know they will be entirely afloat by the time breakfast is over. At the Skippers' meeting, Tad announces that, to mix things up a little, the first hour of the day's leg north to Westview will be rowing only. This will favour Bus Bailey, Tuvaaq and Bear, and the more energetic of the dinghy crews. It will not be so good for

Bus Bailey, Hornpipe and Tuvaaq in Malaspina Strait

the heavier boats or a single-hander like me who is only good for a sustained speed of about two and half to three knots.

The weather is clear again and the wind is forecast to be light and variable for the day. Sure enough, after the rowing hour is over, there is only a light south wind that soon dies away. I can see ahead that past a patch of calm, a north breeze is setting in, as the various boats ahead are heeled over and beating into the wind. When my following breeze dies away I row through the calm patch into the north breeze and raise all sail.

It is a beautiful day of bright sunshine and relatively flat seas. The fleet separates on long tacks upwind across Malaspina Strait, working towards Grief Point just south of Westview. I keep to the mainland shore as I get closer to Grief Point. I count on flatter water behind the Point and I figure that the wind will curve around the point and give me a better slant. The wind does indeed curve around the point and the water does flatten out a little. I have guessed right for once and I gain a place on one of the Mower Dories who crossed to the Texada Island side. Around the point I lose ground again as I have to tack offshore to avoid a tug and log boom close in to shore between me and the destination at the government harbour. The breeze dies away in the last half mile and I row in. The government docks in Westview are nearly full of commercial fishing boats which necessitates that we all raft up, four deep, to other boats. There are public showers at the head of the dock and it is pure luxury to wait in line for a turn under the fresh water to wash away the salt and sunscreen.

Tuesday is the cook's night off, and we are thrown on our own resources for supper. Most of us end up at a Mexican restaurant recommended by the locals. By an amazing coincidence of timing, their new liquor license, which they applied for some time ago, arrives between the time of the first crews ordering their food and the later crews. The laggards like me get to have a Corona with their supper while the early birds don't. Back down to sleep on the boat, I rig the tarp over a line between the masts, without battens and with the ends tucked under a couple of oars to make a small tent. Although not much room, it works fine to keep off the dew and is less trouble to rig.

* * * * *

In the morning the day dawns clear again and the forecast is for light and variable winds. It is already warm in the morning, holding a promise of getting fried by the sun later in the day. Our destination this morning is Lund, not too far away. The day starts off calm, with everyone rowing, but a light north breeze comes up, allowing everyone to tack northward, much like the day before. The breeze only holds for an hour and half before sputtering out to calm, after which we are all back to rowing. The shore moves by painfully slowly in the heat and Lund doesn't seem to get any closer until suddenly it's there. At the end of this first leg, I nip a Wayfarer at the finish line and am quite a way ahead of one of the Mower Dories, whose crew decline to do as much rowing in the heat. I am hot and dehydrated by the time I get to the concrete breakwater that serves as outer mooring. I sit in the shade, eat lunch and rehydrate, passing up the potential delights of strolling around Lund.

There is an evening short sprint leg, rowing-only, between us and our destination for the night, the Copeland Islands, only about two and half miles away. The start horn goes off and I lay into my oars but can't keep up with the two-person boats or the longboat or the umiak. This leg is just made for Colin in Bus Bailey and he finishes first or second.

The anchorage at the Copeland Islands is beautifully sheltered and has a great view to the northwest. The water in the Strait of Georgia warms noticeably as you get near to this part of the Straight, as the tidal streams from north and south around Vancouver Island meet up just north of here. As the summer wears on, the water gets warm enough that swimming is no longer an exercise in staving off hypothermia. The kids from the longboat have a great time swinging from a topping lift on the mother ship into the water and climbing out and doing it again. I don't know where the kids get the energy, as they have been rowing that heavy boat all day. At dusk I rig the tarp and drift off to sleep in a very quiet bay with the night air still warm.

* * * * *

The night was peaceful, aside from a few mosquitoes - which zeroed in on my ear of course. The destination for today is north to Eveleigh anchorage, on the edge of Desolation Sound, just outside the very popular yacht anchorage of Prideaux Haven. The rule for today's stage is sailing-only for the first two hours. As there is a light southwesterly breeze at the start, meaning a broad reach, this pleases me. I do well right from the start and I'm lying third as we round Sarah Point and head east to Eveleigh. The day's tactical challenge is whether to go south or north around Mink Island, which lies across the direct course. I opt for south, hoping that the southwesterly/westerly breeze will funnel along the island and hold through the pass at the east end of Mink Island.

The wind holds as a following light breeze until the pass, but it is not strong enough to overcome the wind shadow of Mink Island in the pass. As it dies away, I take up the oars and begin to notice the ebb tide which is setting through the pass against me. Meanwhile, one of the Wayfarers, who got into the pass ahead of me, catches a brief wind slant and scoots through. No such luck for me - I fight against the ebb in nearly calm air. It feels like rowing through molasses, but eventually I get clear. The wind is so light for the remainder of the distance to Eveleigh that it is a toss-up whether sailing is faster than rowing. I end up rowing the last mile and am nipped at the finish line by the second of the Mower dories. Most of the other boats took to their oars earlier and are in ahead of us. This day, the Umiak is first in.

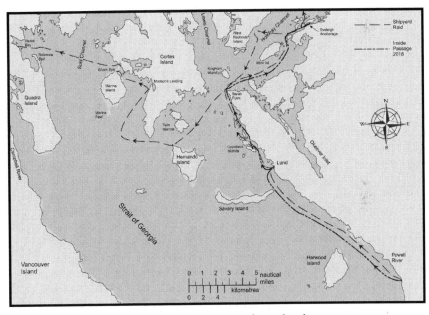

Powell River to Quadra Island

Once anchored, the day is still very hot. The water looks inviting and I jump over the side for a swim to cool off. As I come back to the boat it occurs to me that I have never before tried to scramble back on board from the water. I am not sure I can do it. After hanging off the gunwale awhile and thinking about it, I throw one leg over the side, keep my weight low, and roll in. The boat is just stable enough. The evening turns absolutely calm and it remains warm until after dark. The clear skies far away from the city lights mean there is a spectacular view of the stars.

* * * * *

It remains calm throughout the night and it is warm in the morning as the sun rises and shines through the gap in the trees at the east end of the anchorage. The anchorage is beautiful in the morning sunshine, and sitting eating breakfast on the mothership, drinking coffee and chatting with the other raid participants and supporters in anticipation of the day, it seems to me that this life is pretty sweet. At the morning skippers' meeting, we learn that distance to be covered over the day is nineteen miles to Manson's Landing on Cortes Island but is to be broken into two legs. The first is to be a longish morning leg retracing part of the way we came the day before, as far as Sarah Point, then on around the south end of the Twin Islands to a stop at the spit on Spilsbury Point at the north end of Hernando Island. The second is to be an afternoon leg after lunch west and south around the shoals and bell buoy at the south end of Cortes Island, then north up to the government dock at Manson's. Winds are forecast to be light and variable again, much like the day before.

At the start, once we clear the anchorage we find a light head wind from the west southwest, but it is enough to give us good sailing. The fleet scatters across the channel to the West Redonda Island shore, crossing tacks, as we make our way back to Sarah Point. There is more wind than the day before, at least as far as the point. I occasionally have to reef as it puffs up, just about driving the lee rail under during the puffs, then shake the reef out again as it drops. While this is necessary to keep the sea on the right side of the hull, the reefing and unreefing definitely costs me time. Past Sarah Point, in the early afternoon, the wind begins to fall lighter. The more weatherly[64] boats who get there first hold the wind further towards Marina Island. I can see them ahead rounding the Twin Islands to head for the spit. With the breeze steadily dropping, I am still ahead of the Umiak, but the afternoon is getting on. Just as the wind is dying away altogether and I contemplate a switch to oars, Tad comes along with the clean-up boat, towing the Umiak and telling me to hook up too for a tow to the spit. We have a long way to go that day and he doesn't want to delay the restart for the afternoon leg too long. I sit back and enjoy the breeze created by the tow.

As we wait for the next start, the wind picks up again, this time from the south. This means that all the boats are on a reach at the start as we round Spilsbury Point and head west towards the bell buoy. The shoals extend a long way out from Cortes Island, and while they are obvious on the chart, they are invisible from the water. It feels like we are heading to the middle of nowhere. We have a great sail with plenty of wind to move us to the buoy, and we all round it in fine style, with not much of a spread between first and last boats. Once round the buoy the wind begins to slacken again. The keeners take to their oars sooner to maintain speed, the rest of us hang on to our sails a little longer and take up our oars later. We all row the last couple of miles to the anchorage in front of the government dock at Manson's Landing.

The summer high pressure system is still in place and the evening is once again calm, warm and clear. The fleet anchors among the existing boats spread out along the shore some pull their boats onto the beach and camp ashore. I misjudge my anchoring spot, and I am too close to another boat when the tide swings us. Of course I only notice this after I have the tent rigged and everything set up for the night. I have to get up again, take the tent down and anchor a little further away.

* * * * *

It is Saturday and the last day of the Raid. On waking I look past my feet out the end of the tent and don't see any water, only sand and rocks. Looking over the side, I see that I have misjudged the depth where I anchored and have only about eighteen inches under my keel. While this is enough to float the boat now, the tide is still dropping and will ground me out shortly. Clearly I have to move. Although it is an hour at least until breakfast, I head over to the mothership in hopes that the coffee will be on early. It is, and the cooks are busy fixing breakfast. I pitch in to help peel and cut the potatoes for hash browns. Soon, breakfast is ready, the other boats begin arriving and the day is truly underway. I am a little nervous about today. I experienced a significant blow while on a kayak trip in this area several years ago on the stretch of water between Cortes and Quadra Islands, which is completely open to the Strait of Georgia to the south. On last years' Raid, this apparently was one of the windiest legs of the entire Raid, and one of the boats capsized.

The day is also to have two legs – a late-ish morning start for a short sprint to Shark Spit on Marina Island for a lunch stop, followed by the last leg across to Heriot Bay on Quadra Island in the afternoon.

There is a northerly wind at the start blowing into Manson's Landing. It is uneven enough that, like the day before, I have to reef a couple of times in the gusts. This loses me ground to the boats that don't have to reef. I eventually decide that, since the destination is dead to windward, I can make better progress by rowing, which I do, and get into the spit ahead a couple of the other boats – it feels good not to be dead last. The day is warm and sunny as we wait for the other boats to come in. We beachcomb, rest and talk, and tend to the boats on the rising tide. As we have lunch and listen to the weather forecast, it seems that the wind is blowing strongly from the northwest in Johnstone Strait, the other side of Quadra Island, not too far away. This aligns with the light northerly wind we are experiencing over the spit. During lunch, however, that wind dies and then unaccountably begins to blow from the south, and fairly briskly at that.

The afternoon start is to be a very short run to the narrow passage north round the spit, then a reach across the south end of Sutil Channel towards Heriot Bay on Quadra Island. I start out with just the mainsail up, as it is too strong for both sails. The wind gusts up and down the next hour or so, keeping me busy reefing and unreefing, losing ground to the boats that can carry more sail. Finally the wind settles into a steady eight to ten knots from the south. This suits me fine, and with all sail set, I make good time, a steady four knots. It is a wonderful sail the last four miles across Sutil Channel in the bright sunshine and blue water and, although I am dead last by now, I don't mind at all. The wind holds right until the tip of Rebecca Spit, a mile from Heriot Bay. Once past the spit, the wind drops off and a big powerboat wake shakes what wind there is right out of the sails, leaving *Hornpipe* wallowing on the wake.

I pull across the last mile to the finish line just outside the government dock and just ahead of the ferry coming in from Cortes, get the finish horn blast from Tad, and my raid is over.

It has been a terrific eleven days. I learned a lot about the boat in a short time and met some great people. The weather for the most part was terrific, notwithstanding too much wind for my comfort on Sunday and Monday. The only rain I saw was the first day as I set out from Sidney to take the boat up to Silva Bay. We covered a lot more ground than I likely would have if I had been single-handing during the same days, as I tend to be more cautious when on my own. I likely would have started sooner in the morning and been off the water sooner, perhaps avoiding the worst of the strong winds that we had Sunday and Monday. As for the competition aspect of the raid, I tied for seventh overall, which I consider a not-too-shabby performance for an old guy like me single-handing a new boat. I learned that my boat would likely be more competitive in a raid if it had a crew of two. The extra weight, hiked out to windward, would mean that sail could be carried longer. Two oarsmen would likely mean a rowing speed of closer to four knots than two and a half, which would make a considerable difference in the rowing-only legs and light air sailing plus rowing. In sum, it was a great time and a great event with like-minded people. I was glad I took part and glad I experienced a new section of coast.

Gulf Islands by Sail and Oar

Haro Straight at eleven in the morning and the skies are gloomy from the low cloud, the wind is beginning to rise and there is more swell than I counted on, rolling in from the Juan de Fuca Strait to the southeast. Have I made a mistake?

The day starts out well enough, the first of the week that I've managed to carve out away from work for a short cruise in the Gulf Islands. The morning is clear at my house but by the time I load the gear into the car, drive down to the ramp at Cattle Point in Oak Bay and get the boat launched, low marine cloud moves in from the southeast. I am a little worried, as Oak Bay and the south end of Haro Strait are open to the east entrance of the Strait of Juan de Fuca. The Strait is a wide body of water where the weather can change suddenly. With the cloud coming in, perhaps the forecast is wrong and there is some high wind on the way. I row away from the ramp by ten and have a good reach under all sail and a moderate southeasterly breeze across to Ten Mile point. The tide will be rising all day. It should be an easy passage northward through Baynes Channel, which is notorious for its currents and tide rips. There is a favourable current when I get to the channel, but there is still some weird waves and slop where the current through the channel meets the water coming around the east side of Chatham Island. Running on a broad reach now, *Hornpipe* is moving well and we are soon through.

Once into Haro Straight, there is a reasonable amount of traffic around, with always a boat or two in sight. I'm alongside Zero Rock. The breeze is variable and rising, and just at the point when I wonder whether I have too much sail up, the breeze begins to drop. Nearing James Island[65] and Darcy Shoal, the sun manages to break though from the west. The clear patch of sky over the

Hornpipe on a reach

land pushes back the cloud over the water. The sun sparkles on the water and puts an altogether different complexion on the day. It looks a lot more cheerful now and my tension from earlier melts away. Where I want to go, down Sidney Channel between James Island and Sidney Island, is straight downwind. *Hornpipe* isn't at her best on a downwind run with both sails up. In that configuration she rolls and wants to gybe the mizzen sail. Instead I bear off about twenty degrees and alternate gybes downwind, filling the mizzen and main both on each gybe, and although I travel farther I make better boat speed. The breeze freshens again through Sidney Channel. The anchorage at Sidney Spit, which is about fourteen miles from the launch ramp, draws abreast at one o'clock. I calculate that I averaged over four and a half knots along my course, including the extra distance for the gybes.

Approaching the end of the Spit, I catch up with a thirty-six foot sloop. On this point of sail and in this wind speed, I overtake him. This tickles me as he is exactly twice my length. Mind you, he is not flying a spinnaker or drifter, just a large genoa and the main sail. Past the lighthouse on the Spit, the wind shifts a little to the east. Now Portland Island/Princess Margaret Marine Park, my day's destination, is dead downwind once more. I find that I have to sail toward Forrest Island then gybe towards Coal Island. Through the gap at the Little Group Islands, the wind starts to drop and the water gets very sloppy again from the tidal action through this constriction. The wind continues to drop which means that I can't sail as directly downwind. I have to head up more to keep the apparent wind up and the sails filled. However, I am in no hurry and there is now lots more boat traffic to be on the lookout for. I stick to sailing, where I can more easily see forward, rather than break out the oars. I eventually drift in to the main anchorage at around four o'clock. I feel good about this first day. The sailing was challenging and the bad weather that I feared never materialised. There is now a dinghy dock on the west side of the bay, added since I was here last, which is very nearly twenty-five years ago, now that I come to think of it. I stop at the dock briefly to read the sign, which tells you that you can't land any boats but dinghies at the dock. The sign also points out the designated campsite in the old farmyard meadow at the head of the bay.

This island has an interesting history. After thousands of years of occupation and use by First Nations, some of the first non-native settlers in the late 1800s were Hawaiians, who called themselves Kanakas at that time. There is still a Kanaka Bluff on the west side of the island. In more modern times it was a sheep farm and was then donated to the Province. The Province made a present of it to Princess Margaret, who kept it for a couple of years before giving it back to the Province to be used as a park. In its first years as a park, it had feral sheep that roamed free, destroying much native vegetation before they were culled.

I row over to the beach, but not before I crunch directly on to one of the few below-water rocks on the beach. I hit directly on my polyethylene keel shoe, and fortunately no damage is done. Up on the meadow, I discover a mini village of tents that turns out to be a University of Victoria summer archaeological field camp.

They are there to map middens and other First Nations sites. I come back to the boat to try the depth off the beach, thinking to set the boat out with the clothesline mooring and camp ashore. However, the water is shallow quite a way out, beyond the reach of my line at low tide. I'll have to sleep on the boat at anchor.

After supper on the beach and a short stroll around part of the island, I move the boat out and set the anchor. I string the line between the masts and set up the tarp and sleeping platform on the thwarts. While I sit reading before I turn in, I discover a vice of the boat that I didn't notice last year when sleeping on the boat. There is still a little breeze from the south sending ripples into the bay. The boat seems to get sideways to them – there is not enough windage aft with the tarp rigged to keep the boat pointed into the wind I suppose - and hit some kind of resonant frequency with the ripples. It then rocks and rocks out of proportion to the size of the ripples before it hits a maximum amplitude, when it settles down. It does it again on the next set of ripples. As it is nearly dark, and I have no better anchorage to go to, I decide to live with it and turn in wondering whether I be able to get any sleep.

* * * * *

The rocking keeps me fitfully awake until about ten thirty, after which the breeze and ripples must have died, because I don't remember much after that. Awake again at six thirty, I row into the beach to cook breakfast and make my morning shot of caffeine. Nobody from the archaeology field camp is up yet. The sun rises well north of east and it does not yet reach this south-facing beach, backed by tall trees above the tideline. It is cool in the shade but calm and it is a very peaceful start to the day. I leave by eight o'clock in a calm with a high overcast sky. There are not many boats out but I soon begin to see Harbour porpoises, at about the same place as last year on my row up to Gabriola Island for the start of the Shipyard Raid. They are shy creatures that don't spend much time on the surface and you don't hear them blow unless you are in a quiet boat like a rowboat or a kayak. I wonder to myself whether the porpoises are territorial[66].

The current off the east side of Portland Island is still going south, in spite of the tide having turned to flood. It seems there's a reason they call them tidal predictions. Still in the calm, I row past Beaver Point on Salt Spring Island. There are lots of campers in the park there, which is a land-based park with no easy access by water as it is too exposed and rocky. Moresby Passage is the scene of lots of ferry activity, both the big ferries to Tsawwassen on the mainland and the smaller ferries to the Gulf Islands. There is enough room for me to avoid them and they produce such a long period wave from their wake that they are not a problem for smaller boats unless you are really close. When the wake passes underneath me, I feel like I am going up and down on an elevator. Around Beaver Point, it is still cloudy and calm up Captain Passage. Finally there appears to be a breeze ahead north of Prevost Island in the opening leading to Trincomali Channel, if I can get to it. I'm getting hungry and while it is still calm I stop rowing and drift while I eat lunch and watch the scene. After lunch, a few puffs make themselves felt from the northwest and I can raise sail. I'm able to tack through the channel north of Prevost into Trincomali Channel, but not much further. I resign myself to a long afternoon of beating upwind, but at about two o'clock the wind drops and the sun comes out. It falls to a flat calm and I have to drop the rig and go back to the oars. There is lots of boat traffic about now, including three Navy boats. These are the junior officer training vessels which replaced the old minesweepers that were used for that purpose in my day. Clearly they need the training, because they come way too close to me, don't slow down and leave too big a wake. I don't quite get swamped but it is a near thing.

I keep rowing in the heat and the sun, having no alternative. I keep hoping for the daytime heating to produce some kind of breeze to cool off or sail in. It doesn't materialise though and I wearily arrive in late afternoon at Conover Cover on Wallace Island. Wallace Island is another marine park that also had a brush with celebrity. It was owned for many years, from the 1940s to the 1960s, by David Conover. He, among other things, took the first publicity photos of Marilyn Munroe. She also visited the resort that Conover operated on the Island. After later ownership by a group from Seattle, who tried to develop the island but couldn't because of lack of fresh water, and then by a couple from California, the island was eventually acquired by the Province, except for some land still privately held.

The Cove is busy, with a number of boats anchored stern-to the mooring rings set in the rocks ashore. The dock is almost full, but, determined to avoid last night's rocking at anchor, I manage to snag a spot that is left when a visiting day boat departs. Of course, as soon as I dock, the hoped-for breeze from the southeast comes up and begins to curl into the cove. I am done for the day but the breeze provides a break from the heat. I guess my boat looks small and vulnerable next to the other boats at the dock, for I soon have a supper invitation from the couple on the Catalina sloop next to me. They are from Galiano Island and are also hosting friends of theirs who have kayaked over from Galiano. At first I'm reluctant, not wanting to sponge, but they say they have run out of ice and the food will spoil if not eaten. Well, that is a different story, anything to help out and keep food from going to waste! Supper is of much higher calibre than what I planned and is accompanied by homemade wine which is actually very good. After supper, our host brings out his guitar and I break out my harmonica and we have a bit of a sing-along.

Raccoons are an issue on Wallace Island and they have become habituated to boats on the dock at Conover Cove. People have fed them in the past and now they associate boats with food. People warn me that with my open boat I will be a target for them come darkness. I carefully stow my food dry bag underneath the sleeping platform, figuring that they will have to go through me to get to the food, and then turn in, wondering how I will fare with the masked bandits. Sure enough, after dark, a whole family of raccoons comes sauntering down the dock as if they own the place, growling and tussling with each other.

Still, they don't seem to be bothering me and I drift off to sleep. Suddenly, I feel a motion and noise on the boat and look aft to see the big male tugging at my life jacket. At that point it dawns on me that I've left an opened power bar wrapper tucked into the mesh pocket of the life jacket and that must be what he is smelling. I chase the raccoon back onto the dock and put the wrapper away, but now the damage is done. The raccoon is sure I have more food where that came from. I try to get back to sleep but he keeps coming back and dropping into the boat. I get out one of my large parachute flares to use as a cudgel, but he is too quick for me, just dancing out of reach every time I take a swipe at him. Finally, he drops down off the dock onto the middle of the boat just outside the tarp. I connect with a good two-footed boot from inside the sleeping bag that lifts him back to the dock and that seems to provide enough discouragement. After that I am left in peace for the rest of the night.

* * * * *

In the morning it is late before I get underway, nearly nine o'clock. There is no wind at the start as I row along the length of Wallace. I go through the pass at Chivers Point and wave to the kayakers camped there as I go by. Once through the pass, a slight but welcome breeze comes up, from the direction of Porlier Pass and Georgia Straight. I raise sail but the breeze is quite light and almost heading me. I persist and favour the starboard tack along the Secretary Island shore, figuring on a lift as I get closer to Porlier Pass. That's in fact what happens and my experience for the next few miles is almost exactly a repeat of last year in the same place. The wind builds to the point where I have to tuck in a couple of reefs in the main, and I blast along on a reach. Alas, it doesn't last, and I have less than an hour's sailing before the wind dies alongside Reid Island. Back on the oars I row until about noon and stop for lunch. Boat traffic is steady but not heavy. The afternoon continues hot and calm as I row right up to the anchorage on the south side of Pirates Cove on De Courcy Island, which I reach mid-afternoon. Pirates Cove is quite a popular stopping place for yachts but the open cove to the south is not as busy, and provides better access for kayakers and small boaters. It has a good campground among the old growth Douglas Firs.

The island has a colourful history. The most notable inhabitant was Brother XII, a charismatic cult figure who set up shop on De Courcy in the 1920s and 30s. He talked passing boaters out of their money and occasionally convinced them to join him. They were there to survive the Armageddon they were sure was coming. Eventually internal stresses, precipitated by the cruelty of Brother XII and his main mistress, a Madame Z, led the followers to bring a court case against him to recover the money they had donated. They won the court case but before the money could be awarded, Brother XII absconded with the money and disappeared, along with Madame Z. For a long time after, rumours persisted that he had buried the money on the island, but no one ever found it if he did.

Once again, after I stop, having rowed far enough for the day, the breeze comes up. I set up the boat on the clothesline mooring and take my camping gear ashore and set up camp. I awkwardly manage a wash under the campground pump and it feels good to get the salt off. Aside from half a dozen boats at anchor in the cove and the usual crowd of boats in Pirates Cove itself, the only other campers are two novice women kayakers who paddled over from Vancouver Island near Cedar. I feel like I have done an honest day's work and I feel very content as I finish the evening sitting reading on the beach in shorts and t-shirt in a gentle breeze. I don't bother to listen to the marine weather forecast that evening, which provides me a sounder sleep than I would have had if I had listened to it, judging from what happens next morning.

* * * * *

In the early morning it is apparent from the sound in the trees overhead that the wind has risen and strengthened from the northwest during the night, although the south facing cove is relatively calm. I finish packing up the camp and reel the boat in and stow the gear. After undoing the shoreline setup and retrieving the anchor and float, it is shortly after eight. As I start to row out of the bay and into the channel, it becomes obvious that the wind that I heard in the trees is much stronger than it had first appeared. My original thought is to just put up the main, but as I look at the wind and sea state, I decide to be conservative and just put up the mizzen in the centre mast position. With just this scrap of sail up, we fill away and romp off southward. Once out from the shelter of the island into the centre of the channel, either the wind gets stronger, or more likely, I can now feel the full effect of the wind. I realize that it is at least twenty five knots, maybe more in gusts, with three to four foot waves. The boat is overpowered with even just the mizzen, surfing and coming near to broaching occasionally. I put the reef in the mizzen, something I rarely need to do, and re-hoist it. That proves to be about right but if I could reduce area even more, I would do so. I give a brief thought to the two women kayakers, who are planning to cross back over to Cedar today in order to catch the music festival there this evening. With their self-admitted limited skills, I wonder how they will fare once they get out into these conditions. I hope that they will have the sense to turn back and wait for lower winds and calmer waves.

I am committed now and fly downwind past Ruxton and Pylades Islands towards the tip of Thetis Island, still surfing now and then. I cover in a short time what took slow hours of toil in the calm yesterday. Past Reid Island, I decide to duck in east behind the Secretary Islands to see if I can find a bit of shelter from the wind that has now a little more north in it. I figure that I can stop in Conover Cove for a lunch break before carrying on to my intended destination for the day, Montague Harbour on Galiano Island. I reach Norway Island, the start of the Secretary chain, by mid-morning. As I get in behind the islands, it is definitely more sheltered, as I expected, but soon the wind starts to drop. I change the mizzen sail for the larger main but the wind continues to drop and I finally put up both masts and both sails.

Soon there is no wind at all, which is not at all something I would have predicted at the start of the day. I take down the sails and get out the oars, but within twenty minutes of starting to row, a breeze begins again, but this time from the exact opposite direction, the southeast! As I set about putting the sails up again, the breeze freshens. Now sailing to windward, I can only carry just the mizzen, set in the mid-boat mast position. I tack directly upwind now, in about fifteen knots of headwind. With only me aboard as ballast fifteen knots is usually just about the limit where I can usefully sail *Hornpipe* to windward. It soon it proves to be the case here. At one point I make three tacks back and forth between the tip of Wallace Island and an off-lying rock reef, only to find I have not gained any distance to windward at all. There is too much leeway and the waves kill my forward speed.

With no choice, I take to the oars and begin rowing directly to windward, to head for Conover Cove, the nearest reasonable destination. It is hard work and painfully slow, and as I am close to the shore I can measure my progress in terms of feet. I don't make much more than three feet with every stroke. But even three feet is progress and after about an hour and three quarters, I'm able to cover the remaining mile and turn the bow into the Cove. What a difference! The temperature shoots up, the wind doesn't reach into the harbour, and anybody in the cove that hasn't been out there would wonder why I look tired. It is not yet one o'clock, but Montague Harbour is too far too windward and is out of the question at three feet per stroke. I am done for the day. Just before I make it to the Cove, a big powerboat that was anchored in the south cove of De Courcy that morning pulls in ahead of me. I dock just ahead of them. The owners, who saw me leave in the morning, are there to greet me.

"How did you make it all the way here in that little boat?" the man asks. "I had my smallest sail up, with a reef in it," I say, "That's only thirty-three square feet. Even so, I was surfing occasionally."

"I'm not surprised," the man says, "we even found it pretty rough going in our powerboat and it's thirty-six feet long."

While I am eating lunch, a big Tollycraft pulls in ahead of me, followed by their friends in a Catalina 28 sloop, who are also interested in my boat. The north wind that I awoke to was much stronger in Pirates Cove where the Tollycraft had been moored, stern-to. In the middle of the night their stern line parted and they dragged their anchor. Apparently other boats dragged as well and it was a disturbed night there for everyone. Soon, the owners of the Catalina break out a box of wine and we sat drinking it on the dock in the lawn chairs the Tollycraft carries - there are some advantages to sheer size in a boat. They invite me to supper and this time I have no qualms about accepting, as barbequed Alaskan salmon is on the menu. Supper turns into a potluck affair between three boats, four if you count *Hornpipe*, although I can't contribute much, and it is wonderful.

In the evening, I make sure there are no loose power bar wrappers about and have no trouble with the raccoons, even though they make their nightly patrol down the dock. I fall asleep worrying a little about what tomorrow will bring, as I don't fancy rowing to windward any distance if the wind persists. Awake in the middle of the night for a biological break, I find that the sky is clear, and the wind is calm. The bioluminescence in the water is brilliant, like stars below the boat, echoing the stars blanketing the sky above.

* * * * *

I wake before six and can tell that the wind has switched to the northwest from the southeast overnight. Fearful of yesterday's pattern, I decide to get up and go as soon as I can, thinking I can get down Trincomali Channel and at least around into the opening of the harbour on Salt Spring Island before the wind switches. That way, I will have a bailout option by running down into Ganges harbour if the wind persists from the south. In preparing to make breakfast, suddenly my camp stove, an old MSR Whisperlite, won't hold pressure. I take apart the pump, expecting that the cup leather has dried, but discover that the cup is made of rubber and appears to be good shape. I oil it anyway and it still won't hold. I conclude that it has to be the check valve, for which I have no spare. This is a major crisis. Apart from not having hot cereal, it means no coffee! I'm forced to make do with a cold breakfast of gorp, dried fruit and a power bar. I finish up, pack the boat, and pull away from the dock just after seven. Out in the channel, there is about ten knots of wind from the north, just enough to push me along, with both sails set, close to hull speed. I gybe downwind at a good clip, port tack favoured slightly for opening to the channel. There are a few clouds about, but it is mainly sunny, a little cool and there are not too many boats out yet. I make it to the entrance of Captain Passage north of Prevost Island in a little under an hour and half, well over four knots average speed.

The breeze seem to be holding, enough that I think I will try my luck and see how far south I can get before the wind shifts – perhaps to Portland Island. The breeze goes a little light through Captain Passage but starts to pick up again near Beaver Point. There is more boat traffic now, including one elderly sloop flying only a jib, which I pass easily. I turn the corner at the point and the wind shifts a little too, more from the north. The wind picks up even more and I'm making such good progress, it is time for a decision. I have limited provisions that don't need cooking meaning supper will be a cheerless affair without a stove. I will have to end the cruise early. I decide to head straight for the boat ramp at Sidney, as the ramp at Cattle Point where I launched is out of bounds because of the tide against me in Baynes Channel. Down through Moresby Passage, the wind begins to be variable but still mostly northwest. Past Coal Island and the gap at the Little Group, I make the turn to head for the public ramp just south of the Washington State ferry terminal, close by the town. It is completely clear now, but on this last run, the water is very choppy and confused from all the boat traffic coming and going from Port Sidney and Tsehum Harbour. Downtown Sidney looks different from the water since the last time I was this way. I think back to all the changes from when I first saw it more than thirty years ago.

I arrive at the boat ramp at noon. I covered over twenty-one miles in four and three quarter hours, at an average speed of near four and half knots. This is pretty good going for a boat with a waterline length of just sixteen feet. I phone to be picked up and while I wait for the trailer to arrive, I am entertained by a steady stream of boats launching and retrieving. While I eat lunch in the sunshine I reflect on the week. It's been a good cruise, even if cut short by the failure of the stove. It proves once again that exotic destinations are not necessary for good small boat cruising and that even this relatively settled part of the coast is full of interest.

* * * * *

It is four years later and during a long, hot August dry spell, I am determined to get out for a cruise in the Gulf Islands again. I've converted *Hornpipe* to a yawl rig by building a smaller mizzen mast that steps in the stern-most mast position. That position was designed to only hold the original mizzen as a mooring point for a boom tent. I built a Norwegian-style push-pull tiller to get around the new mast. This cruise will be a shake-down of sorts for the new rig, as I have only been out on short day sails with it to date.

I launch at the public ramp in Sidney in late morning under a hot blue sky, in windless conditions. The heat of the sun is relentless as I row and I am glad of the excuse to stop for lunch on the beach at Sidney Spit. The water is so still that I don't even have to pull the boat up the beach to prevent it from drifting away, it's just grounded, motionless. Looking back towards Vancouver Island, the sun drains the bright colours out of everything in view. There are a few shorebirds working the beach but the seagulls seem to find it too hot to fly. I persuade myself I can feel a breath of air as I finish lunch, and as I push off the beach I raise the sails, but it was a false hope. There is not enough pressure to move the sails away from where they hang limply against the masts. As I row north past Forrest, Domville and Brethour Islands at least the tide is with me, unlike the last time I came this way, and I have no trouble getting through the pass. I am headed for Bedwell Harbour and after slogging along for nearly four miles, which seems to take forever, a faint breeze from the northeast makes itself felt over my right shoulder. I stop rowing to make

Moonrise over Bedwell Harbour

sure that what I am feeling isn't just the wind created by rowing, and, joy of joys, the breeze is real, if light. I raise the sails and head off. In fits and starts as the breeze falters and recovers, I sail towards the entrance to the harbour, where it finally dies altogether among confused tidal currents.

I row around the point into the harbour only to find a wind blowing right out of the harbour. I didn't expect this, but I should have. It is a nearly text-book example of gap winds, caused by funneling and channeling of wind that is forced to flow between two islands or land masses. This phenomenon is explained in the excellent Environment Canada publication, Marine Weather Hazards Manual. I carry this with me, but it is one thing to read about something like this and another to recognize ahead of time when it is likely to occur. It is another good lesson about the vagaries of the conditions caused by the coastal topography.

Since it is only about a mile to the beach at Beaumont Marine Park, I don't raise the sails again, but row in against the wind. As I row past the Marine Host boat tied up to the Park float, they tell me that the wind has been blowing like this in the harbour all day. My clothesline mooring technique is rusty and it takes me nearly half an hour to get set up. The campsites here are good but there is no freshwater supply. No matter, I have plenty on my first day out. I am the only one here and I think I will have the entire campsite to myself tonight, but as I sit after supper on the beach away from the mosquitoes in the dying wind, four kayakers come in. The evening ends with a lovely full moonrise over the Pender Island hills enclosing the bay to the east.

* * * * *

The gap wind flowing out of the harbour is back in the morning when I leave, as I head further up the harbour to the narrow passage between North and South Pender Islands. I am rowing again because the harbour is too narrow to sail at this point. Rounding Ainslie Point, I find more ebb current that I expected but, by rowing my hardest, I can just squeak through under the bridge. There is a tense moment when, just before the bridge, I hear a shout behind me "We're going to run into you!" I turn and see a powerboat with a woman on the bow holding a boat hook, rapidly bearing down on me, in the grip of the current. "You're the one with the motor," I yell back as I stop rowing, "Use it!" They shift the motor into reverse, hit the throttle and slow enough to slide around me. They had come barreling into the channel at far too high a speed and not left themselves enough room to manoeuvre. What would they have done had I been a powerboat larger than them, instead of a small rowing boat?

Through the channel and into Port Browning beyond there is still some wind. I am hopeful of being able to sail up Plumper Sound but when I put up the sails, I find I am being pushed back by the ebb tide faster than I can sail, the wind is so light. Yesterday's heat is back, only more so. The ebb tide in Plumper finally turns to flood and I am sure that I will be boosted right into Navy Channel. When I get there I discover that the tide in Navy Channel actually floods from both ends toward the middle and I am forced to work the back eddies along the shore to make any progress. Once through Navy Channel I find some relief from the heat in a gentle breeze that is enough for me to sail another mile and half before it dies.

The traffic in Trincomali Channel alongside the east side of Prevost Island is thick with ferries, power yachts, sailboats motoring, work boats, tugs and fishing skiffs. The water is very churned up by all this activity and it is difficult to settle into a steady rowing rhythm. I grind my way up Trincomali Channel in the slop and finally reach the entrance to Montague Harbour but it still requires another three quarters of an hour of steady rowing to get to the park. I have never seen Montague this busy. Every mooring buoy is taken, the rest of the bay is full of anchored boats and even the beach has virtually disappeared under the high tide. It is a minor miracle then to find a *Hornpipe*-sized space open at the Park dock. I take it as a sign that I should stay there. I tie up and pay my ten bucks for the night. The air stays hot into the evening, although it is slightly cooler under the trees. There is a lot of dinghy traffic to and from the boats to the dock but it tapers to almost nothing after darkness settles and, under my boom tent, the night is quiet. I fall asleep looking forward to be able to sail on the forecast north wind tomorrow.

* * * * *

Yesterday's sun is gone and I'm late getting away in the morning. It is still calm, with the forecast wind nowhere in sight. Under a few sprinkles courtesy of the overcast sky I immediately notice the contrary ebb tide once I row out of the harbour. I head over to the Galiano Island shore to see if I can work the back eddies. The water is smooth this morning and I fall into a zen-like state as I row, only breaking out of it when I eventually notice a light wind coming out of the north. I immediately raise the sails but it is a wicked snare, as the wind disappears as soon as I get them up. I lose ground while attempting to sail and have to make it up rowing again. Retreat Cove eventually materialists abeam and I pull in out of the current to find a vacant spot at the public dock to tie up out of the boat wakes for a lunch break.

Along the Galiano shore north of Retreat it is mostly steep-to with many undercut sandstone formations. Houses here are all up on top of the cliffs, leaving the sandstone rocks at the tideline free to be used as haul-outs and parking places for Harbour seal pups while the mothers are off foraging. I see many pups here, all looking as cute as stuffed toys as I row past them. I stopped late for lunch and it is another twelve miles to Pirates' Cove, where I thought I might go. That seems to me to be farther than I want to row the rest of the day and I switch my destination to Conover Cove instead.

The tide has turned to flood by now and as I cross over to Wallace Island, I have to aim up-current in order not to get swept past Panther Point on its southern tip. It works and I find that I actually compensated more than I needed to. Around the point a light north wind comes up, but I am so close I just row the rest of the way to the cove, turning in to the entrance in late afternoon. There is a spot, just exactly *Hornpipe's* length, on the inner dock and I take it. People already there tell me the raccoons are as bad as ever but the park has now installed a metal food cache ashore. This allows kayakers and open boaters to put their food beyond temptation. I go for a walk to the point at the north end of the island, intending to stop along the way for a wash at the well. When I reach the well it is now capped, without explanation. I'll have to do without a fresh water wash.

* * * * *

Finally some wind! Today didn't look promising at the start. It began to rain overnight and it rained heavily enough that I discovered a flaw in my tarp/boat tent arrangement. I rig a line, taut between the two masts, and stretch the tarp over that down to the gunwales, with three lengths of plastic pipe bent into hoop shapes to give enough shoulder room. The rain overnight soaked into the ridge rope and traveled down under the tarp to the low point, right above my sleeping bag, where it began to drip on me enough to wake me up. With my sleepy brain in the middle of the night I couldn't think of any way to stop it. As a work-around I resorted to draping my Gore-Tex jacket over the sleeping bag to divert the water to the side. It worked and I went back to sleep. Waking in the morning, it is still raining. I have to set up the breakfast cooking gear on the aft seat, beyond the tarp, but I put up my umbrella to keep the rain off the proceedings. I am not at all sorry to see the rain. It has been so dry and hot for so long that is a delight to feel fresh water falling from the sky. The rain stops as I get underway late, rowing north along the shore, working the eddies to avoid the full effect of the ebb current. I stay inside the Secretary Islands until the pass south of Norway Island. Rowing through into Trincomali Channel I find a south wind. I quickly raise the main and surge off north but find I have misjudged how much wind there is. I drop the main sail and put up the old mizzen, which I still carry as a high wind sail. There is no loss in speed and I am much more in control. The rain starts again and once settled in to the downwind run and no longer generating heat from rowing, I rapidly cool off. I layer up progressively and sit back to enjoy the run. As I am sailing along, several porpoises or dolphins, of a type I don't recognize, surface briefly beside me. Their fins are too big and too curved and their blow is too loud and explosive for Harbour porpoises. Their backs are a smooth grey, which rules out Dall's porpoises[67].

Nearing Pylades Island, the wind begins to drop and I shift back to the larger main sail. The wind continues to drop but retains enough power to carry me into the south beach at Pirates' Cove. I rig the clothesline mooring, get my gear ashore and set up camp. By this time the rain has stopped, although it is still cloudy and cool. Pretty hungry by late afternoon, having missed lunch during the excitement of sailing, I cook an early supper. I go for a walk under the towering Douglas Firs that surround the two coves and which comprise the park. The Gulf Islands have become so developed that the parks which preserve some of the original forest are all the more precious. I can't help but wonder what these islands were like before the coming of European settlers, when the only human presence was the various First Nations villages, which lay much lighter on the land.

Listening to the familiar voice of the Coast Guard Continuous Marine Broadcast, I hear that the wind is forecast to switch around to the north in the area of the Strait of Georgia south of Nanaimo. The wind out in the Strait is not always the same inside the Gulf Islands but if it happens it will be good news, as I am at my turn-around point for this trip. A northerly wind, combined with the south-going ebb tide, will push me back south. I go to bed early and fall asleep immediately.

* * * * *

Overnight it is quiet, except for some mice making exploratory excursions between the fly and the inner tent, their soft scutterings briefly waking me with sounds out of all proportion to their size. At six o'clock when I get up the wind has not yet showed itself but I begin to pack up and make ready to leave. This morning I am clumsy and uncoordinated for some reason and it takes me twenty minutes just to coil and stow the mooring line. As a result, I don't get the early start I had planned on. Despite the late start, I feel good as I row out of the cove under the bright, but not completely clear, sky. It is cool for mid-August but the rowing keeps me warm as I move past Ruxton and Pylades Islands. Just past the islands, the wind comes up, not from the north as predicted, but from the south, along with a fog bank. It is about ten knots, more than enough to sail in. I raise the sails, get out the GPS, put on layers and settle down for a long cold beat to windward in the fog. I don't sail for long before the wind begins to fitfully diminish. I persist in sailing for a couple of hours but eventually, alongside Reid Island, the wind dies away altogether. I drop the rig and start to row but after about twenty minutes, the wind comes up again. Back up go the sails and I sail a couple of miles almost to Chivers Point on the north tip of Wallace Island where I lose the wind again. I drop the sails and row through the pass, which I would have had to do even if there was wind, as the pass is too narrow to sail through. Through into Houston Channel, a light wind comes up from the south again, but I am less than two miles from Conover Cove, where I am headed. I just keep rowing alongside the sandstone formations that line the shore, reaching the cove in less than an hour.

I am back where I was two nights ago but this time the cove is full of sailboats, not power boats. The same little stretch of dock, too short for most larger boats, where I was before, is open and I happily tie up there again. The cloud has thinned out to a high, hazy veil, which doesn't do much to block the sun. Out of the breeze in the channel, it is hot in the bay and I go for a walk under the trees along the centre of the island. In the shade it is very comfortable and I feel that contentment that comes from having put in a good effort and reached my destination for the day, with nothing pressing, nothing that has to be done, for the rest of the day. The quiet of the island, away from the sounds of traffic and machinery, is a balm to my soul.

* * * * *

It starts to rain just as I turn in and I fall asleep as the rain gets heavier. I am not worried as there is no wind to blow it in the ends and I am dry and snug. In the middle of the night, the water drips down from the saturated ridge rope again. It is calm but still raining when I get up and as I cook breakfast with the stove on the stern seat just out from under the tarp, it feels like it is going to be a long soggy day. Rowing in the rain is almost always a futile exercise in trying to keep dry. With rain gear on, you are protected from the water falling from the sky, but then you get wet from the inside, as even the best Gore-Tex rain gear is not vapour-permeable enough to allow the sweat from exertion to completely evaporate.

My goal today is to get down the east side of Salt Spring Island to the home of my friends Peter and Mary in Musgrave Landing. As I row out of the cove and across Houston Passage, the rain tapers to a stop. It leaves behind an overcast sky with low clumps of cloud patchily obscuring even the more modest hills on the islands around me. The dreary start to the day seems to have dispirited all the pleasure boaters as I am the only boat on the water until I round Southey Point. There I see a tug towing two chip barges, coming in from Porlier Pass, no doubt heading for the mill at Crofton. Commerce doesn't wait on good weather and I wonder where the crew of the tug started and when, to be arriving this early. I imagine a long, long night, with the crew trading watches, keeping an anxious eye on the radar in the rain, on the lookout for other vessels. I don't envy them their job in this weather but they are probably glad to have put the night behind them and to shortly be tying up. I hope they get a chance for a good breakfast and at least some rest before they have to head out again with empty barges in tow.

As I row past the light on Grappler Rock, the memory comes to me of the first time, after moving to Alberta, that I had returned to the coast on a sailing trip. We were sailing south well outside of the rock when we spotted a small sailboat, motoring with the sails furled, heading north inside of the rock. It is very shallow there and sure enough, we heard a crunch as the boat ran aground and stuck. We heaved-to, I jumped in the dinghy and rowed over to see if I could help. I found a young man and his girlfriend in a boat he had borrowed from a friend for the upcoming weekend. He admitted he had no sailing experience, wasn't sure of the draft of the keel, didn't know much about tides and had no charts aboard, only a road map of the Gulf Islands. He at least had the presence of mind to go below and see if there was a hole in the boat and if water was coming in. There wasn't, thankfully. The outboard didn't generate enough thrust to get them off. I took their anchor and rowed it out, and took the line back to the boat. They attached it to a sheet winch and pulled themselves off. There wasn't much more I could do for them except to advise them to travel outside of any light or buoy close to land and only travel when the tide is up, if they could. Finally, if they make it back safely, I advised them to acquire some charts and take some lessons.

I carry on rowing as the tide turns in my favour, making good time along the shore and across the bay at Vesuvius. There a wind rises from the southeast and I raise sail. It is a welcome relief to be sailing, getting the best out of the boat as I begin tacking towards the north entrance of Sansum Narrows. I quickly arrive off Grave

Point and the wind strengthens, bringing with it a chop out of the narrows. I tack across the entrance and back again but I haven't gained any ground to windward. I put the boat about and try again, with no better result. In this chop, I can't seem to point any closer than sixty degrees off the wind and I am not getting any closer to my destination. In frustration I drop the rig and take to the oars again, rowing directly upwind in the chop. It is hard work and it takes me well over an hour to cover the mile and a half of this part of the narrows and turn aside into Maple Bay for a breather.

By this time and at this rate, I will certainly miss the slack at the southern part of the narrows off Sansum Point. I will have to spend the night in Maple Bay. It occurs to me that it is Friday afternoon, and Mary, who works in the city during the week, might be arriving in Cowichan Bay where Peter will pick her up in their boat for the short trip to their house. I might be able to persuade them to come and tow me to their place. I pull out my cell phone and call Peter and find that indeed, he has just picked up Mary and they are just about to head out. A short time later, their boat pulls up to the public dock where I am, and I take their lines.

Peter jumps out and says, "How are you?" Mary says, "Hi stranger, long time no see!" "I'm doing great," I say, "except that it took me way longer to get through the north part of the Narrows than I thought."

"We went to a couple of the marina docks first," Peter says, "before we figured out you must be on the public dock."

"I probably wasn't as clear about it as I should have been," I say, "It's good to see you both." "Let's get a towing bridle rigged," Peter says, "I think we'll make it a two-point bridle."

He quickly rigs the bridle and we head out and down the narrows, keeping the speed low enough not to swamp *Hornpipe*. We have a great time catching up over dinner in the lovely house they have built[68] overlooking the bay.

I get a late start in the morning, lingering and chatting over Peter's pancake breakfast, but it doesn't really matter, as the tide doesn't turn to ebb until mid-morning. The morning is overcast when I set out, but there isn't much wind. I am convinced at first, looking at the crab pot buoys, that there isn't much current in my favour, and am prepared to be irritated at imprecise predictions, but then, noticing how quickly I am actually moving past them, I decide that there must be a fair amount of current after all. There is surprisingly little boat traffic on this Saturday morning and it feels as if I am further north somewhere instead of in the middle of one of the most popular boating areas on the coast. As the morning wears away, the early feeling of relative solitude dissipates as the boat traffic increases.

When I turn out of Satellite Channel and into Colbourne Passage, the boat wakes turn the water into a lumpy obstacle course. I now must pass the BC Ferry terminal at Swartz Bay on the south side of the passage and of course I have arrived just as the large ferry to Tsawassen is leaving and two other smaller ferries also manoeuvre for position in the tight space in front of the terminal. The current is now running strongly, setting east. I row hard to stay close to Piers Island and to avoid being swept into the ferry lanes and there is a tense twenty minutes while I am not at all sure I can stay out of their way. Finally, I am past and I turn into the public dock past the terminal for a rest and some lunch. In hindsight, I should have taken the time to go the extra distance around the north of Piers Island and avoided the terminal altogether.

Leaving the dock, there is a bit of easterly breeze and I have hopes of being able to sail through Iroquois Pass but it is not strong enough. Once through the pass the breeze is altogether absent – the famous Sidney wind hole – and I carry on rowing. Rowing past Sidney Harbour, there is a lot of boat traffic coming out and going in causing a constant chop from wake. It is hard to get into a rhythm in the wakes but once past the harbour, the wakes subside somewhat. I see a few sailboats farther out who seem to have enough wind to sail but is calm near shore where I am rowing, until I am nearly at the dock. I row into the dock mid-afternoon and call for the boat and trailer.

While I am waiting, I think about the trip. I have encountered less wind than any other sail and oar trip I have taken. I have probably rowed 95% of the distance. What little wind there was, was either too light or contrary or both, and most of the time I made better speed rowing. The one strong headwind I had, the chop prevented me from making headway. I am definitely not happy with *Hornpipe's* performance in that situation but don't yet know what to do about it. Despite the lack of sailing and despite the summer boat traffic, it has been a great trip and a great break. At this moment, I feel the truth of the old bumper-sticker slogan, "a bad day's sailing is better than a good day at the office."

Broken Group by Sail and Oar

I'd last been to the Broken Group in 2008, right at the start of the big economic recession. That summer, there were fewer people in the islands than I had ever seen in more than fifteen years of visiting there. I am not sure what I will find this year. The Broken Group can only be accessed by boat. There are several ways to get there if you are kayaking, but one of the most common ways for experienced paddlers is to drive to the campground at Toquart Bay and launch from the beach there. I figure it will also work well for my cruise in *Hornpipe*, as there is a small marina (two floats and a launch ramp – no other services) associated with the campground, which is popular with recreational fishermen.

The last ten miles on the drive to Toquart Bay are on a gravel road that is an active logging haul road. The road takes a beating from the big trucks and is frequently very rough with big potholes. I am nervous for my trailer and boat, but this time the road has been recently re-graded and by going slow, I make it to the campground without mishap. This is a better accomplishment than I knew. Later that night, a small bus, delivering clients to the dock to be picked up and taken to a fishing lodge, limps in the last two miles on a flat front tire, having holed it on a sharp rock on the road. The driver has to call a 24 hour tire service from the nearest town that has one, Port Alberni, to come out and change the tire. The tire mechanic uses manual tire irons. It looks like a lot of work and I am impressed with how quickly it is done.

I arrive at the campground in late afternoon and it is even cloudier than on the road, and cool with a bit of fog around, and completely calm. It is over six miles to the nearest island in the Broken Group and I figure, what with launching and loading the boat, and rowing all the way there in the calm, that it will take me the better part of three and half hours, maybe four, to get there. I decide to stay in the campground overnight and launch the next morning. I amuse myself that night talking to the fishermen and admiring their catches of coho, spring and Sockeye salmon[69]. The fishing seems to be good. I also answer a lot of questions about *Hornpipe*, as I am a rarity. The standard rig at the campground seems to be a ¾ ton truck with a camper on the back pulling an eighteen to twenty foot sport fishing boat with 150+ horsepower outboard motor on the back. Altogether at least $125,000 of investment to chase at most a couple of hundred pounds of fish for a week. I just don't get it. On the other hand, they probably don't understand why anyone would choose to travel in a small open boat with only sails and oars for propulsion and no motor.

* * * * *

Overnight, the weather remains cloudy and in the morning there is still low cloud and bits of fog around. I am in no hurry to get going as it is still calm, which means rowing. I launch the boat, load it and row away from the dock on the dot of nine thirty. I row in the calm over to the Stopper Islands and through the channel between them to find a light breeze on the other side. It's coming straight towards me from Lyall Point, which I have to get around. Still, the breeze, light as it is, looks like it is going to stay. I optimistically raise sail and ghost along for an hour with the breeze dropping to a puff or two. Finally, just before the point, the last puff dies away and I give up and take to the oars to get around Lyall Pt. Once around the point, the breeze starts up again and up go the sails. I head off on a close reach towards Hand Island, the first island in the Broken Group you reach when coming from this direction. Ahead, on the south side of Hand Island, the *MV Frances Barkley* goes past, heading towards Ucluelet. It's like seeing an old friend. On this reach, I start noticing that I am having trouble getting the main to set properly and there seems to be more weather helm[70] than the last time I had the boat out, but with the light breeze that is blowing, I ignore it. Just in the lee of the island, what there is of the breeze once more dies away. I put the oars in their sockets and row around to the south side of the tombolo[71] that connects the main island with the small island that has the designated camping area. As it is about lunchtime by now, I pull up to the beach to find a number of kayaks drawn up and tents set up.

Over lunch, some of the very low cloud lifts and the breeze starts filling in a little from the southwest. Getting under way again, I row away from the beach far enough to get clear of the rocks and raise sail. This time there is enough breeze coming through the Tiny Group of islets that I am able to fetch the entrance to the Dodd Island anchorage on two long tacks. On the second tack, it finally dawns on me why the main is setting badly and why I have weather helm. Somehow that morning I managed to set up the main mast in the centre mast position instead of the forward position! The centre position is fine with just one mast up, but with the mizzen up as well, the centre of effort of the combined sails is way too far aft and I am sheeting the main to the wrong mast track. It is a forehead-slapping moment – how can I have been so absent-minded and unobservant?

As I approach the entrance, the islands make enough of a wind shadow that there isn't enough wind to sail through it, and I have to row the last third of a mile to the campground on Dodd. In all my years of coming to the Broken Group in kayaks, I never stayed at this particular campground. My rationale was that just off the beach of the campground is one of the favoured anchorages for larger boats. There used to be a problem with bigger boats anchoring here and running their noisy generators. The Parks staff now encourage boaters to anchor a little farther along the anchorage, away from the campground, which has mitigated the problem, apparently. In any case, the campground isn't very crowded. I find a little secluded little spot for my small tent up in the trees and decide to stay for the night. The tide is dropping to a low in the late afternoon with the next high at about eleven at night. I figure on letting the boat ground out on the low, letting the tide move it up the beach all evening and then ground it out overnight again on the retreating tide. The sky is getting lighter, with some almost-sunshine to warm up the beach, but not enough to heat the land and develop any significant amount of sea breeze, the usual summertime condition.

The wildlife is still pretty wild here. While sitting and resting, leaning against a beach log, a Fox Sparrow[72] comes scratching along, kicking up the detritus gathered against the log. He hops right behind my boat shoes that are propped up drying against the log and then right behind me as I sit there. I am clearly just another beach obstacle to him, not a dangerous human. I do a little beachcombing and am impressed with the nice golden colour of the Rockweed[73] on the rocks on the point and the colour of the sea stars that have jammed themselves under rocks to avoid getting eaten by the seagulls. A few more paddlers pull in as the day passes and a couple of boats motor in to drop anchor but it never becomes crowded and thankfully no generators are heard to disturb the anchorage. The evening passes quietly and I go to bed with the sun.

* * * * *

In the morning I sleep in, amid the dead quiet under the trees. When I finally do get up, the morning is almost a repeat of the day before, grey with low cloud and almost no wind. I take my time over breakfast and coffee and watch the kayakers getting ready to depart, answering questions from them about *Hornpipe*. I have no particular destination in mind for the day, which in many ways is the best itinerary to have. I wait until the tide has risen to where the boat sits and I push the boat down the beach to the water to launch. It's a lot easier pushing the boat downhill than dragging it uphill.

I don't have a destination in mind for the day. I think I'll row out between Willis and Turtle Islands to see if there is any wind there, and from which direction. When I get there, I can see a breeze ruffling the water off to the south past Turret Island. At the end of Turret Island the water opens up quite a bit to the south and there is between five to ten knots of wind blowing from the southwest. It looks to be an easy sail upwind to Effingham Island

and the campground next to it on Gilbert Island. I put up just the main as I am not in a hurry and I'm not sure what the sea state will be in the channel. At first it appears I don't have enough sail up but the breeze fills in and steadies. I find I can fetch a point a little west of the east point of Effingham Island. The sky is still overcast as I cross Coaster Channel and it doesn't take long to get to Effingham on the starboard tack. I tack over to port to head west toward the campground on Gilbert, but the wind starts to lighten up, contrary to all expectation for afternoon winds. I tack ever more slowly up towards Gilbert until I am finally becalmed about half a mile from the campground. I row into find the campground almost deserted – only one other tent there. I beach the boat and go up to check the camping area under the trees where I find a good camping spot next to the rock face at the south end above the beach.

Shortly after that a group of eight young guys in kayaks pull in to the beach. They make a great deal of hullabaloo unloading the kayaks and setting up their tents. I think to myself, why do the young make so much noise? Was I like that at that age? I really don't remember but if I was, I was probably oblivious to it. It is probably just high spirits and I am just turning into an old fart with no tolerance. Mercifully, the noise doesn't last long as they all go out again for some late afternoon fishing. The clouds start to lift a little in the afternoon and opens up to a couple of hours of sunshine. I am glad to be done for the day, although I have only rowed for an hour. I seem to have strained my right forearm – probably from repeatedly lifting the bow of the boat up as the tide came in yesterday. I don't have anything to lift it with except the bow eye and the painter attached to it. I make a note to myself to figure out something that will give me more leverage and put less strain on my arm.

The day ends with the young guys, after having a few drinks, deciding around midnight it is a really good idea to go swimming – something they don't do earlier as that water is damned cold when you're sober! The bioluminescence of the water is good, as

Gilbert Island

the exclaiming over the resulting light show goes on for quite a while. I finally resort to ear plugs and drift off to sleep.

* * * * *

The previous night I did a repeat performance of dragging the boat up the beach and letting it ground out. The high tide is to be an hour later, but the night is calm and the beach shallow. The last hour of the boat moving up with the tide will mean that the boat will settle out nicely as the tide drops, with the painter tied off to a log ashore. When I get up in the morning though, the outgoing tide has carried the boat sideways for some reason, not straight out, and the boat grounded out partially on some bare rock poking up out of the sand. With the high density polyethylene keel shoe, this doesn't cause any damage, but it does mean I can't just shove the boat straight out into the water. I scratch my head a bit wondering how to deal with it. I remember another little cove I know of at the back of the campground and go to collect some driftwood poles to use as levers and skids. By lifting one end of the boat a time and shoving a pole underneath, I am able to move the boat sideways enough to line up with the sandy part of the beach.

After the late night, I didn't get up early and that, combined with moving the boat, means it is late morning before I manage to leave. The sunshine from yesterday afternoon has disappeared and the day is grey again, without wind again. I row around a couple of the smaller islands just to sightsee and stop at Dicebox Island, intending to have lunch and gawk at the sea cave around the corner from the landing beach. Although the landing beach at Dicebox is not directly exposed to the open ocean, the other side of the island mostly is, and the swell refracting around the end of the island causes quite a surge at the beach. As a consequence, the boat is grinding on the smooth gravel on the beach and I have to keep jumping up to tend the boat. I feel I can't leave the boat long enough to go look at the cave. Lunch is interrupted and hurried and immediately afterward I shove off again.

I set off to find out if the sea lions that normally sun themselves on the rocks seaward of Wouwer and Batley Islands are in residence. Out from behind Dicebox, to the north, there is a little breeze that carries me over to the channel between Wouwer and Batley. At the entrance to the narrow channel, the breeze blows directly through it. It's too narrow to sail and I have to row through and out to the rocks. There are the sea lions, right on cue. Unlike the more urban sea lions found in some harbours in California and Oregon, these guys get nervous if you approach too closely and they dive into the water. Sometimes they will swim right up to your boat and look you over from close range. I have never enjoyed having something the size and weight of a Volkswagen, with teeth, surfacing next to my boat and looking belligerent. Out of caution, I stay well off, listening to the din. From viewing the sea lions, I had planned on sailing the few miles to the campground on either Clarke Island or Turret Island, but the wind falls calm. My right forearm lets me know it really doesn't like this as I row. I am relieved when, after about a mile, a nice little five-knot breeze comes up. It gives me a broad reach almost to the beach on Clarke Island.

After last night's result with the boat grounding, and given that high tide is another hour later again, I set up the boat on the clothesline mooring. In setting up the clothesline, the challenge is to get the anchor set far enough out to be at the full extension of both the clothesline and the shore tether. If you just row out to the end of the clothesline and drop the anchor, by the time the chain and line straightens, you have too much slack in the clothesline. I finally get out the extra fifty feet of polypropylene line I carry, attach that to the end of the clothesline, row out to the end of the polypro and throw the anchor out as far as I can. I reel in the polypro, then clip the clothesline through the buoy on the anchor line to the bow eye on the boat. After all that, there is still some slack in the clothesline. The trouble is, this beach shallows out and the boat might still not be far enough out at low tide in the early morning. I might have to figure out a plan B.

More kayakers pull in to the beach over the course of the afternoon and the resident mink entertains us, in constant motion while hunting crabs among the rocks. Clarke Island has one of the most picturesquely situated campgrounds and beaches, which gets both morning and evening sun, when there is any. There was a privately owned cabin on the flat above the beach, long before the islands became a park. The lawn is still there but all that is left of the cabin is a crumbling stone fireplace. The composting toilets of the Broken Group are surprisingly interesting. With such intensive use in the park, the camping has to be confined to seven campgrounds to reduce the impact. You can imagine the potential sewage problems that could result. Fortunately, more than twenty years ago, the parks service had the foresight to build good composting toilets at each campground. The upper parts are built of rough cedar and they have solar powered exhaust fans. Each one has had some craftsmanship and creativity applied to the construction of the approach ramp and the result is quite attractive. Successive generations of kayakers have built shell and driftwood wind chimes and other ornaments to decorate the toilets. After all this time, some, like this one on Clarke Island, have developed their own natural green roof of moss, ferns and salal.

Everyone else I have talked to on the beaches so far has seen whales while they are out on the water, except me. They describe the acrobatics and feeding behaviour they have witnessed but I haven't even had a glimpse yet. I begin to think they are actively avoiding me when, just before supper, a humpback cruises past about half a mile away. Finally, I get to see my whale for the week. The day ends with me swallowing some ibuprofen before turning in. My right arm has developed a swollen red lump about six inches long above the wrist and the tendon makes a crunching sound when I move my wrist. I'm not a doctor but even I know that is not normal.

* * * * *

Plan B for the boat grounding out turns out to be really simple. I calculate, from the time and range of the tide overnight, that the boat will indeed ground out on the rocks, even at the end of the clothesline. I realize I need to get up in the middle of the night and reel the boat into the sandy part of the beach on the dropping tide. It turns out that three thirty in the morning is about right. When I get up then, although it is still cloudy, the full moon above the clouds provides enough diffuse light that I don't need my headlamp at all to see what I am doing, even to untie the knot that keeps the clothesline from shifting. Later in the morning, when I get up after sunrise, the tide has retreated to reveal both the float and the anchor now exposed above the water on the sea bottom, but the boat is safely where I left it in the night. My arm is actually a little worse than last night – more swollen and more sore whenever I move it at all. This definitely puts a crimp in my plans to see more of the islands if I have to do any rowing. Together with the observation that there is actually some wind this morning, unlike the other mornings, brings me to the decision to make a long day of it. I'll try to cut the trip short and sail back to Toquart Bay. Not knowing exactly what I have done to my arm, I don't want to risk making it worse to the point where I can't use it at all.

By the time I pack up and re-stow my mooring set-up, it is about eleven before I get underway. There is about eight to ten knots of wind coming from the south. It is perfect for sailing on a close reach to the west end of Turret Island – just right for only the main sail. It is enough to push me along comfortably at a little more than four knots and I make good time across the channel. Past Turret Island and approaching the Tiny Group from the west the wind drops a little but I am still moving faster than I could row, especially with this dud arm. Once I thread the needle of all the rocks in the Tiny Group I get out the fixings for lunch and put my feet up while I drift along eating as the wind continues to drop. The clouds thin out a little to let some heat through from the sun and the view of the mountains of Vancouver Island from my restaurant table is very fine.

After lunch and after the busboy has cleared the table, I shift the main to the forward position and raise the mizzen. This increases the speed a little, but where I want to go, around Brabant Island to Hand Island, is directly downwind. This is not *Hornpipe's* best point of sail, instead I begin gybing downwind. The breeze drops lighter and lighter until finally, past Hand Island, it drops off altogether. I lower the sails and get out the oars but only row for about ten minutes before I row into the wind again coming in Loudon Channel from the open ocean. I raise sail again and am off on a reach past Lyall Point and the salmon fishermen clustered there, to where I can turn the corner and head for the gap between the Stopper Islands. I hold the breeze right into the channel between the Stoppers, but that is it.

I row through the channel and find the slightest suggestion of a catspaw of wind on the other side and raise sail in hope but am sadly disappointed when even that suggestion goes away. So, back to the oars and with gritted teeth, I take up rowing again. I have a marked tendency to row in circles because of the weak arm. I lower the rudder and set it to counteract my unbalanced effort. In that weakened state I row very slowly all the way back to the marina in a flat calm, arriving in late afternoon. Once there, the marina is very busy with returning fishermen, and I sit drifting, waiting for two more boats to be pulled out before it is my turn. In three quarters of an hour I am on the road for the long drive back to Victoria.

Despite having to cut it short due to the arm injury, it is a good trip. Having so little significant wind for so long and so little sunshine must be some kind of a record for the area. The Broken Group, which was beginning to feel familiar when travelling by kayak, presents different challenges and looks different when viewed from a small sailing boat. It is the way many of the original European settlers would have got around and I feel I understand them a little better.

* * * * *

It is the following summer and I have been invited to join a small group of other sail and oar enthusiasts for a trip to the Broken Group. I have never met any of these sailors, except through an online forum, but from their writings they seem decent enough that I think it is worth taking a chance. I hadn't seen all I wanted to see last year because my arm and I am keen to go again. The rendezvous point is the Toquart Bay campground, the same place I launched from last year. Its main redeeming feature from a small boat perspective is that it provides a launch beach for kayaks wanting to paddle the Broken Group. It is the closest launch ramp for sail and oar boats wanting to get to the Broken Group and Barkley Sound.

I'm the first to arrive at the campground. Shortly after I get my tent set up, a small convoy of the other sailors pull up and stop next to me. The man in the lead vehicle jumps out and extends his hand, "I'm James," he says, "it's great to finally meet you in person not just virtually."

"Likewise,' I say, "this must be Rowan, your Oughtred Sooty Tern," as we look at the boat on his trailer.

"Sure is," James says, "and here come the other reprobates." "I'm Tim and that's my boat Big Food" says one, "and I'm Eric and that's Bandwagon," says the other.

"Great!" I say, "Let me help you get set up in your camp spots. I really want to have a closer look at all your boats. This is going to be terrific week."

We troop over to the office to register, only to find that the dead hand of liability insurance reaches even this remote corner. We are told that non-powered boats are not allowed to be launched at the marina – power only. When we ask why, we find out that is the result of an unfortunate accident five years before. They tell us a kayaker paddled/was sucked into the propellers of a big power boat at a marina launch ramp, and subsequently lost his legs. The insurance companies reacted by banning kayaks and canoes from marina launch ramps in British Columbia, perhaps all of Canada[74]. The campground isn't quite sure where to pigeon-hole us sail and oar boats, being neither fish nor fowl from a liability perspective, but in the end give us the benefit of the doubt since we are there, and allow us to stay and launch our boats. It is too late to launch and get over to the Broken Group this evening, but the salmon steaks Eric brought for supper compensate for not getting out sailing immediately. The weather is not looking ideal, with showers or steady rain predicted, but it holds off until the middle of the night.

* * * * *

In the morning, James is the first to launch and get underway in Rowan, intending to do some fishing outside the closed area of the Broken Group. Eric, Tim and I get going somewhat later, in the rain. Rendezvous is nominally lunchtime at Hand Island, the first possible campground and a good beach to stop. Once underway, we find about five to ten knots of headwind, which carries us to the channel between the Stopper Islands, where the wind dies, requiring the oars to carry us through the gap between the islands. A light headwind picks up again after that and after several tacks to clear Lyall Point, we are able to turn the corner for a nice reach over to Hand Island, arriving there about twelve thirty. James arrives at the beach about an hour later to clean a rockfish he caught. After lunch we sail over to look at the shallow lagoon between Jarvis and Jacques Island, home of eel grass, moon snails, bat stars, sea stars, and various other bottom dwellers. I am sad to see that their numbers are much reduced since the last time I was here. The wind that greets us for the sail over to the campsite on Gibralter Island is fluky and gusty but it gets us there without having to row.

The wind sweeps in gusts across the campsite beach at Gibralter Island when we get there, making me wonder about the suitability of the island as an anchorage. The state of the overnight tides are such that we can leave the boats to dry out on the beach overnight. We opt for the dry-out, except for James, who anchors out anyway and sleeps aboard his boat. James' crab pot yields enough crab for appetizers for supper and we end the first day in contentment.

* * * * *

The night passes quietly with no rain and the wind drops a little overnight. Talking about what we want to do, over breakfast, we set the destination rendezvous for the day as the campsite on Gilbert Island, near Effingham, towards the outer edge of the Broken Group. The day starts to brighten while we eat breakfast and by the time we get going at about ten o'clock, it is partially sunny. By this time the wind starts to pick up again and it is blowing right through the pass near the campsite. I row through the pass against the wind over to a white sand beach in the lagoon-like setting on Dempster Island that I remember from my visit here with Debbie and Norris years before, and after a false start, find the entrance. James joins me and later Tim comes in but Eric never finds us. We look at the tide pools and admire the setting then move out, intending to stop, perhaps, at Keith Island for lunch. By the time we get there, though, the wind has picked up more and is blowing right onto the beach, ruling out a stop. I change my rig down to the main mast in the centre position but find that as I get out into the main channel for the reach to Gilbert, I am dipping the lee rail more than I like in the gusts. Down comes the main and up goes the mizzen in its place. That is just right for the gusts, though a little underpowered for the lulls, but I am willing to give up overall speed for keeping the gunwale above water. We later estimate the wind at about eighteen knots. Prior to this, I am gaining on Tim in Big Food and Bandwagon, but Eric in Bandwagon passes me after I change to the mizzen, even though he has a reef in.

From this point it is a close reach, verging on a beat at times, all the way across Coaster Channel to Gilbert Island, starboard tack all the way. James forges ahead – it is ideal conditions for Rowan with just one reef. I find a groove and I start to catch Eric. Tim finds the conditions to be exactly wrong for Big Food in terms of the period of the chop and the sail area he can carry and he falls behind. James goes back to sail alongside him. As we get closer, I can't quite fetch the light on the small island guarding the bay in front of the campsite. In order to get around it, I have to throw in a short tack and then carry on, with a close reach to the campground. We have been seeing another small lug yawl sail and oar boat in the distance in Coaster Channel and it converges on the campground at the same time as us. It turns out to be Chris from Delta, BC, in his Welsford Walkabout. He's been out six days and is anchoring in various protected small coves around the Broken Group. It is unusual to have this many sail and oar boats in this area at once. Last year I was a decided rarity with *Hornpipe*.

By the time we land, it is time for a late lunch for me. About three quarters of an hour later Tim and James come in. It was a great sail, fast and challenging, although the beautiful sunshine at the start of the sail gave way to low cloud by the time we arrive at Gilbert. We rig our clothesline moorings and set up our camps and James sets out his crab trap. We walk the trail through to the cove on the other side of the island and come back with enough firewood for a fire that evening. Gilbert Island campsite is normally crowded but the only other people there today is a couple who are kayak camping with two very young children. What a great way to introduce them to an active life, I think. As they grow older, it will just seem normal. Around the fire we talk about what we have seen and experienced during the day and the finer points of similarity and difference between our boats. As I have little experience with these types of boats compared to the others, I find it very instructive.

* * * * *

In the morning, the crab trap yields enough fresh red rock crab to provide an appetizer for breakfast and to allow James to begin to assume his newly-bestowed title of Crab Slayer. Having not packed a cleaver, his technique becomes refined over the week, eventually ending up with the rock-as-anvil plus sharp-rock-as-cleaver method. As I elected to let my boat sit on the beach overnight, I have the task of getting it down to the low tide mark when it comes time to leave. In the soft sand, this is more work than I remember at the same cove last year, but the two small kids help by carrying the roller sticks from bow to stern - they are eager to be part of the exercise.

We set the day's rendezvous for the campground on Turret Island, one that I haven't been back to since my initial visit by canoe nearly twenty years ago. The plan is generally to go out into the open ocean and look for whales and sea lions. I am a little later getting underway and go east and south of Austin Island, just drifting along in their lee, really. Once past Austin I find about ten knots of wind and sail out into Imperial Eagle Channel before turning back towards Austin. I am just tacking back upwind between some off-lying rocks when a grey whale surfaces a couple of times not two boat lengths from me - as close an encounter with a multi-ton animal as I ever want to have. It is thrilling, nonetheless, to get a close look at the mottled skin patches and barnacles that distinguish these whales.

The sun is starting to break through again and I tack upwind to Dicebox Island. I stop there for lunch in the cove on the lee side and go to look at the sea cave around the corner. After lunch

I go looking for the sea lions that usually can be found west of Wouwer and Batley Islands. The channel between them is directly upwind and the wind is stronger and I have to reduce sail to a double reefed main and full mizzen. The sail area is about right but the reefed sail doesn't allow the boat to point upwind quite as well. I think I might be able to sail through the narrowest part of the channel between the two islands, but at the last minute, it is too narrow and I am making too much leeway. I drop the sails and row upwind to the usual sea lion hangout. They aren't there – maybe they stepped out for lunch – so I raise sail again and bear away north for Turret. It is another fast close reach across Coaster Channel in ten to fifteen knots of wind.

I arrive about three o'clock, in the sunshine under masses of cumulus cloud to find both the campground and the little cove empty. I commandeer the best fire pit/beach log kitchen setup and set my boat out on the clothesline mooring. A couple of kayakers come in next and it turns out that I know them – the world is a smaller place than we think. The family from Gilbert Island also comes in and finally, about five o'clock, the other sail and oar boats arrive. After much messing about with moorings and anchors, we get settled for the night. James again elects to sleep aboard on Rowan under his new cockpit tent. It clears

Turret Island

off completely by about seven o'clock as we sit around the fire talking about boats and other trips taken.

* * * * *

We awake in the morning to find our little cove swaddled in thick fog and a kind of ethereal stillness. The fog muffles any sounds that we make. We can't even hear the usual sound of waves on rocks that follow you everywhere in the Broken Group. The forecast is for clearing by late morning but we are in no hurry to get going until we have visibility and wind. There is more crab for breakfast, courtesy of the Crab Slayer. Our original plan was to head across Imperial Eagle Channel to the Deer Group over near Bamfield, outside of the Park, as it appeared the winds would be favourable. It is a four mile crossing and it is totally exposed to the open Pacific. The crossing is not a big deal if the weather is moderate, but the afternoon winds can build pretty quickly to very strong.

The fog lifts before 11:00 am, and we weigh and get going by about 11:30 am. Out of the cove, we find bright sunshine over the islands and about an eight to ten knot breeze from the southwest. While it is clear over the Broken Group and Vancouver Island to the east, out over the ocean the fog is still thick. The fog pours in like a river on both sides of the Broken Group, obscuring the Deer Group and also on the other side of the Broken Group in Loudon Channel towards Ucluelet. We decide to head over to Effingham Island, the potential jumping-off point for the crossing, to see if the fog might lift by then. We sail across Coaster Channel once more and get in behind the wind shadow of Effingham. We can see that the fog is being refreshed from offshore by wind like a conveyor belt, being pumped in as fast as it is being dissipated by the sunshine further in. James immediately sets to fishing while the rest of us drift around looking for wind. I have lunch while waiting and James rows over to announce he has caught three fish which will make a promising foundation for supper. We all have a short conversation on the radio and decide that the fog isn't going anywhere soon. The Deer Group is out for today and we switch destinations to the Dodd Island campground. The wind is back by now and we have a good reach across to the east side of Turtle Island, then some tricky but rewarding light wind sailing through the passages to the campground beach. There are a few kayakers there and a few more come in but there is plenty of room at this campsite. James comes in later, having proved to himself, by sailing around it, that Dodd is in fact an island. The fish that he caught yielded a fillet for each of us. Mine, greenling pan-fried with a little oil, is superb.

* * * * *

James' crab trap yields more crab for breakfast. We decide that we can get used to this and that James is a handy fellow to have along on these trips. It looks like today is going to be a repeat of yesterday, fog-wise. We plan instead to go over to Wiebe Island, near Effingham, and look into the fantastic tide-pool formed there by the circle of rocks at its south end. Then perhaps we might sail around the outer side of Dempster and Nettle Islands. James is first underway, as usual, with the rest of us following soon after. The winds, or more properly, breezes, are very light, generating challenging light-air sailing to get through the channels and over to Wiebe. When we get there, the low cloud lifts enough that we can see the Deer Group. We decide to attempt the crossing, especially as there appears to be more wind out in Imperial Eagle Channel. We set our rendezvous as the Ross Islets and one of the reported campgrounds there. Not all of us have paper charts for the Deer Group. I only have what is on my GPS chart for that area, good for close-in but the screen is a little small for getting the bigger picture.

James points his boat higher to windward, aiming for a pass west of Diana Island. The rest of us head straight for the pass west of Sandford Island. I have full sail up and am making three to four knots, pulling ahead of Big Food and Bandwagon. Towards the far side of the channel the wind increases and I hang on to all sail, hiking out on the rail to stay upright. As I approach the pass on a reach in the southwest wind, my speed is now regularly six knots. Any more wind or a longer crossing and I would have had to reef, but as it is I am able to turn the corner and run downwind very quickly into the lee of Sandford Island. I drop the sails and row around the Ross Islets looking for a campsite. I look at a couple of spots further on but come back to a tidy little sandy cove on Sandford. The campsite has clearly been used many times, as there are tent pads back in the bush and a crude picnic table and kitchen shelter set up. I set the boat up on the clothesline mooring, then Tim and Eric come in. We set up shop on the beach, to avoid the mosquitoes in the bushes.

James comes in a little later, sailing his boat right up to the beach. As he hops out, we can see he has something in his hand. Catch any fish?" Eric asks. "No, but I caught this pack of beer in Bamfield, where I stopped in," James says. "What a terrific sail!" he says, "What about you guys?"

"I just avoided having to reef, but if it had been any farther or the wind got any stronger I would have had to," I say.

We have a good supper and build a fire to keep the damp away, as it is a little blowy and misty, almost rainy, but we are snug in our cove in the lee of the wind.

* * * * *

Despite the threat of rain last night, it doesn't materialise. The winds are light in the morning but it is still solidly overcast. The day's rendezvous is Hand Island again which will put us in a good position to return to Toquart Bay Saturday, our last day.

James is anxious to do a big sail around the outside of Effingham and Benson and Clarke Islands and he leaves early. Eric wants to look into Bamfield and he leaves next. Tim and I, being less gung-ho, or in my case, being nervous from previous experiences of being caught out by big winds on other crossings, want to get across Imperial Eagle Channel as quickly as possible. Once out from behind the Ross Islets, the wind is strong enough that I have to put a double reef in *Hornpipe's* main and Big Food needs a single reef. Even with the reduced sail area, *Hornpipe* is moving at five knots at first. Halfway across the channel the wind starts to drop but I leave the reef in, as I am still doing three and half to four knots. The four mile crossing to Sechart Channel takes me less than an hour. Big Food comes in a little behind me and we stop at a sandy cove on Reeks Island for lunch. After lunch we row into the wind through the channel to the inside of Nettle Island, and then through a narrow pass to the north of it, where I discover an uncharted rock. Fortunately, I am only rowing at about one and half knots at the time and run straight onto it with the rub strip on the keel, and no harm is done. If the tide was another six inches higher I would have floated clear over it. The sea life on the bottom is clearly visible in the pass and it includes one of the biggest Sun Stars I have ever seen.

Through the passage, we raise sail again in Sechart Channel and ghost across to have a look at Sechart Lodge, now a source of rental kayaks and a starting point for many kayak trips to the Broken Group. By this point, we can see Eric coming into the Channel from his crossing. We carry on by oar through the central passage of the Pinkerton Islands and note a couple of float houses tucked away in tiny coves there. It looks to me like it would be a great life in the summer but very damp and grey in the winter. We meet with more wind on the crossing to Hand Island directly to windward. I misjudge the strength of the wind, guess wrong on the sail combination at first, and I fall behind Big Food. Eventually I put up the main in the centre position with a single reef and that proves to be just right. There are lots of kayakers on Hand, also staging for their last day. Again, as with nearly every other day, we get the question of "what kind of boats ARE those?" James comes in with two good sized ling cod that he caught. Once again we have a gourmet supper courtesy of James' fishing skills.

* * * * *

Saturday morning, the last day, dawns calm. We aren't in a hurry to get started, since we will be rowing. The crab trap does its duty once again. The Dutch oven comes out and we have hot biscuits and fresh crab for breakfast. Reluctantly we pack up and begin the long row back to Toquart Bay. It remains calm right around Lyall Point, where we are treated to a humpback whale show – one adult and a calf at least, perhaps more. The whales repeatedly surface and breach. It is a spectacular sight. At the entrance to the channel between the Stopper Islands, a zephyr from the south makes itself felt. In hope, I raise sail and ghost and pirouette slowly through the channel without having to row. By this time, Big Food and Bandwagon have caught up to me by rowing but I am determined to keep sailing. Once out of the channel, a nice breeze comes up from the north, to windward, perversely, but it is great sailing. Rowan sails round the east end of the Stoppers and emerges into the channel ahead of me. Finally, whether rowing or sailing, we all converge on the ramp at Toquart in the last of the breeze which dies away just as we get there.

By the time we get the boats hauled, we are reluctant for the adventure to end, and it is really too late to contemplate the drive back over the Island for those who have to catch the ferry. We decide to carry on into Ucluelet, get cleaned up, have a good meal in a restaurant and hoist a brew or two to the voyage. This we do, with the added bonus of finding that the weekend is "Ukee Days" in Ucluelet. At the campground we are treated to a concert from down the road, whether we want it or not. The town is busier with tourists than usual and we have to pass up our first choice of restaurant, but where we do end up is just fine. A post-supper stroll down to the fishing docks yields a purchase by me, from a first nations fishing boat based out of Bamfield, of several chunks of smoked Sockeye salmon to barbeque once I get home. It was a great week of sail and oar boating with new experiences in an old haunt and I made good new friends.

The Broughtons by Sail and Oar

A couple of years after the sail and oar trip to the Broken Group, the same group of sailors organize a trip to the Broughton Archipelago. Eric was there many years before, as was I a couple of times by kayak, but Tim and James have not been there. The area, although well-traveled, is decidedly more

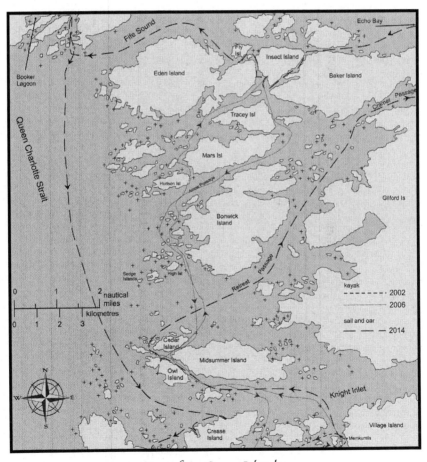

Broughton Group Islands

rugged and remote than the Broken Group, with bigger distances, stronger currents, bigger tides and generally higher winds. It is the beginning of the second week in September, when the chance of the weather turning from summer conditions to autumn gales starts to increase. We aren't sure what we will encounter, but we are game to try.

I have also modified the sail rig on *Hornpipe*, from its original ketch, to a yawl rig. I have built a much smaller mizzen mast set further aft on the back deck. The overall sail area is reduced, but I hope that the rig will be easier to set up, stow and reef. I am looking forward to seeing how the new rig will actually perform. We arrange to meet at the Alder Bay Resort, north of Beaver Cove, where we will launch for the trip. We all arrive at Alder Bay in late afternoon and set up in the adjacent campsites assigned to us. We go down the road to Telegraph Cove to the restaurant there for supper. Over supper we get caught up on who's been doing what and discuss our plans and hopes for the coming week. We're all excited to sail in this area but probably also a little apprehensive about potential bad weather, although nobody will admit it.

We launch on a Saturday morning and leave the resort shortly after nine under brilliant blue sky with not a cloud to be seen anywhere, not even over the distant mountains of the mainland, and on an absolutely calm sea. James, ever hopeful, has his fishing rod out over the stern as he rows. It feels good to be setting out in such ideal weather and the sight of our four boats rowing along in such wide open waters feels like the beginning of a quest. It's not much more than a mile across Johnstone Strait to Cormorant Island but as we row south past Beaver Cove, the Strait widens out. There is definitely a feeling that we are in big country, compared to the Broken Group. A lot of water moves through this area and the tidal current can reach three knots, even here where the Strait is wide. This day, though, we have a gentle flood tide helping us along until we get to Weynton Passage, where much of the water that flows in Johnstone Strait finds its way in from Queen Charlotte Strait to the north. At this junction, in spite of the gentle current, the water is very disturbed, with a lot of whirlpools, rips, overfalls and general tidal weirdness. Eric and I are leading and get into the rips first. We get part way through when three humpback whales suddenly show up and put on a show, blowing and surfacing. It is magical to see, so soon into the trip.

A faint breeze comes up from the southeast and James thinks he can sail, but he is moving so slowly he falls behind the rest of us who are rowing. We finally get through the tide rips and I stop rowing, intending to drift and have lunch. I am caught in a huge back eddy and losing ground. I cut lunch short as I have to take up the oars again. Tim and James are catching up rowing when they feel a breeze again, from the northwest this time, and they raise their sails. The breeze finally reaches me and I raise my sails too, and then Eric does. We all have a great sail down alongside Hanson Island past Weynton Passage. Within a few minutes of beginning to sail a few orcas, including a lone male with his impossibly tall straight dorsal fin, comes right through the middle of our group of boats. It is a captivating and unforgettable sight, with the light following breeze, the backlit sails, the sunlight winking and flashing off the facets of the wavelets and the tall dorsal fin of the orca rising out of the centre of a larger, brighter patch of water that rolls off its back. Seeing the orcas so soon after the humpbacks, and so early on our first day, feels like a good omen for the week ahead.

We arrive at Blackney Passage a little early for predicted slack but the water looks still already and Tim and I start through. The wind tails off and both of us drop our sails to row. Eric and James are convinced there is still enough wind to sail and spend a lot of time tacking back and forth to get through the pass. Meanwhile Tim and I row through and find more humpback whales at the exit to the pass, including one that breaches right clear of the water and smacks back down with a loud percussive boom. There is a good breeze after the pass but while Tim puts up his sails again I just carry on rowing as there isn't far to go before we enter narrow Whitebeach Pass. We find an ebb current coming against

Orca among sail and oar boats in Johnstone Strait

us out of the Pass. We row past a beach on the north side where years ago I had heard that a cougar had come out of the bushes and surprised a group of kayakers who successfully drove it off. It is a silent reminder to stay vigilant when ashore. Once through the narrowest part it is just a short pull to the campground beach at Mound Island, where I find a group of four kayakers already there. James and Tim come in much later, having successfully stopped to catch three fish between them, which furnishes the basis for supper. At the end of the day, with the boats set up on their moorings, we sit on the beach in the calm under a clear sky watching the tide rise while a bat flits about, reducing the insect population in the quiet darkening air above us.

* * * * *

Fog steals in some time after dark and throughout the night we can hear fog horns of the many ships and boats transiting Johnstone Strait three miles away. We wake to find the fog still with us but it isn't very thick and there is no rain with it. James was sick overnight. He suspects it is a bug he picked up from his wife, a teacher, who picks up everything from the kids at the start of the school year. On top of that he misjudged the depth when he anchored and woke up with his boat completely above the water and the stern hung up on a big rock. As a consequence we don't get a quick start as we have to wait for the advancing tide to float his boat. We move out around quarter to eleven and laze along the south side of Mound Island in the morning calm. A light breeze then comes up and we are able to raise the sails and ghost along the rest of the way to Memkumlis where we stop for lunch and a look around. The village is a lot more overgrown than when I was last here seven years ago. Tom is no longer here giving tours and the docks that were in place around the corner are also gone. The fallen totems, with their depictions of bear and wolf, that were so visible when I first stopped there with my kayak, are now barely recognizable as totems. Although it is inevitable and what the carvers intended, it is still a little sad to see.

It is still cloudy, but the fog is lifting and it is brighter when we leave Memkumlis, heading for Owl Island. There is a good stiff one-reef wind in our faces as we point west out Kingcome Inlet. We have good sailing, tacking upwind with the current in our favour, all the way to the campsite at Owl. The sun comes out at about three o'clock adding to the good mood from sailing. The campground beach at Owl is not ideal for our boats, being too stony to easily ground out and there are big tides predicted for overnight. It is a busy campsite, with quite few kayakers already in residence. Our arrival caused a bit of a minor sensation, as it did earlier at Mound Island. While kayaking is very common and popular in this area, small sail and oar boats are obviously not. A couple of the kayakers are very interested in the design of the boats, how we have come to build them and what it might take to acquire similar boats themselves. We point them at Eric, the professional boat designer/builder among us, as potential future customers for him. James is still feeling off and retires to his boat early. Tim, Eric and I have supper on the beach before they move to their boats to sleep. I put up my tent and sleep ashore as it is too windy for me to sleep on the boat. My boat tent (just a tarp) is too open and it won't be comfortable in that much wind. The sun disappears after supper and the wind strengthens.

* * * * *

The morning dawns cloudy with a fairly stiff northwest wind. The conditions are right for a downwind sail across Spring Passage and up Retreat Passage northeast to Echo Bay. We have a short but challenging row upwind in the slop to get out around from the channel in front of Owl Island. I sit for a few minutes in Spring Passage gauging the wind coming in off Queen Charlotte Strait, feeling a little nervous about how much wind there is and how gloomy the day looks. I decide the wind is strong enough that I only need to put up my old ketch mizzen sail, which I still carry to be used as a sail for high winds. It is a good decision. With our sails raised and sheeted in, we rocket off across Spring Passage towards Retreat Passage at nearly hull speed. The wind turns the corner with us into Retreat and follows us right up the passage. Further along the wind continues to build, the waves soon follow suit and it becomes boisterous enough that I have to round the boat up into the wind to put a reef in the sail. Just at that point Eric, who already has one reef in, puts in his last reef. We carry on at full speed with the occasional semi-surf, fully engaged in steering the boats and watching sail trim. Although it takes the whole morning to sail the dozen miles to Echo Bay it feels like no more than an hour passes.

We row into the calm of the bay past the busy commercial marina and store to the old British Columbia Parks dock. The continuing starving of British Columbia Parks budgets, which has been going on for decades, has caused Parks to forego any maintenance or upgrading of the dock. Instead, they put up a sign that says the dock is officially closed and that any use is at your own risk. The dock is still usable, although a little decrepit. There are a few other larger boats already there, who have also decided the risk is worth taking. Echo Bay is a beautiful little place. On the north side of the bay, a handful of float homes of the residents, from extremely modest to more elaborate, are tucked up against a cliff that towers dramatically above them, The cliff is coloured tan, reddish, brown and grey and has small trees clinging to crevices in the rock. At the head of the bay, to one side is a shell beach in front of the old school, which is closed down now for lack of children. On the other side is a small stream that empties out into the bay, running with water even at the end of a dry summer.

After lunch we walk around the end of the bay, through the calm of the forest, stopping to sample the ripened Salal berries in the open sunny patches. We go up to see Billy Proctor's museum and met Billy Proctor. Billy was born in the 1930s and grew up and worked in this part of the coast all his life. He has seen its economic and social ups and downs, its moods and knows its people. His story is beautifully told by Alexandra Morton of Echo Bay in her book *"Heart of the Raincoast."* It is an honour to meet Billy although we don't get to talk to him long as there are lots of people waiting to also make his acquaintance. We carry on to the store where Eric and Tim buy some bottled water, as they are running low and there is no other source. The rest of us walk back while Tim stays on the dock with the water and Eric rows over to fetch it and Tim. The crab trap yields several of legal size for a mouth-watering protein main course for supper. Eric, James and I set up our tents to sleep ashore, under the spreading branches of a group of cedar trees. The night wind in the top branches of the trees is not as strong as forecast and merely acts as sound masking, and I sleep soundly, untroubled by any worries of dragging anchors.

* * * * *

We get up early, while it is still dark. While I am packing up with only my headlamp for light, I absolutely cannot find my sleeping bag stuff sack and must pack the sleeping bag in the dry bag without it. Cursing the darkness and my ineptitude, I carry my gear down to the boat. We row away from the dock on calm water and under cloud so low it is almost fog. There is about a hundred feet of clear air below the cloud as we row along the north shore of Baker Island at the edge of Fife Sound. Out in the Sound a few humpbacks surface, briefly, but don't reappear. A little wind comes up as we reach Davies Island in the channel. Given the strong winds of yesterday I am sure it presages stronger winds to come. In the passage leading to Insect Island, the flood current is running strongly against us but there are a couple of bays to provide back-eddy relief and allow us to get through. I am ahead of everyone else and arrive at the beach in late morning. Eric and Tim come in about half an hour later. James comes in after noon, having spent time fishing. He caught a small ling cod, a bullhead and a small coho salmon. Tim's crab trap that he set out earlier yields a good-sized crab. James cleans the fish for a late-lunch fish fry, on top of the lunch I have already eaten earlier. It seems I always can find an appetite for freshly caught fish.

I make myself a pot of coffee to compensate for the coffee I missed in the morning and while I am sitting enjoying it the sun comes out. I decide it is warm enough that a good wash is in order. I dig out the soap and brave the cold water for a brief (very brief) swim and a hair wash. When I undress for the swim, the stuff sack for my sleeping bag falls out of the bottom of my pant leg inside my boot, where it got caught up when packing in the morning, solving the mystery of its disappearance. Eric also decides a swim is a good idea and he is tougher than me as he stays in longer. After the wash I feel quite civilized but very lazy and just lounge on the beach with my book. Tim is more ambitious and goes out fishing while James goes out for an exploratory sail around the nearby islands. James surprises us in late afternoon by reaching into the hatch of his boat and pulling out sticky rice, a package of Nori seaweed and a small bamboo mat. He sets to work, cooks the rice, cleans the fish and soon provides us with sushi made from the salmon he caught. It makes a connoisseur's appetizer to the fish entrée supper of the fish that Tim caught. The finest restaurant on the coast could not deliver us a better meal than the one we have on the beach.

* * * * *

My camp spot up on the rocky point at the south end of the little bay has a great framed view through the trees of the hills on

Gilford Island. The others, who spent the night on their boats, come up in the morning and we sit in the sun over a relaxed breakfast. James makes biscuits in his Dutch oven and we dawdle over coffee before reluctantly packing up. Once underway it is calm and out past Fly Island into Fife Sound there is a suggestion of a breeze, enough for me put up the sails, but it doesn't last and I soon take them down. It is brilliantly sunny and calm all the rest of the way along Fife Sound. Rowing steadily along, it is a day to appreciate the wildlife and the scenery. A pair of Western Grebes and a pair of Common Loons swim by me at close range, not at all disturbed by my quiet passage. The patches of snow that still linger on the high ridges of the mountains of the mainland to the east contrast with the dark green of the forested lower slopes. Humpback whales are everywhere in the Sound this morning, surfacing and blowing. I feel electrically alive, aware of the exertions of my own body and of the connection to the life and the sea and land around me.

Our destination is Cullen Harbour, which guards the entrance to Booker Lagoon. I get there first and find that the site where we planned to stay, a marked campsite on Tim's recreation map, is a non-starter for our boats. By the time the others arrive, the state of the tide is perfect for going through the small channels to Booker Lagoon. In we go and find a little shell midden on a small rocky island just inside the passage. We stop there for Tim and James to clean more fish they caught. Meanwhile I sail over to the far end of the lagoon to check out a couple of other spots on the chart that look like they might offer potential beach camp sites. As is often the case, the chart is not the territory and the reality doesn't match the chart markings. It looks like it will be a quiet night though, and after supper we all anchor out for the night near the midden island to sleep on our boats. The sun sets behind a few sparse low grey clouds and high spreading vapour contrails, colouring them the palest yellow. The calm water of the lagoon perfectly mirrors the low western shore and sky above.

* * * * *

In the morning after a quiet night, we get up early to be out the lagoon pass before breakfast, in order not to lose the ebb. The clear night sky has cooled the air and wrung the moisture out of it, covering every surface with heavy dew. The sun is up but does not yet have enough heat to evaporate the water as I pack up the tarp, and I must put it away very wet. We find that the pass that we came through yesterday afternoon is in full waterfall mode from the ebbing tide. If it was a river we would call it Class II white water. Sitting, bobbing in our boats above the cascade, looking downhill to the other side, Tim says, "I don't like the looks of that. I think I'll wait for a while until the situation calms down."

"Tim," I say, "the tide outside the lagoon is dropping faster than the water can drain out of the lagoon. It will get a lot worse before it gets better as the height difference between the two gets greater."

Eric, who has been sitting quietly listening to this, suddenly pulls on his oars and points his boat down the centre. He is caught by the current and shoots through in a moment. Adrenalin and heart pumping, I go next. Giving a short pull on the oars to centre the boat, I am drawn into the central chute with a rush and in seconds I am through and swirling around in the eddy at the bottom. Tim follows. The three of us pull out of the swirls and into calm water beyond and rest on our oars. A few minutes later we hear "Woo-Hoo! That was awesome!" as James comes shooting out from behind the tip of the island that protects the pass. We raft up together for a brief breakfast before setting off.

On setting out we have another good humpback whale show, with whales diving under us and surfacing just yards behind us where we have just been. We hope that they are aware of our presence and will avoid us. If it comes to an encounter between a multi-ton whale and our little boats, no matter how inadvertent, we will definitely be the losers. It dawns on us that it will be a very good idea to get moving and away from the possibility of a collision.

The sea is mirror calm again, with only faint puffs of air every now and again to tempt us into raising sail and drift downwind for a while, slower than rowing. James, as he frequently does, heads off by himself, towards the western shore of the island group to the east and we soon lose sight of him. We are headed for Crease Island and since it looks like we will be rowing all day, the shortest distance is a line straight across Queen Charlotte Strait. Remarkably for this big expanse of water, this part of the Strait is quiet this day. After a few hours of rowing, our three boats have separated a little. Except for the wake from the boat's passage, the other boats do not appear to be moving. I am reminded of the lines from Coleridge's Rime of the Ancient Mariner: "as idle as a painted ship upon a painted ocean."

We keep on rowing, sinking into a kind of kinetic reverie, the rhythmic motion of leaning forward, dipping the oars, pulling back and out and leaning forward again becomes automatic, leaving the mind free to wander. My reverie gradually dissolves as I slowly become aware of a noise in the distance. At first I can't identify it. It sounds like a curling, breaking wake from a powerboat, except that no boats have gone by for hours. Then as the sound gets closer, I suddenly see that the sound is coming from a large group of Pacific White Sided Dolphins[75], spread out nearly from horizon to horizon. They are travelling fast, surfacing and diving again, arcing briefly above the water with a short blow every time they break the surface. There are so many I can't count them but I figure there must be several hundred of them, maybe many more. I stop rowing and stare, enthralled, not knowing where to point the camera. I have heard of these super pods but have never seen one before. They may be hunting, as periodically one or the other of them will veer to one side with a splash, dive and then surface again. I am thrilled when one swims within a boat length of me, just under the surface, where I can see its grey body with white markings and see the powerful pumping of the tail that propels it. Within a couple of minutes they have passed by and the sea is quiet again. It is a thrilling experience and I feel privileged to have witnessed it. It takes me another few minutes to rouse myself and begin rowing again.

After that exciting interlude, the rowing gets very tedious under the hot sun. We toil along and eventually get to the promised beach on Crease Island just before mid-afternoon high tide. The beach is a narrow pebble one with a few tent spots behind it in the trees. There are a couple of kayakers already there with their tent pitched but they are just getting in their boat and leaving the beach as we come in. We wonder what has become of James and he finally comes in a couple of hours later. He was anchored in a small cove to the west, having initially misunderstood the rendezvous. We get a fire going, James bakes some Dutch oven blueberry muffins and after supper we sit, talking companionably, until dusk. James elects to go back over to his cove to sleep on his boat at anchor while Eric, Tim and I camp ashore. As the scant light of dusk gives way to darkness, the kayakers still haven't returned. We are a little concerned, and although it is only a few days past full moon and the night will be relatively light, paddling at night is riskier than daylight, should anything go wrong. There is nothing we can do about it though, and we go to bed. We need an early start to get through Swanson Passage west of Crease Island with a favourable tide.

* * * * *

When we get up at four o'clock to move the boats, the kayakers are just coming in, after having been out all night. God knows where they have been. Perhaps they were caught by the current and couldn't get back until it changed. We don't find out as they go straight to their tent without speaking to us. We pack up, get the boats off the beach and row around to find James. It is still dark when we row into the cove. At first we can't see him, only a large power boat anchored in the middle of the outer cove. Pulling around that, we find him further in, anchored securely. He is still asleep and we wake him as we bump alongside. We stream the three other boats astern in a breeze coming out of the bay and have a little breakfast in the dark. Tim boils water for coffee on his Jetboil and we sit quietly in the chill, slowly coming to life as the caffeine works its magic. As it starts to get lighter we think we had better attempt Swanson Passage as soon as we can, in case it won't go and we have to go around either Crease or Swanson Islands. We find that the tide is already running against us as we enter the passage but we find some back eddies along shore to help up move forward. Through the narrowest part there are no eddies near shore, as the shoreline is steep. There is no choice but to put our backs into it and power through, slowly. We rest for a few minutes in the little cove to the southwest of the pass once we are through. Then, since we have lots of time to wait for slack at Blackney Pass, we row around the corner to Freshwater Bay. There I find the kayakers we met on Insect Island, who are being picked up by water taxi. I talk to the taxi boatman who gives us tips for getting through Blackney on an ebb-to-flood turn. After the water taxi leaves with the kayakers, we tie up to the kelp in the bay and have a rest and a snooze in the sun. Exploring the shore is out, as the beach full of large rocks is untenable for our boats while the tide go outs.

With a couple of hours to go before slack, Eric, Tim and I set out to cross towards Parsons Point. The wind is still calm but there are lots of swirls, eddies and cross currents from the tide as we move across the end of Blackfish Sound. When we get to Parsons Point we find James up against the cliff under the point. He was fishing earlier but moved over to tie up to the kelp, as we did. While we were sitting in the sun and are warm, James was sitting in the shadow of the cliff and is feeling the chill. We aren't there for long before it is almost time to move. The general wisdom for getting through the Pass in an engineless boat, according to the water taxi boatman, seems to be to hug Parson Point until slack, then stay close to Cracroft Point as the current turns to flood. Tim is impatient and sets off early to work the eddies around the point. The rest of us soon follow. As we come abreast of the entrance to Baronet Passage we find a breeze out of the west, from Johnstone Strait. One after the other, we all raise sail, James leading. We slant off towards the Vancouver

Waiting for the tide near Blackney Pass

Island shore and Blinkhorn Peninsula, pursuing different reaching strategies. I elect to stay close to the Vancouver Island shore, thinking that if the wind strengthens, I will have at least a little protection from the worst of the waves. The others tack right up the centre of the Strait. The breeze remains relatively light from the northwest though, never getting any stronger. We all arrive at the peninsula more or less at the same time although I am last in. Eric, Tim and I decide to let the boats ground out again overnight while James anchors out.

James caught a large ling cod that weighs about twelve pounds when gutted. We build a fire and while it is burning to coals suitable for grilling, James produces four cans of Guinness that he has been saving, as an aperitif to our last-night feast. James grills the cod over the fire on a grill made of branches and I make a big pot of garlic rice to which Eric adds sautéed pepper and onion. James makes Dutch-oven corn bread and also sautés some cabbage and carrots. A fire on the beach in the calm of a later summer evening is one of the world's best appetizers. At that moment, I don't think there is anyplace else that any of us would rather be. The fire is welcome in the chill evening after supper as it is brilliantly clear again, cooling the air around us.

* * * * *

We need to get up early to get the boats off the beach into the water before the retreating tide strands them. A four forty five wakeup call sees us packing up gear and getting the boats ready. The boats are actually just above the water because the slope of the beach is so shallow, and it is a bit of a wrestle to get them off. *Hornpipe* is especially difficult as she is so bow-heavy, but with the three of us we manage. Then I anchor, Eric and Tim raft up to me and we make breakfast and coffee while the sky lightens. There is a moment of excitement when Tim accidentally knocks over his lit Jetboil onto the floorboards of his boat and the liquid fuel surges out of the burner and flares up. Tim calmly scoops up some seawater with his coffee mug and douses the flames. The whole incident only took seconds, and there is no harm done. It could have been ugly - a fire on a boat can do a great deal of damage. Tim, Eric and I pack up our breakfast things and row out of the bay to the point of the peninsula. James remains at anchor as he plans on taking a day or two more to visit Alert Bay, and maybe even Port Hardy.

It is a brilliantly clear and calm morning again. There is no sign of the predicted fog, only a few wisps of cloud at the southern horizon, tinted delicate shades of pink, with hints of orange to contrast with the fading blue of the sky above. The ebb tide pushes us quickly north along past Blinkhorn and Istell Peninsulas and Telegraph Cove. At Beaver Cove, enough of a breeze comes up to tempt Tim and Eric into putting up their sails, but I figure it is only the remnant of the night breeze that won't last, and don't bother. The wind lasts just long enough to allow Tim to catch up to me before it dies away. As we finally row into the dock at Alder Bay, it is still calm and sunny, just as it was when we left the bay almost exactly a week ago. It was an exhilarating week. We had far better weather than we have any right to expect for the time of year. We experienced some wonderful and challenging sailing, rowed for long days and saw plenty of wildlife. I think we all feel blessed to have had the chance to experience this small and intriguing section of the coast.

Inside Passage South

I had owned and cruised *Hornpipe*, my Alaska 18, for about four years, when I started pondering the idea of designing a new sail and oar boat. After all the work I put into building *Hornpipe*, why was that? Well, she is a fine boat, but after four summers I found that there are a few features I look for in my ideal boat that *Hornpipe* doesn't have. *Hornpipe* carries a lot of sail area for her length and beam. While this allows her to sail on a mere suggestion of a breeze, where others will be rowing, it also means that I have to reef earlier than other boats designed for the same mission. The setup for shifting masts, which increases the number of possible sail combinations, calls for a certain amount of athleticism that doesn't come as easily as it used to. *Hornpipe's* long straight keel, while making for good tracking, also makes tacking an exercise that needs care. I also can't sail to windward in the kinds of winds I would like to be able to. I was not happy with how *Hornpipe* loses ten degrees of windward pointing ability as soon as the water gets a little rough. I convinced myself that it is due to inadequate daggerboard area and thickness, a shortcoming which is not easily remedied. When sleeping aboard at anchor, the interior arrangement requires setting up a slat bed at the level of the thwarts. This puts the bed above the roll centre of the boat, which means that in any kind of wave action, it is like trying to sleep atop a beach ball – you feel like you are going to roll off to either side. It also means that the boom tent sticks up rather high above the gunwales and creates a lot of windage. The result is, on windy nights the boat tends to sail around restlessly on the anchor line. The high boom tent is also colder because it is more exposed. In short, I concluded that a boat that has more form stability and requires less work to reduce sail area would be a better sail and oar boat. A larger, thicker centreboard would allow better performance sailing to windward. A different interior arrangement would let me sleep on the floor boards. An interior with enclosed stowage would both keep the gear dry and provide more positive flotation in the event of capsize.

So, why didn't I just pick an existing design and build that? There are lots of other designs out there intended for this type of use. The one that has the capabilities I admired the most is the Sooty Tern, a double-ended lug yawl designed by Iain Oughtred of Scotland. My friend James built the first one and I've seen its capabilities first-hand. It came down to the size of my garage, which serves as my workshop. It's not long enough to accommodate a boat that long and wide. Also, I am not especially enamoured with the aesthetic of a small double-ended boat. I have nothing against them, particularly, I just don't prefer them. I do like the aesthetics of a wineglass transom. I also have never had a problem with overtaking seas overtopping the transom stern of *Hornpipe*. That included the experience of sailing downwind in thirty-four knots in the Strait of Georgia during the Shipyard Raid. Avoiding that problem is the usual rationale given for a pointed stern.

I started designing a boat of my own that would have the characteristics I wanted, and which could be built in the space I have. I posted my thoughts on my first effort an online forum devoted to wooden boats. I got back a lot of feedback, some of it useful, some of it not. I tinkered away with the design for another couple of years, but hadn't made the commitment to building it. Then my friend Tim announced that he had commissioned our friend Eric to design a new sail and oar boat that he would build. He intended to take the completed boat on a trip from Seattle to Alaska up the Inside Passage. That was the spur I needed. I was considering doing that trip myself and I asked Tim if I could join him. He said yes but I knew I would want my new (not yet built) boat for the trip. Although I had designed the hull of the new boat with computer software, which supplies renderings that you can manipulate, it is not the same as physically looking at it in three dimensions. I built a scale model of the hull of my new design to see how it would look and to see if there were any glaring faults in the design. I was glad I did, as I wasn't satisfied with the shape of the hull in the forward sections near the waterline. I thought they were not full enough to prevent the boat from rolling the bow down when heeling over under the press of sail. I made a few changes to address that and decided it was refined enough to begin building.

The new boat would be eighteen feet long, five feet four inches wide at maximum beam and would be rigged as a balanced lug yawl. She would have built-in buoyancy/stowage in the ends and have a pivoting centreboard. The hull would be built of glued-lapstrake marine plywood, the same as *Hornpipe*. Most of the other wood for structural pieces would be Douglas Fir. The transom, thwarts and benches, which would have a varnish finish, would be Sapele, an African hardwood. The rest of the boat would be painted.

I began the build at the beginning of 2015. I had made the decision a couple of years before to start winding down my consulting business, but that took time, as I had several multi-year commitments. However by the spring of 2015 I was down to half time, effectively, and was able to spend more time on the boat. With the benefit of the experience of building *Hornpipe*, this build went faster. I finished the new boat in mid-June of 2016. The final step before launching was to bolt on the carved nameplate. I named her *Fire-Drake*, which is the 18th century sailor's archaic term for a meteor. In addition, J.R.R. Tolkien, in his book "The Hobbit," also appropriated the term for the dragon in that book. I liked the etymology of both of these meanings. Besides, I was never a fan of serial boat names, so I ruled out *Hornpipe II*.

I just have time for one quick overnight trip to check that the new boat sails and rows well enough, before getting ready for the Inside Passage trip. I launch from Sidney and go a few miles north to Portland Island. I spend the night there on the boat, underneath the new cockpit tent that Peter, my local boat canvas guy, made for *Fire-Drake*. It is every bit as comfortable as I hoped it would be. I sleep on the floorboards alongside of the

Fire-Drake launch day

centreboard case, out of the wind and feel like I am rocking in a hammock. The next day, with a clearing sky and a moderately strong breeze from the south, I have a chance to see how *Fire-Drake* will sail to windward. It is a two-reef breeze for my new boat and there is a nasty chop. I am thrilled to find that when I harden in the main sheet, *Fire-Drake* heels over only about fifteen degrees and charges ahead. She points well and shoulders aside the waves, and almost no spray comes aboard. As I tack upwind, I am gratified to confirm that my calculations and design choices have paid off. It doesn't appear that there will be any significant changes I will have to make. The only thing I do not have time to do, in the rush to get ready, is to do a capsize test. The reason for this test would be to confirm whether my flotation tanks/storage chambers will keep the filled water level below the centreboard trunk in the event of a capsize.

* * * * *

Two weeks later at the end of June on the public dock in Sidney I say goodbye to Kathleen mid-morning and row out in the morning calm and sunshine, heading north. If all goes well, in about six or seven weeks Tim and I will arrive in Prince Rupert or even Ketchikan. It will be very much a journey from the known to the unknown, from the familiar waters of the Gulf Islands to the less peopled waters of the north coast. Perhaps most importantly, it will be a shift in mental space from the familiar story of short trips to the unfamiliar narrative of an extended expedition.

I am filled with both anticipation and trepidation. Anticipation of accomplishing a major act of small boat voyaging, which, while it has been done many times before by others, is still not a common or easy thing to do. Anticipation of experiencing parts of the long, primeval coast between the settled south and the Alaska border that I have never seen before, in one continuous thread. Trepidation at whether we will encounter overwhelming seas, impassable currents, weeks of rain, gales or storms. I have a deep respect for the ocean, its power and capricious moods. The sea cares nothing for humans and its casual disregard can kill you if your vigilance slackens. The weather, especially on the north coast, is the biggest unknown. There is potential danger from being caught on crossings or open stretches by weather which might be too much for our small boats to handle. The very act of setting out to travel on the ocean in a small engineless boat is inherently risky. Still, daily life on land is not without risks, though we are inured to them through familiarity. Most great reward does not come without at least some risk. We will need to balance prudence and boldness. For the major open water crossings we will need to decide when to move when the weather allows and when to bail out or stay put when conditions become too dodgy. I am, however, sure of my skill and ability to do this trip. Decades of sailing, studying seamanship, gaining experience kayaking and small boat voyaging leave me with the confidence that I am up to the challenges ahead.

It remains sunny and calm as I row north past Sidney Spit, where a Harbour porpoise surfaces alongside, a good omen for the start of the trip. Past Forrest Island I turn northeast to head for Bedwell Harbour on Pender Island. Just when it looks like it will be a long hot row that will take the rest of the afternoon, a light southeast wind rises. I stand up the masts, raise sail and set off on a close reach. The wind is fitful for the first few miles past

Moresby Island and into Boundary Pass, then it steadies into a moderate breeze. It is a delightful sail in the sunshine and there is lots of boat traffic to engage my interest. Boundary Pass is busy with a large container ship followed by a bulk cargo ship. Each makes the dogleg turn at Saturna and Stuart Islands, which carries them from the Strait of Georgia to Haro Strait and on to Juan de Fuca Strait and the open Pacific. Fortunately, my course keeps me outside the shipping lane and out of their way. The wind strengthens as I turn into Bedwell Harbour and it quickly blows me the mile downwind to the beach at Beaumont Marine Park. This is the site of the rendezvous with Tim, who has sailed up from Seattle. Tim is joined by our friend James. James has moved to Singapore since our last trip together, but he has returned with his boat out of Anacortes to join us for the first few days or a week of our trip.

I set up *Fire-Drake* on the clothesline mooring, but Tim and James have not yet arrived. I get out the cell phone and call Tim. He and James have arrived at the resort across the bay, cleared customs and are, predictably, in the pub sampling the local brew. Half an hour later they arrive at the beach. James is recovering from a cold and has a bad cough. Over supper on the beach we get caught up, set our plans for the morning and retire to the boats to sleep. I phone Kathleen to let her know I have made it without mishap. I confirm that the new satellite tracker that I bought for this trip is working, including the text messaging feature. As I drift off to sleep and think about the whole trip ahead, it seems a little daunting. I remind myself that, if I approach it one day at a time, I can do it. Today is a good start.

* * * * *

The morning dawns cloudy, with enough wind coming right into the harbour that we have to row out against it. Once we round Wallace Point at the mouth, it becomes a light tailwind that pushes us north along Swanson Channel. It is lazy sailing, under the gradually clearing skies, and it is deeply satisfying to be sailing in company with two other similar boats. It feels like the adventure has truly begun. The wind holds until we reach the north end of Prevost Island at Trincomali Channel, where it dies away altogether. We drop the sails and take up the oars. We work in the heat on glassy water under the high sun until about half way across the channel, where a cool southeast wind suddenly comes up. This is not only a welcome relief from the heat, it means that we can sail again. Up go the masts and sails. We have a fast sail the rest of the way across the channel and up the harbour to the beach at Montague Harbour Marine Park.

After supper, still suffering from the effects of his cold, James goes to bed early in an attempt to recover. Tim and I decide to take advantage of the bus service that the Hummingbird Pub runs on the Island. It picks up boating visitors from the campground and takes them to the pub and back. The best part of the visit to the pub is the bus ride itself. As the bus pull up and we get on, the driver says to me, "Here's your tambourine," and to Tim, "Here's your maraca." "What are we going to do with these?" I ask. "Just be patient. You'll see," says the driver.

At that point we notice that he has a tambourine taped to the centre of the steering wheel and cymbals and cow bells mounted above the windshield. After few more people get on at the next stop, the driver turns on some vintage rock 'n roll and cranks up the volume. He proceeds to sing along and accompany the songs with a drumstick on his percussion instruments while we join in. It is a hoot. The driver, Tom Tompkins, aka "Tommy Transit" explains how he has made it his mission to engage people on what would ordinarily be an encounter-free bus ride, in order to end social isolation. A retired city bus driver, he now drives the Hummingbird Pub bus in the summer tourist season and does motivational speaking in the winter. It is a marvelous encounter.

* * * * *

The next morning does not have a promising start. We get a late start to wait for the rising tide to float our boats, which have ground out over breakfast. It is overcast when we set out rowing and it soon turns to drizzle and rain. The mood is entirely different when you think you may be rowing all day in the rain. You definitely don't look forward to it the same as on a sunny day. The rain is just water after all, but it is harder to remain dry and comfortable when you are generating your own moisture inside the waterproof clothing that is attempting to keep the water from the outside getting in. The rain and discomfort don't last long. After about three quarters of an hour, enough wind comes up from the southeast that we are able stop rowing and set sail. We sail over to the west side of Trincomali Channel and up the west side of Wallace Island to have a look at Conover Cove as we go by. The wind holds, the rain stops and the clouds gradually clear away. Approaching the beach at the south end of Pirates Cove Marine Park on De Courcy Island, it is obvious that the south-facing cove is too exposed to the south wind to allow us to anchor there for the night. We turn around and sail back out of the cove and around the point towards the more sheltered cove in the north side of the Park. Coming around the point, I feel a thump on the boat's bottom and I suddenly lose steering control. Looking over the transom, I can see that I have hit something, most likely a submerged log. The collision pulled the rudder downhaul line out of the rudder, and the rudder is just floating, not biting in to enable me to steer. I drop the sails for the short row to the cove. We row in the entrance and up to the head of the cove where we can anchor farther in than all the big boats that are already there. We raft up together and I borrow a needed tool that I don't have, remove and disassemble the rudder and soon have it repaired. We eat supper while rafted up and sit and talk about the day. The anchorage becomes more crowded as more boats come in. It is a very popular anchorage and it can be very hard for deeper draft boats to find a place to anchor if they arrive late in the day.

* * * * *

We head out next morning for the turn of the tide at False Narrows, about four miles north, which is predicted to occur at about eight thirty. We leave the anchorage at about six thirty in order to give ourselves plenty of time. We needn't have worried.

It is partly cloudy but calm as we row up the west side of Pylades Channel along the De Courcy Island shore. There are summer cottages on this shore but there aren't many people stirring this early. The absence of people makes it seem as if we have the islands to ourselves this morning. We arrive at the entrance to the Narrows at the tip of Link Island about half an hour early. Since there are more cottages on the shore here we anchor in the shallow water to wait. As the tide ebbs, the dropping water level reveals more and more life on the bottom below us. We can see eel grass, various kinds of seaweed, crabs and small fish. There is a wonderfully mellow feeling that comes while waiting for the tide when you know you have done everything you can to get into the right position and there is nothing left to do but wait for the world to turn and the moon to drag the ocean up or down. You're in a safe place and the prospect of action is before you, but you have been granted a space to simply contemplate and appreciate the world around you, in a way that our increasingly virtual existence doesn't allow. Tim calls this "chilling out" and it is to become a significant feature of our trip ahead.

Just when it looks like we are going to ground out, it is time to leave. The water in the Narrows is slack as we get into the most constricted part, but the current soon turns in our favour. By this time, there are a number of people on the shore on both sides of the Narrows, strolling along the beach, walking their dogs and investigating tide pools. It is a lively scene but we can't gawk for too long as the channel is very narrow and other boats show up to transit the pass. As we exit, a very faint breeze comes up from behind us and James optimistically decides it is enough to sail. Tim and I carry on rowing and soon leave James behind, with his sail up but barely moving. Tim and I stop for a breather and a snack – breakfast was a long time ago. While we drift, the breeze fills in a little more and James catches up to us. We also raise our sails and slowly set off. The wind at first is just enough to push us along to the zone of no wind, where we slow and stop and the wind fills in behind us. This happens several times along Northumberland

Channel but at last the wind increases to a steady, but light, breeze and carries us into the public dock at Nanaimo[76].

After a shower at the public docks, we troop off to the local chandlery to pick up various items that we have found a need for but don't have. I buy a new pair of fingerless gloves for rowing, as my old ones that I've had for many years are too worn and are not protecting my fingers from blistering. Next order of business is to find a pub for a beer, followed by an early supper at the restaurant next door. The wind, which picked up after we got in, dies down again by the time we row across the harbour to Newcastle Island, the marine park. We intended to anchor out in Mark Bay but discover notices on posts telling us that it is illegal to do so. There are a number of mooring buoys further out in the bay, many of which are available, but the rates seems outrageous. There is a permitted anchorage to east of the dock between Newcastle and Protection islands, but it is quite exposed to northerly winds, and it doesn't seem like it will be either comfortable or safe in our small boats. On rowing in to the public dock, we discover that the cost of tying up at the dock overnight is actually reasonable, so we opt to do that. It will also be the safest place to be if the northwest winds tomorrow become as strong as forecast.

* * * * *

Now we endure two days of waiting for the northwest wind to moderate or shift. We wake the first morning to a wind of fifteen to twenty knots. Any potential cross-Strait destinations for us are either a direct beat to windward or a close reach. We just can't do it safely in wind that strong. Any crossing of the Strait of Georgia is not to be taken lightly, especially in a small open boat. The fetch is long and the sea state builds quickly. Setting out with two or maybe three reefs in the sail at the beginning of a crossing is just not prudent. You can't be sure the wind won't get stronger during the crossing – predictions are never that precise – and if it does you have no fallback plan, no further reductions in sail area that you can make.

The first day is a Sunday of the Canada Day long weekend. The docks at Newcastle are full and the harbour ferry brings many visitors and picnickers over for the day. James and I go for a walk on the trail around the perimeter of the island. The trail takes us up over the bluffs on the east side and brings us out to the north side. There we have a good view of the white-capped waters of the Strait and the snow-capped mountains of the mainland across the Strait, only slightly obscured by a little haze on this otherwise sunny day. Newcastle Island has an interesting history which is in some ways a microcosm of the history of many places on the coast, involved as it is with major industries and groups that are important on the coast. It is known as Saysutshun (Au' si:em siyeyu) by the Snuneymuxw First Nation people who used it as a base for the spring herring fishery before European contact. The first evidence of European use of the island you come across when you set out on a walk is an abandoned pulpstone quarry. The island's sandstone was first quarried in the 1870s for building projects, including San Francisco's US Mint building. Later, in the 1920s, as pulp and paper mills begin opening up on the coast, stones for grinding wood chips into pulp are required and the island's sandstone was suitable. The giant hole saw that was used to cut out the four foot diameter stones still sits abandoned in the quarry.

The main story of the European settlement of Nanaimo comes with the revelation, by the Snuneymuxw Chief Che-wech-i-kan, that there is coal on the island. The story goes that he was in Fort Victoria in late 1849 to have his gun repaired. When he observed the gunsmith using coal and was told how valuable it was, this quality of coal having to be imported from England, he said he knew where there was lots of it. He was told he would be rewarded if he could prove it. When he returned in the spring with a canoe-load of coal, the Hudson's Bay Company clerk Joseph McKay looked into it. The result was that the first coal mine shaft was sunk on the island two years later, employing the Snuneymuxw as miners early on. Later, as the mine expanded, workers from England were brought in and other shafts were sunk. Unfortunately, the Snuneymuxw people didn't really benefit much from this exploitation of the resource on their land. Instead, the mines made the fortune of one of the richest men in British Columbia at the time, Robert Dunsmuir. This was the start of a significant industry in the Nanaimo area based on coal. The industry was also the source of labour troubles for decades. Accidents claimed the lives of workers, resented Chinese workers were imported and there were strikes caused by dangerous working conditions. The strikes were suppressed by the owners with the help of strike-breakers and suppressed by the authorities with militia. The remains of one of the mine shafts can still be seen on the northwest corner of the island. Newcastle Island was also the site of a herring saltery and shipyard, largely run by Japanese immigrant fishermen, until they were shamefully rounded up and interned at the start of the World War Two. Another major name in the development of the Canadian West, the Canadian Pacific Railway, came into the picture in 1930 when they bought a farm on the island and built a tourist resort. They operated it until they sold it, because of declining revenues, to the City of Nanaimo in 1955. The City couldn't make a go of it either and sold it to the Province, for a dollar, in 1960. It was then turned into the current park, which is currently managed by the Snuneymuxw in a collaborative management agreement with the Province and the City.

✱✱✱✱✱

About midnight the second night, I'm woken up by a frantic-sounding woman's voice, sounding like it is coming from very nearby. "Help! Help! There's a raccoon on the boat and I can't get him off!" the woman says. Sounds of scuffling and low growling. "Wait! It's OK, nothing to worry about – go back to sleep," the woman says.

"Are you OK, do you need help?" I say. "No, no, everything is fine. Go back to sleep," she says.

Next morning the woman apologizes for the helpless female moment (her words), but the raccoon got under their boat tent.

He was after some juice in a box, and wasn't initially intimidated by the fish gaff she was brandishing, but eventually he was persuaded to leave by a whack on the nose.

The next day the wind is still lively and from the northeast. It is blowing eighteen to twenty knots already at Entrance Island at five o'clock in the morning. This pretty much rules out a crossing of the Strait. James decides that, with the limited amount of time he has, he can't risk coming with us further north and potentially getting stuck waiting for a favourable weather window to get back across. He decides to head for Silva Bay on the Strait of Georgia side of Gabriola Island. Tim and I are on the northeast side of Newcastle when we see him thrashing his way out of the bay towards Entrance Island. He is clearly bucketing up and down a lot and having trouble making progress. We see him put the boat about and head back. As Protection Island obscures him from our view again, that is the last we see of him. Tim and I amuse ourselves by taking the ferry across to town and discovering a downtown micro-brewery.

* * * * *

On the morning of the third day at Newcastle the wind has moderated to a forecast ten to fifteen knots, still from the northwest. This is down enough that we figure we can make some progress to windward and maybe get to Schooner Cove, north of Nanoose Bay. This will put us on a better slant for the crossing the following day, when the wind is forecast to switch to the southeast. We row around the back side of Newcastle to Departure Bay, to get a head start on the beat to windward. We raise sail and begin the beat out of the bay. Although the wind isn't terribly strong this morning, there is about a three foot chop left over from the wind that was blowing for the last two days. I put in a reef and am making good progress with *Fire-Drake*. I am pleased with how well she goes to windward in these conditions (one of my design objectives achieved) but Tim is having difficulty. He radios me, we put into the lee of a small point and drag the boats ashore to wait for conditions to moderate. It soon starts to rain. The beach is much flatter that we initially thought and soon the boats are high and dry as the tide goes out. We have lunch and putter about the beach. The rain eases off and the skies begin to clear but we are still stranded by the tide. By the time we get off the beach mid-afternoon, the northwest wind has almost gone and we have to row. After about an hour of pulling, the wind begins to come up from the opposite direction. We raise sail and soon we are scooting along downwind in delightful sunshine with the wind over the starboard quarter. The waves haven't had time to build up and the water is relatively flat, a dark indigo blue. It's a welcome contrast from the rain and the gloom earlier.

By late afternoon the sunshine heats the land and the wind turns into an afternoon thermal, strengthening considerably. It seems like no time at all before we sail right into the Schooner Cove marina, dropping our sails just inside the stone breakwater across the entrance that protects it from the sea. The breakwater protects the marina from the waves but it is quite exposed to the wind. The wind whistles across the little bay all evening and sets the halyards clanging against the aluminum masts of the sailboats at the docks. On the plus side we are able to shower and do laundry. We turn in late wondering whether we will be able to make the crossing of the big water tomorrow.

* * * * *

It is clear in the morning when we get up. The wind is light to moderate from the southeast and the sea state is low, nearly smooth. We can't ask for better conditions to make the crossing. Just past the end of the breakwater, we are able to raise all sail. Once settled in, the point of sail to the south end of Lasqueti Island is a broad reach. In the seven to ten knots of wind that is blowing, it's ideal for our boats and rigs. We are able to maintain four and a half to five and a half knots of boat speed. It is an exhilarating sail, with the sun beaming down out of a cloudless sky and the sea throwing up flashes of light from the wave tops and faces. With each plunge into a wave the bow of the boat throws glittering drops of spray into the air ahead, like a handful

Crossing Strait of Georgia in perfect conditions

of jewels carelessly tossed aside by a magnanimous potentate, repeated time and again with no end to his wealth. Both the sailing and the boat's motion get a little more lively as the wind increases when we get further into the crossing. Mostly it is a case of the sea state catching up to the wind. It is only about ten miles to Young Point on Lasqueti. After about two hours we round the point, drop the sails and pull into Rouse Bay for a breather, to eat lunch and figure out our next move. We look at the chart and decide that we can make it to Pender Harbour. It will require beating to windward for two to three miles at the start to get around Upwood Point at the southern tip of Texada Island, but then it will be downwind.

It is decidedly lumpier beating to windward but I am still tickled with how well *Fire-Drake* handles the chop and powers to windward. I find that I point higher and sail faster than Tim in his boat. It takes us several tacks to clear the point and I get there first. I am finally able to ease the sheets and bear away for Pender Harbour. We are now running a little off directly downwind. On that point of sail Tim's boat is faster, and he soon catches up and passes me. The sailing is once again wonderful and the entrance of Pender Harbour soon appears. We turn in and find that the wind follows us and blows us right up the centre of the harbour. The water of course is flatter, with almost no fetch, and is sheltered by the surrounding hills. We steam along quickly, taking in the sight of the deeply indented and convoluted shoreline of Pender Harbour with its several small settlements, many docks and boats.

Pender Harbour is sheltered in all weathers and it is likely this feature that led the Shishalh tribe of the Coast Salish people to make it their winter headquarters. As busy as the harbour is now, archaeological evidence suggests that the population was actually greater, before contact. This didn't last though, as a smallpox epidemic in 1862 wiped out nearly all the people. A residential school was established in the harbour by Catholic missionaries a few years earlier specifically to convert the people from their traditional way of life to a European one. We are still living with the after-effects of that disastrous policy. Unlike Nanaimo with its coal, there was no single major industry driving the white settlement of the area, rather it was a combination of fishing, logging and farming in the early years. It was a tough go much of the time, so much so that in the late 19th century, the area was known as Hardscratch. Gradually things improved and the harbour become a regular stop on the Union Pacific steamship route. In the 20th century, Pender Harbour became popular with yachtsmen and vacationers, as it is to this day. The depression of the 1930s hit the area hard, but there were relief camps established in the area, and the men in them extended the road up from Sechelt by 1936. After that it opened up more and more to permanent settlement.

The wind pushes us right up to the public dock at Madeira Park, where we tie up for the night. The grocery store there furnishes us with fresh vegetables that are the chief ingredients of a stir fry supper that we make on the picnic table at the head of the dock. The sun is still out and the wind is diminished a little and it stays warm right into the late evening. We go to bed hoping that the wind the next day isn't going to be as strong as forecast.

* * * * *

The cloud moves in overnight and sits low on the skirts of the hills and mountains enclosing the bay. It is a little misty when we set off from the dock. We row the mile and a half out to the harbour mouth as there isn't enough wind to sail. There is still no wind at the mouth but there is a significant slop coming up Malaspina Strait from the south, out of keeping with the lack of wind. That should have clued us in. I carry on rowing out past the islands that guard the bay, figuring the wind will fill in eventually, while Tim follows maybe a quarter mile behind. Sure enough, the wind arrives with a bang, rising from calm to about twenty knots in a matter of seconds. I put a single reef in the main sail and raise it, only to find that is too much. I drop the sail again and tie in a second reef. I have just raised the sail again when Tim hails me on the radio. "I think this is too much wind to start the day in," he says. "The weather is likely to get worse and we won't have many options if we are starting out with a couple of reefs in already." "I think you are right," I say. "We ought to head back in. I'll turn around and join you."

By this time I have gone downwind more than a mile from the harbour. To get back to the harbour mouth I have to tack back against the wind. Because the apparent wind is always stronger when you are sailing into it than running with it, I tie in the third reef and start to beat back upwind. The wind is very gusty and I am not making much progress. The sail with three reefs in it is about right for the gusts, but when the wind slackens off, there isn't enough sail area to power through the chop. I hobby-horse uncomfortably along, then, with a last blast, the wind dies altogether, leaving me flopping about in the lumpy waves. I drop the rig and begin rowing. It is hard work in the ragged, uneven slop as I can't get a rhythm going. As the boat is thrown around, the oar is buried deeply on one side, and I can't move it, then on the other side the oar slices the top off a wave, getting no purchase. Slowly I finally make it past the off-lying rocks north of the last island, where the wind comes up again, just enough to sucker me into raising the sails, before it dies away. I drop the rig once more and take up the oars, with The Who's *"We Won't Get Fooled Again"* running through my head. A hard pull later I eventually get back to where Tim is waiting, having been spared all the drama and work, and we row back into the harbour.

On the way back in we think we will look at the alternate government wharf shown on the chart at Gerrans Bay. When we get there we find no room, less shelter and no facilities, as it is clearly intended for commercial fish boats. We abandon the search here and head back to Madeira Park. The rain arrives during the row back there and comes down steadily as we tie up to the dock. We set up our tents to keep the water out of the boats and go up to the coffee shop, where we listen to the four o'clock forecast. There is now a gale warning for the Strait. Merry Island, just to the south and Grief Point near Powell River to the north, are both reporting twenty-five to thirty knots. We made the right decision. When supper-time rolls around, the rain eases but still threatens. Not fancying setting up the cooking gear in the wet when there is an alternative, we walk up to the Grasshopper Pub. We have supper there, snug inside while the rain arrives and pours down. It quits by the time we finish and we have a dry walk back.

The next day the rain stops but the wind remains high, more than twenty knots in the morning. We go for walks, go for coffee, sit at the dock and periodically check the conditions, but the wind doesn't drop all day. We find out that we can't stay another night at Madeira Park. There is a wooden boat festival planned for the next day and they want the dock space. When we point out that our boats are wood and engineless, built and used in the spirit of classic wooden boats, we are told that we don't qualify, as we are too new - they only want old wooden boats. What can you do in the face of such discrimination? We pull across the harbour to Garden Bay where we find a warm welcome, showers, supper and beer at the marina pub. I go to bed and sleep soundly until about three in the morning when I wake to the mighty bangs and crashes of a thunderstorm, accompanied by rain of truly biblical proportions. My tent, made of supposedly waterproof material, gets saturated and begins to leak, first along the seams and then generally everywhere. I dig out my bivvy sack, unroll it, stuff the sleeping bag inside and set up the hood, which is awkward as there really isn't enough room. But, it does keep me dry and I drift off back to sleep.

* * * * *

The rain tapers off by five o'clock and I get up at half past six and have breakfast. It is calm then but the winds are forecast to be about ten to twenty knots from the south in the morning and getting stronger later in the day. It looks like we will have a good window to get north to Powell River. Tim still hasn't got up by seven thirty. I wake him and suggest we get going to take advantage of the window. He agrees and we pack up and get moving by about eight thirty. The calm lasts until we row out past Pearson Island when the wind comes up suddenly, not unlike two days before, only not as strong or as gusty. I put a reef in the mainsail, raise it and set off after Tim, who beat me to it. Off we go, swooping along on the waves, with the following wind pushing us at hull speed and sometimes more. Within half an hour, the wind increases again. I round up, drop the rig and go straight to the third reef. The sail with three reefs in it is still plenty of area as the wind is above twenty knots by now. We haven't gone very far and clearly it is going to get worse. I radio Tim and suggest that we seek shelter in Cockburn Bay just ahead, where I was with the Shipyard Raid seven years before. We hang on, sailing fast and occasionally surfing on top of the waves and turn the corner at Cape Cockburn. Within a few boat lengths the wind drops right off next to shore where we are. The wind roars overhead and we row along in the calm water to the head of the bay. The cloud of the morning has broken up into large clear patches surround by towering thick cumulus clouds. They have grey undersides where they are between us and the sun, but they are brilliantly white with crisp edges away from the sun. In the bay it is so sunny, beautiful and calm that it is hard to believe it is blowing hard just a mile away.

There are only a few houses in the bay, on the north side, and right at the head of the bay there are no buildings. On the south side, near the head where it opens up a little I set the anchor, Tim rafts up to me and we get out the fixings for lunch. Just as we do so, a woman comes down to the dock opposite us, on the north side and calls out, "Hello!"

We answer back, "Hello, how are you? Beautiful day!" She replies, "Come on over and stay on our dock. It will be easier than anchoring." "We'd be glad to," we say, "we're just tucking in to lunch and we'll be over after that." "Fine! Tie up to the dock when you're done," she says.

We row over after lunch and as we are tying up to the dock, the woman's husband comes down to greet us and invite us up for coffee. He introduces himself as Paul and his says his wife's name is April. Over coffee we talk about the trip we are making. I mention that I was here before, during the Shipyard Raid, with all the other Raid boats. When I talk about my previous boat, *Hornpipe*, and how I played the harmonica in the evening that time, April says she distinctly remembers the boats and the harmonica playing. April and Scott tell us about their life here. They have owned the land for about thirty years but only started building the house at the top of the hill five years ago. They have a smaller single room building at the head of the dock, now April's studio, which was their original house. They have several outbuildings, including a large shop, where Paul has a chainsaw mill that he uses to cut lumber from salvaged logs. They invite us for supper. As we sit down to a fine spread of roast beef, potatoes, vegetables, she tells us how she took the large roast out of the freezer that morning, before we arrived. She thought to herself that it was really going to be too much for the two of them. Then we arrive – karma! April tells us we are their first dinner guests in the new house. Supper is a very convivial occasion indeed and we linger over apple pie April made and stay talking afterwards. Paul and April tell us a little about the various kinds of wildlife they see, including a pair of resident Ravens that have become quite used to them. They tells us of local history, which has it that the head of the bay is the site of a massacre of the local Shishalh people by the Haida, long ago[77]. The head of the bay is now thought to be cursed, with every subsequent owner and commercial venture eventually coming to a bad end. Finally, when we can keep our eyes open no longer, we thank April and Paul for their unlooked-for hospitality, which we deeply appreciate, and go down and turn in.

* * * * *

In the morning, the sky clears and we find everything covered with heavy dew. It is early when we leave and the sun is adding golden colour to the tops of the hills on the south side of the bay. The sun hasn't yet made it down to water level as we set out. Looking over the transoms of our boats, facing east as we row out of the bay in the calm, the hills are reflected in a perfect mirror image. Coming out from underneath the shadow of the hills we are immediately blinded by the low sun as it shines directly into our eyes, but at least the heat starts to dry up the moisture in the boat. Outside the bay, we haven't gone too far when a light wind rises from the northwest, the direction we want to go. We put up the sails and start tacking upwind. The sky overhead is blue, there is a tattered band of low cloud intermittently obscuring the tops of the mountains on Texada Island to the west and the low rippled waves are a deep burnished denim blue. It is another great day to be alive. A single simple task to accomplish – sail to the best of my ability to get to our destination to windward, perfect weather to do it in, and all the time in the world. It is wonderful sailing, even if we aren't moving very fast.

As the morning hours tick by, the wind increases to the point where we have to take in a reef in the sails. The sailing become a little more challenging and, like a few days earlier, I am to windward of Tim. We have only made about six miles by noon and are approaching Scotch Fir Point at the entrance to Jervis Inlet. Tim radios and suggests we take a break to see if the wind will moderate, as it is forecast to do. We pull into McCrae Cove, raft up together and have lunch while the wind blusters overhead in the trees ashore alongside us. We lounge and drowse in the sun, and the wind finally eases a little about three o'clock. We set out again, with a single reef in the sails, but we soon have to shake it out as the wind falls lighter. The wind stays steady for the rest of the afternoon and into the evening as we beat upwind towards Grief Point. Westview, our intended destination, is just a couple of miles past it.

Since the beginning of the trip, I've been bothered by a wrinkle in the foresail, running from the throat to the clew, which no amount of adjustment of the downhaul tension or sheet would eliminate. After staring at it for more than ten days, thinking about it off and on and letting my subconscious work on it, I think of another adjustment I might make to the clew outhaul. I did that while we waited for the wind to moderate and to my satisfaction, it works. The sail now sets with a nice airfoil curve from luff to leech and I seem to have found the groove for going to windward. I am also using the GPS that afternoon, by setting Grief Point as the destination then using the subsequent Velocity Made Good (VMG) function to show me the fastest point of sail to windward. I discover that the fastest point of sail is not as high as the boat will point, but about five to ten degrees off that. It also shows me that the difference between the attaining the best VMG and not is pretty fine. For best velocity to the destination I have to constantly pay attention to steering and sail trim. All very technical but what it means in practise is that I sail a little farther, but much faster, and get there quicker. For a sailor, this is all deeply satisfying.

Along about seven o'clock, I lose sight of Tim, who was about a mile behind me. It turns out that he ran out of wind about then, off Albion Point and had to get out the oars. I am a little further out in the strait and hold the wind until quarter to eight. I too have to shift to rowing, about two miles short of Grief Point. By the time we reach the point, the sea is as smooth as a mill pond. A shaft of sunlight from the setting sun way off low in the west, makes a beautiful yellow glow on the horizon under the grey of the clouds that has started to move in. Lovely as it is, it heralds the end of useful light for rowing. We are still nearly an hour's row away from Westview. Not being keen to row it in the dark when there is still boat traffic around, we turn in instead to a little marina just south of Grief Point, built out from the gravelly shore with rock breakwaters. The marina normally caters to small runabout sport fishermen, but there is room for us, and we are happy to find a haven for the night. We are tired from the long day and hope to be able to have supper in the adjacent pub, but it is Sunday night and they closed early. The liquor store is still open though. We go in to pick up some supplies and come back down to the boats to make supper on the dock. We attract one curious onlooker who sits and talks to us all though supper and well into the darkness about our boats and our journey. He starts by asking whether we are part of that year's R2AK (Race to Alaska) which started in Port Townsend mid-June. We tell him that we are definitely not racing, that our style is more of an "Every Pub to Alaska" cruise.

* * * * *

The next morning provides a light breeze from the south as we leave the marina and sail around Grief Point. It takes about an hour to cover the two miles to the public marina and we manage to miss the entrance to it, going past it to the commercial docks. We have to turn around and beat back the half mile, in a freshening wind, to the public dock. The rest of the day is a kind of "make-and-mend" day[78], in Navy parlance. I do not have a dry suit and have decided that, after discussing the merits of them with Tim, who has one, it will be a good piece of kit to have. It will be especially useful if we get into really prolonged cold, rainy, windy weather further north on the coast. I know from my previous trips just how unpleasant that can be and I am determined to acquire one. I think Powell River might be big enough to have an outdoor store that will carry them. After calling and tramping all over town, we determine that none are to be had. We do take the opportunity to lay in some fresh produce, likely the last for a while, and pick up some more useful items, including a couple of cans of waterproofing for my tent and a wind jacket for Tim in a truly livid shade of safety yellow/green. I also do a load of laundry at the nearest laundromat, which isn't too near. As I walk back to the marina, it starts to rain and the wind picks up. Tim made the executive decision to stay put and paid for our moorage for the night. It turns out to be the right thing to do as the wind picks up even more before it begins to abate. We finish the day with supper at a Thai restaurant.

We set out next morning in air that is totally still and on water that is totally flat, without even a ripple. The sky is covered with nimbostratus clouds with dark grey bottoms where they are thickest, interspersed with brighter patches. The sea is smooth and sluggish, the colour of molten lead. The steam from the mill at Powell River rises straight up to join the low cloud and the mill noise easily reaches us as we row past, a mile away. We soon leave the mill behind and carry on towards the channel between Harwood Island and the mainland where we find a very light following wind. It is enough to tempt us into raising sail and we sail along, no faster than rowing, but without the effort, as the sky gradually lightens and the clouds gave way to scattered clear patches then full sunshine. I take the opportunity to charge my electronics battery with the solar panel and to set out the remainder of the laundry, which hasn't fully dried. We drift slowly north, with a brief period where we have to resort to oars again. We begin to notice a steady parade of boats converging on the channel, likely heading north to Desolation Sound.

At Lund, we stop in for a break and to check out the town. It is more than thirty years since I last walked around it. It has become considerably busier and more crowded since then. We have to raft up outside two other sailboats that look as if they haven't moved in months. After a pleasant stroll around the town, a stop at the general store, the bakery and the ice cream stand, we head back to the boats to leave. The harbour master lady promptly accosts us and points out we have overstayed our one hour free stay grace period by ten minutes and that we will have to pay for a half day's moorage. I pay but it seems a trifle too rigid to me, given how much the town's businesses depend on passing boaters. Rules are rules I suppose, but such zealousness in enforcing them doesn't recommend the place for a return visit.

A brisk south wind outside the harbour blows us quickly north the couple of miles to the Copeland Islands. There we find a tiny cove-within-a-cove, surrounded by steep rocks and trees, to anchor our boats out of the wind. During supper I manage to upset a pan of pasta on to the floorboards but, unwilling to start again, I scoop up what I can, add more water and finish cooking it while I clean up the remaining mess. It turns out surprisingly well, and I hope the boiling kills off whatever germs might have been on the floorboards. In the evening I apply some more seam sealer and waterproofing to my tent, hoping to have a drier night in the next heavy rain.

* * * * *

We seem to be settling into a pattern of calm mornings with cloud that clears later. That is what we find as we head north along the Malaspina Peninsula and around Sarah Point, bound for Desolation Sound. Except for a brief puff or two, the wind stays calm and the sun is very strong as we row across the mouth of Malaspina Inlet. The boat traffic is even thicker than yesterday, with all manner of sail and power boats motoring to and from Desolation Sound and into Malaspina Inlet. I rest on my oars, remove another layer and wait for Tim to come up. We raft up and just float while we have lunch and watch the passing parade. It is so hot that when I go to retrieve the tube of lip sun block from the front pocket of my life jacket, which has been sitting on the floorboards, the goop has mostly melted! I stuff what I can back in the tube and put the tube below the hatch in the aft compartment, where the water keeps it much cooler, in hope that it will solidify again.

Alongside Mink Island, enough wind comes up, from dead ahead, that we are able to sail for a while before it dies away again. On the oars we make our way through the pass east of Mink, where I am pleased to find a freshening wind, although our destination is dead to windward. I optimistically raise sail and find I soon have to reef. Tim opts to keep on rowing into the wind around the back of Otter Island. I make several tacks, but the wind is very gusty and, being reefed for the gusts, I don't have enough sail for the lulls. I make such poor progress that finally I concede the victory to the wind and take to the oars again. It is hard work rowing directly into the wind and the chop. It takes me an hour and half to cover the remaining mile and a half to Eveleigh Anchorage, just west of the more popular Prideaux Haven. I find Tim already anchored and I raft alongside for supper and social hour. As the evening comes on, the wind drops, a serene calm settles over the bay, and we have a fine view of the distant Vancouver Island shore to the west.

* * * * *

We are heading for the "back door" route along the north section of Vancouver Island. The most direct route a boat going north can take is up Johnstone Strait. For a small, engineless boat, this may not be the best choice in the summer. The Strait is notorious for the strong northwesterlies that funnel down it during the typical summer high pressure weather pattern. Combined with very strong tides, especially at Seymour Narrows, the sea state can become quite severe, to the point where it is difficult to make any progress or it is dangerous if you do proceed. The alternative is to wind your way through the channels and tidal passes among the islands between Vancouver Island and the mainland. This is the route we are attempting. Our days to come will be regulated by the passes and tidal currents. We have decided to come the back way for a few reasons; neither of us have been this way before, we think the scenery will be interesting, we hope to avoid the worst of the northwesterlies in Johnstone Strait and it will be challenge to negotiate all the tidal passes in engineless boats. We can move through the passes at slack and move along the channels when the tide is in our favour. Actually, slack is a misnomer in most of these rapids and passes, as there really isn't a period where the water is actually slack. The term used in the Tide Tables, "turn," better describes what happens, as the current goes from one direction to another in a matter of minutes, with no period of calm water.

We get away from Eveleigh Anchorage a little earlier than usual, as strong winds are forecast for later in the day and we want to make some distance before they rise. Low cloud moves in from the east, but we can see clear sky in the distance over Vancouver Island. It remains calm the three miles across Homfray Channel to the entrance to Waddington Channel between East and West Redonda Islands. We row steadily up Waddington and notice a drop off in boat traffic compared to yesterday. Although this is still Desolation Sound, perhaps this channel is simply not as popular as other areas of it east and west. After three and half hours of rowing a slight breeze comes up from the south, enough to persuade us to raise sail. We begin to see clear patches open up in the low cloud and the high tree-clad slopes and tops of the islands to either side reveal themselves. A waterfall high up on East Redonda tumbles down the upper hill and vanishes into the trees again. The breeze only lasts half an hour before it drops again, but it was a good break from rowing. At Shirley Point a breeze starts up from the north, convincing me to sail upwind, while Tim carries on rowing, with his fishing pole out in hopes of catching dinner. I sail for an hour before it dies away again and have to row the last three quarters of a mile to Walsh Cove, where I raft up to Tim for a late lunch. The promised strong wind arrives while we are eating lunch and swirls into the bay formed by the islands guarding it. Since the next move for us will be north into Pryce Channel, where the wind will be much stronger, we are stopped for the day. The wind sets all the anchored boats dancing about on their lines but with our shallow draft, we are further in and less affected. At the back of the cove behind us is a small stream that tumbles down to the beach. I row in to take advantage of this fresh water to wash and rinse my rowing clothes, and shave and wash my hair while I am at it. I feel positively civilized.

We rig the boat tents as awnings and pass the rest of the afternoon lazing about and reading under alternating sunshine

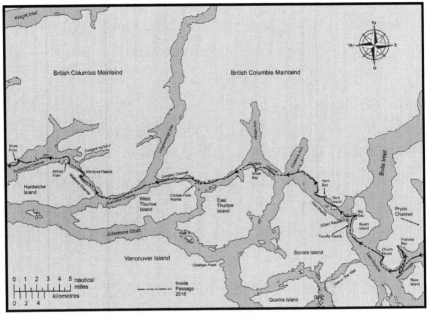

Vancouver Island North Tidal Passes

and showers. The waxing half-moon hangs high in the clear southern sky at sunset while the wind, which hasn't died with the cooling of the day, makes ripples and catspaws on the still bright water in front of the darkening land. It is good to be in a snug place for the night.

* * * * *

In the morning we find a headwind from the north as we row out of Walsh Cove and the last couple of miles up the narrowing north end of Waddington Channel. We anticipate even stronger wind in Pryce Channel but find to our surprise that the wind dies away altogether. Just when you think you are getting a handle on how the weather is affected by high and low pressure systems, daytime heating or local topography, something like this happens to remind you that you still have a lot to learn. It was likely a gap wind. The sky begins to clear earlier than yesterday and, facing east over our boat transoms as we row west, we have a fantastic view of the snow-capped mountains and waterfalls up Toba Inlet

Waiting for wind at Gloucester Point

as they slowly come out from behind the clouds. Had we not had a destination further north in mind, I think we would surely be drawn to those waters to see more.

At mid-morning, a west wind comes up suddenly and we raise sail and begin tacking upwind. We soon find ourselves on opposite sides of the nearly three mile wide inlet as we cross tacks. The wind increases and I find myself on the north side, Tim on the south, when he radios me to say he is stopping at the bay behind Gloucester Point to wait for the wind to moderate. I put about and race across on a broad reach and soon join him. It is an idyllic little bay with a fine gravel beach, crystal clear water, a view east up Toba Inlet and warm sun. There is even a freshwater stream for topping up our water supply. While we are waiting, a couple of old guys in kayaks pull in for lunch. We talk to them a bit. They are both long retired, and admit to not making as ambitious trips as they did when younger, but I am impressed that they are still out doing it when most men their age are thinking about moving into care homes. In early afternoon the wind diminishes enough that we sail out from behind the point and carry on. The wind is erratic the rest of the afternoon, alternately blowing lightly and then dying away several times, necessitating the transition from sail to oar and back again. As we row into Raza Passage north of Raza Island, the wind suddenly comes up again from the southwest, dead ahead. It is exciting sailing, rail down with a reef in, tacking from one side to the other. By six thirty the wind increases to the point where we need three reefs in the sail and are hardly making any progress.

This time, I radio Tim, "We aren't going to get around the corner in this wind and it might be windier in the channel there even if we do manage it." Tim says, "You're right, and it's getting late anyway."

"Frances Bay, just downwind of here, looks sheltered," I say. "Looks good, let's bail," Tim says.

We get a mile into the bay and the southwest wind that drove us into the bay quickly turns into a northwest wind coming down over the gap at the head of the bay between Toba Mountain and the Downie Range. Without much room to tack, we row the last mile and anchor there in the relative calm just off the beach, while the wind booms over our heads. The head of the bay is an abandoned logging show, of uncertain vintage, and there is an ancient and decrepit dock on the west side. Tied up at the dock is the unmistakable hull shape of an old wooden east coast lobster boat, to which an aluminum cabin is added. It is not the most elegant of conversions, but at least it looks seaworthy.

* * * * *

Overnight the wind continues to gust down through the gap, making the boat restless, with little wavelets rocking the boat. The foremast, which I left up, begins clunking against the side of its mast step, keeping me awake. I get up and tie off the halyard to the gunwale, which reduces but doesn't eliminate the noise. I make a mental note to find a suitable piece of driftwood and carve a chock to wedge the mast in place. The wind is definitely lighter in the morning, but the forecast is for big winds in the afternoon. We think that if we row hard we should be able to get around the point to Church House on the other side of the peninsula before the wind gets really strong. We hoist our sails and blow out of the bay on the remaining overnight wind, only to find that the wind dies away just past the entrance to the bay. We row like hell and get around the point where we find some wind still coming down Calm Channel, but we cut inside Bartlett Island and get safely to the bay at Church House.

Church House is an Indian Reserve but no one lives there now. There are a couple of buildings still standing above a gravelly and stony beach, and a good stream near the east end of the bay. The bay is a favoured spot, sheltered as it is from north winds. As the morning turns to early afternoon, the wind dies away altogether. We listen to the forecast again and figure that if we can get across Calm Channel to Harbott Point before the wind comes up, then there is a good chance that we can get through the first of the rapids, Yuculta[79] Rapids, on the afternoon slack. We set out, rowing strongly in the calm and the heat, and make it to Harbott Point in an hour and a half. We are earlier than we need to be and don't want to attempt the rapids until the turn. We tuck in behind the point to rest and wait. Just as we reach Kelsey Point before the rapids, a tug pulling a log boom comes up. We wait until he goes by and pull in behind. There are many other boats also going through at the end of the flood, but apart from just a little disturbed water at Whirlpool Point, we encounter no problems. We can't row fast enough to get through the second part of the Yucultas between the Gillard and Jimmy Jones Islands on the same slack period, but the community dock at Big Bay beckons to us for the night. It is a very pleasant spot in the later afternoon sunshine. The eye is led past the vacation houses behind the docks around the sweep of the bay out to a fine view across the rapids and the mountains of Sonora Island to the west. The calm water around the docks mirrors the rippled reflections of the boats that are tied up and the sun warms the whole bay. The store has showers, and even better, a few fresh vegetables and cold beer. In the evening, after supper, just enough breeze comes up to remove the heat of the day. We are pleased to have made it through the first of the rapids without drama or mishap.

* * * * *

We have to find some place to sit and wait between Gillard Passage and Dent Rapids as we know that it will take us two tides to get through both of them. Tim has the brainwave to phone over to Dent Island Lodge and ask if we can hang out on their dock for a few hours. The Lodge is an upscale resort located in behind Dent Island to the north of the rapids. The Lodge tells Tim that most of the boats that were there overnight are departing. They have no objection to us staying as there aren't a lot more boats expected today and the docks will be empty. We leave the Big Bay dock about half an hour before the predicted turn in Gillard Passage. My plan is to get through Gillard Passage early and use the last of the ebb before the turn to help us on our way to Dent. Once out in the bay we find big eddies that push us first one way and then the other. I have to row very hard to avoid getting swept north of the passage and when I get to the centre, fifteen minutes early, I find that the tide has already turned. It is even harder rowing to get through and then the flood is beginning. Tim is behind me and doesn't make it. He goes north around Jimmy Jones Island. That turns out to be a better move, given the early turning of the tide. He quickly scoots ahead into slacker water while I battle the both the increasing current and the wind that has begun to come up. It is some of the hardest forty-five minutes of rowing I have ever done, but I finally pull into the dock at the Lodge, ten minutes behind Tim.

We now have nearly six hours to wait. The staff at the lodge are very gracious and hospitable, inviting us to top up with water if we need it, and casually mentioning that their restaurant does a very good lunch. We wander the trails behind the lodge and look out past the island to Dent Rapids, which are in full flood. There are some high-powered boats going through, but it looks like they are labouring. Back at the lodge, we decide to take advantage of the restaurant for lunch, as it has a beautiful patio overlooking Little Dent Rapids. Just then a nature tour boat comes in and disgorges a horde of hungry sightseers. As we have nowhere to go, we let that lunch rush go through the kitchen and watch them depart before we go in. We pretty much have the patio to ourselves after that. We have as good a meal as I have had anywhere on the coast, at a cost that is, surprisingly, no more than what you would expect at any high end restaurant. During lunch, the rapids alongside turn into a waterfall as the height difference increases. It is amazing to watch and remember that this is the ocean, not a mountain stream, as the clear green water tumbles down through the narrow gap. The lodge staff assures us that it does go perfectly calm at slack water. We resolve to try going through there rather than out and around to the main Dent Rapids.

The rest of the afternoon passes in alternating sun and cloud with the wind gusting up and dying away. Wary of the early turn in the morning, we get the boats ready to go and keep an eye on the rapids as the predicted time approaches. When it looks like the current is dropping off to nothing, we jump in the boats and row around and through without incident. It is hard to believe it was a roaring torrent just a couple of hours ago. It is now early evening and we carry on about a mile to Horn Bay, a little bay on the north side of the channel. It is about the only sheltered place to stop in the next ten miles or so. We find an old decrepit float home in the centre of the bay that has its mooring lines stretched right across the bay to the shore on both sides – highly illegal. However, the lines are slack enough that we are able to row over them to find anchorage in about ten feet of water inside. We start off rafted up but soon it begins to rain lightly, followed by deep rumbling from overhead and down blasts of wind. This is the arrival of the forecast thunderstorm and I move off, set my anchor and set up the tent. The thunderstorm ramps up in earnest. For a little more than an hour, the lightning flashes, the thunder booms and crashes and the wind gusts and blows as I spin around my anchor. The storm feels like it is really close, and when I time the gap between the lightning flashes and the follow-up thunder, it is less than a second[80]. I am right, it is close. I'm glad we are in wooden boats without any conducting metal. I make and eat supper while all this is going on and wash and set out the dishes on the aft deck to drain. The storm finally moves off with remnant mutterings and grumblings and I decide to turn in early. Our plan is to get underway by about five o'clock next morning to catch most of the ebb tide west along the channel.

* * * * *

When the alarm goes at quarter past four we poke out noses out of the tents to find that it is seriously foggy and as a consequence not very light. We pack up anyway on hope and by five thirty it lightens and thins enough we think we can get around Horn Point, which is only a mile away. We start off but are barely out of the bay when we run into strong back eddies along the shore, slowing our progress. I move out a little to where I am far enough out to get out of the influence of the eddies but can still just make out the shore in the fog. Although I have my GPS on, I don't want to get too far out into the channel, as it is only half a mile wide at that point. We can hear the engines of big boats going by, moving fast. Even assuming they carry radar, no sure thing, I don't know how well that we, in our low, wooden boats with no metal in them, will show up. Getting run over by a big power boat in the fog would ruin the whole day. I creep along just in sight of shore and soon make it around Horn Point but I lose sight of Tim behind me. I drop anchor around the point and wait for him. When he doesn't turn up soon, I raise him on the radio. It turns out that he isn't able to see as well as I do in the fog and is unwilling to lose sight of shore. That close in, he couldn't get out of the grip of the back eddies. He retreated to wait until the fog lifts.

While I wait, I row over adjacent to the point to the rock wall that drops straight down into the water, and have a look at the underwater life there. There are many red, orange and purple sea urchins, a red and brown sea cucumber, a number of yellow sun stars and red-coloured Ochre sea star. The sea stars are an encouraging sight, as apart from a one other sea star back in the Copeland Islands, this is the only other ones I have seen on this trip. Most sea stars on the coast were devastated in recent years by sea star wasting syndrome[81]. It is good to see that they haven't all succumbed and are perhaps making a comeback. Eventually the fog lifts enough that Tim is able to get around the point. By that time, the back eddies are going the other way and he is able to use them to his advantage. He rafts up to me and we eat lunch while we wait for the fog to burn off a little more. It is turning into a fine sunny day above the fog, with no wind. We leave our temporary anchorage at noon and follow the back eddies along the north shore of Denham Bay until we get to Gomer Island, at the mouth of Frederick Arm. There, the tide is still moving against us for the jump across to East Thurlow Island forcing us to anchor once again to wait for the turn in our favour. Looking back to where we have come from there is a still a very thin wisp of fog just above the surface of the water. It is not enough to impede visibility, but it looks like a misty veil obscuring the horizon below the small high cumulus clouds and the bright sky. The sun is now very hot and we rig our tents as awnings for protection. As we wait I have a snooze to make up for the early morning start.

At about twenty past four the tide swirling between Gomer Island and the point calms enough we decide it is good to go. When we get out from behind the island, we can see a towering thunderhead in the west and it looks like it is heading our way. We are headed for Shoal Bay, only four miles away, but it will be a race to see if we can get in before the thunderstorm overtakes us. We pull hard, determined to beat it. My left wrist and forearm, which were bothering me intermittently the last few days, flares up and I just can't pull as hard as I want to nor as fast as Tim, or maybe it is just the age difference. In any case, Tim outdistances me and gets in about ten minutes ahead of me. It only took him about an hour and a quarter. The thunderstorm holds off and we tie up at the government dock in the warm wind that blows out from the land. We go up to the pub to celebrate our safe arrival and also my birthday, which is today. The old US Army Quartermaster freight boat, converted to a charter boat named Pacific Yellowfin, is anchored in the harbour. The pub happens to have "Pacific Yellowfin" Belgian lager, brewed by a Vancouver craft brewery, named after the ship, and which has its picture on the label. Seeing as how it is my birthday, I opt for a double-sized bottle and thoroughly enjoy it as we sit on the patio with the namesake in sight back-dropped by a view of the steep, dark green, tree-clad slops of the mountains enclosing Phillips Arm.

Back down at the dock, I start to make pasta for my supper when Tim comes around (he is at a different part of the dock because of the tight conditions) with an invitation to both of us for supper at the boat tied up next to him. They were out fishing earlier today and caught ling cod, clams and prawns. It is a fine supper and the threatened thunderstorm arrives in the middle of it. It is good to be inside during the heavy rain, swapping stories while in the warm and dry. The evening wraps up at eleven and I fall asleep immediately when I go to bed, despite the noise of the ongoing rain.

* * * * *

It is raining steadily at the hour we have settled on to leave, and the fog is back, although not as thick as yesterday morning. Tim comes by my boat and suggests that today will be a good rest day. Looking out into the thick weather, I agree. I have time for a very leisurely breakfast and do some reading in my tent out of the rain. As the day wears on, the rain tapers off to nothing but the sun never makes a complete appearance. The clouds do thin out and it does get warmer.

The underside of the high, fixed part of the dock is home to a number of Barn Swallow nests and the Swallows seem to be everywhere. Some of the young are still in the nests but others have just fledged. The fledglings are hanging about on all available perches including boats rigging. They mostly just sit there while the busy parents swoop in at intervals to stuff insects down their beaks. It is quite comical, as in many cases the youngsters are larger than their thin, overworked parents.

Later in the day we receive another supper invitation from James and Paula, a couple from North Carolina who are renting the house at the head of the dock. They found the place on Air

BnB but weren't able to form a clear picture of what they were coming to. With their son, his wife and their daughter, they put their gear, including a canoe and kayak, on the water taxi from Campbell River, which cost them rather more than they anticipated, and came out for ten days stay. Supper is a roast rack of lamb and a big pot of lentil soup that was simmering away, accompanied by fresh biscuits. It is another very convivial evening, and I am surprised again at the remarkably generous hospitality we have run into on our trip.

* * * * *

The following morning we do get away early, although there is some patchy fog when we leave, obscuring the mountains either side of Cordero Channel. Half an hour after setting out fog descends, the rain begins and the visibility drops. Now our world contracts to a small circle less than half a mile in diameter and a few hundred feet deep. With the fog and the rain coming down steadily there is nothing to see but the water around us, there is no alternative but to focus on the rowing. We move right over to the north side of the channel to be out of the way of any potential boat traffic although there is likely to be much less of that here. The tidal rapids that we came through a couple of days ago seem to be a great filter of cruising boats. We have seen far fewer boats since coming through Dent and Yuculta Rapids than we did to the south of them. The current pushes us along quickly. Alongside Lorte Island, the fog comes right down to the water again, like it did a couple of days ago. I am ahead and the last sight I have of Tim is his fluorescent jacket disappearing as the visibility goes to near zero. I press on and feel my way at last into the bay just south of Green Point Rapids, the next tidal pass we have to get through. I have a long wait until slack and I drop the anchor in eight feet of water in the middle of a kelp bed about a hundred feet from shore. Tim calls on the radio to say that there is not enough visibility for him and that he will wait until it lifts. I put up the tent, make a late breakfast and linger over coffee, reading while the light rain patters down on the tent.

In late morning, I am still reading when I hear the unmistakable sound of rocks being turned over on the beach. Immediately I think "bear"! I stick my head out of the tent and sure enough, there is a medium sized Grizzly, with blonde fur on its back, dark legs and a lovely cinnamon-coloured head. The bear is very intent on slurping up small crabs from under the rocks and doesn't notice me. Now, just audible over the sound of the light rain on the water, I hear the gentle splash of oars dipping and lifting, as Tim quietly rows up. "That's something to see," Tim whispers, "he's pretty focused on those crabs." "Yeah, he's been there for a couple of hours like that," I say.

The bear pays no attention to Tim or me as I help Tim to raft up. We sit, take pictures and admire the bear for a few moments. "Where did you stop to wait out the fog?" I ask. "I stopped at Cordero Channel Lodge, in behind Lorte Island," Tim says, "the lodge is kind of run down, but they are open and they made me a nice greasy truck stop breakfast, so I was able to sit inside out of the rain." The bear continues to work the rocks along the beach until the rising tide covers them.

Green Point Rapids is another tidal gateway for us on our way north, one where currents can run to seven knots at full flow. It is also narrow, less than 400 yards wide at its narrowest, with not much room to avoid big boats if they are transiting the same time as us. The chart shows a possible alternative, an exceedingly skinny passage between the largest Cordero Island and the mainland shore. This little passage dries out at low tide but might just have enough water for shallow draft boats like ours at high water slack. During the course of the afternoon, while the sun doesn't actually come out, the sky brightens and gets warm enough to dry out the boat. I take the opportunity to apply the last of the silicone spray to the tent, to try to increase its water resistance, which was not complete in the last heavy rain. We raise anchor in late afternoon and row slowly over to the beginning of the small pass. The pass is narrow and twisty, hemmed in by boulders. Perched among the boulders is a large hollow log, with a small tree growing out of one end. It must have been an exceptionally high tide that deposited that log there many years ago as no subsequent tide has moved it. The water surface is smooth and we find that there is still a little flood current, but it is not strong, and we pick our way through around the rocks in just enough water to float our boats. We can hear a big engine on the other side of the island, and when we emerge, we see a large freight boat exiting the main rapids. I am glad we found a back door route and didn't have to dodge the big boat. We row to the other side of the bay behind the rapids, just in the lee of the point forming the north entrance to the bay, and anchor. We hope that it will be sheltered enough for the night.

* * * * *

The night is completely calm and quiet, with no rain, and when I wake at quarter past five, there is high cloud obscuring the sun but also a little low cloud and patches of fog. It gives a very tranquil feel to the morning, but there is not enough fog to prevent us going. We want to get into position to be able to transit the Whirlpool Rapids, more than twelve miles away, at the afternoon slack. We leave about six and are immediately are jarred out of the tranquility of the morning by the boisterous full ebb current tearing down Cordero Channel. With that to boost us, we rocket along the four miles to Loughborough Inlet in less than an hour, rowing easily, until it suddenly feels like we are rowing in molasses. An overfall of outgoing water where Cordero Channel meets the deeper bottom at the mouth of the inlet creates a huge slow upwelling boil that kicks back against the outgoing tide and slows us right down to a crawl. It takes us nearly twenty minutes to get through the half mile transition zone. The rowing gets a little easier after that, but still not as easy as Cordero Channel. My wrist and forearm are acting up again and the rowing seems like very hard work. I am briefly distracted when a pod of pacific white-sided dolphins goes leaping by on the opposite side of the channel, moving slowly into Loughborough Inlet. It cheers me no end to see them. In spite of the hard going, we round the corner at D'Arcy Point into Wellbore Channel at nine, where we find some current in our favour for the first couple of miles. I worry that there will be a lot of wind in Wellbore Channel, as it is not that far from Johnstone Strait where the northwesterlies blow, but it is strangely calm. The last couple of miles along the western shore are against some serious back eddies but we push on, arriving at the bay south of the rapids at ten.

Now comes the wait for the afternoon slack at Whirlpool Rapids. The skies clear before noon and the sun comes out. I roust out the lunch fixings early as the long hard morning drained me of energy. We both put up our tents as awnings for shade. I make a big pot of coffee and lounge on the floorboards and contemplate the world. My view to the south is centred on Tim's boat, a few boat lengths away, just out of the ruffled water that the breeze from around Carterer Point is beginning to produce. To my left is the 3,800 foot peak of Mt. George on the mainland and to my right the smaller, 2,300 foot summit of Mt. Yorke on Hardwicke Island. They frame the long slot of Wellbore Channel, which is blocked at its end by West Thurlow Island, whose shore we rowed along earlier. In looking at the chart, I see that high up out of sight in the centre of that island, just about in line with the middle of the channel, is Wolloomooloo Lake. It is clearly an Australian name and I wonder by what strange pathway it has come to be attached to that obscure little lake on a remote island off our west coast[82]. The sky is now totally clear of the morning cloud and there is a distinct lack of boat traffic. To complete the picture, a Harbour porpoise methodically works its way quietly around our little bay.

The daily northwest thermal wind which comes up in these sunny conditions holds off all afternoon until about half an hour before the predicted slack at six o'clock. We raise our anchors and pull around the point to find that wind dead on the nose. At the narrowest part, which is only 200 yards wide, the wind is accelerated by the nearly vertical side of the hill to the east. It is very hard rowing to make any progress at all and it doesn't get a whole lot easier once we are past the pinch point. We are headed for an anchorage in the lee of Althorp Point. It will not be an ideal anchorage, as the bay is not very large. Most boats looking for anchorage near here head for Forward Harbour across the channel, a deep and well-protected bay. However, we want to make an early start in the morning to get down Sunderland Channel and at least to McLeod Bay before any substantial wind comes up. As it is at least a mile and half into Forward Harbour to the nearest place where we can anchor, we are unwilling to cede that much time to come out in the morning. So, the bay behind Althorp Point it is for us and it takes us a good hour to cover the two miles to it. Once in and with the anchors down, we are indeed sheltered from the wind but we find that some swell curls around the point into the bay, setting the boats to rolling. I take down my foremast to reduce the inertia and lower the centreboard in an effort to dampen the rolling. It helps some and I go to sleep hoping that the wind will go calm overnight.

* * * * *

The day starts out well enough. The clouds move in overnight, which seems to be the pattern for this part of the passage, and it has fallen nearly calm in our little cove. We leave shortly after six and as soon as we get around the point there is a light headwind but there is either no favourable current or it is against us. We are only making about a knot and a half, and the slow speed combined with the thick low cloud makes the morning particularly cheerless. After about an hour, the wind increases enough that we can sail, albeit directly to windward. With the sails up I make good time, much faster than I can row. This feels like progress and despite the dreary aspect to the dim light I feel much better.

I cover about three miles and make it to just past Seymour Island in the centre of the channel when the wind increases to the point where I have to put in a reef. I go through my usual routine of centreing the mizzen, rounding up into the wind and dropping the foresail. I go forward and tie in the reef and raise the sail again. As I move aft to set the sheet and take the tiller in hand, a strong gust of wind comes up and catches the sail. Suddenly the boat heels right over and buries the lee rail deep in the water. I reflexively grab the end of the boom to keep from getting thrown out of the boat, but my butt, the tops of my legs and my torso right up to my armpits are submerged. The gust slackens and the boat pops upright again but it is full of water. I was knocked down but fortunately not capsized. I am too surprised to be shocked by the cold water, and anyway, I put on my floater coat earlier for warmth while sailing. While I am thoroughly wet, the neoprene of the coat is now doing its job. Time seems to slow to a crawl as the adrenaline kicks in. Everything that was loose is floating but a quick glance seems to show that I haven't lost anything. First order of business is to get the sail down so I won't be knocked down again. I slosh forward and quickly drop the sail. I untie the bucket from the pin rail and crouch in the centre of the boat and begin bailing furiously.

While I am bailing I actually have time to think, amazingly. Why did the knockdown occur? I notice the mainsheet is jammed in the cam cleat. Either I neglected to free it when I went forward to reef the sail, or it had a snarl in it that jammed when the gust hit. Either way, instead of the sail being free to weathercock into the wind when the gust hit, it translated the force of the gust into a heeling moment. Being on the wrong side of the boat, I did not have time to react with my weight to counteract it. While I am bailing I also note that my calculations for the size of the buoyancy tanks in the ends of the boat are correct. I wanted enough buoyancy that if the boat is swamped, the water level inside stays below the top of the open centreboard case. If it weren't then water will flood in through the case and you will never be able to bail out the boat. The water level when I start is about three inches below the top of the case, which gratifies me as it confirms that I got it right. I bail steadily and it seems like only five minutes, although it might have been ten or fifteen (I didn't have the presence of mind to look at my watch), when I have the got the water level down to just above the floorboards. This is low enough the bilge pump can take care of the rest. I insert the handle of the pump and set to work. Soon the pump is sucking air and there is only a little water swilling about on the bottom. I go through the boat, picking up and re-stowing everything that was loose or that floated off the gadget shelf. This includes my GPS, camera, VHF radio and satellite tracker. All are waterproof, but it is never a good idea to allow these devices to spend too much time underwater.

With everything tidied away, I take stock of my situation. Tim is nowhere in sight. I have, as usual, outdistanced him sailing to windward and now can't see him at all. I figure that my best course is to head to shelter and get dried out to avoid becoming hypothermic. I raise Tim on the radio, tell him briefly what happened and let him know I am heading for Shaw Point, a bailout spot we agreed on previously. The wind has come up a little more, but now seems to be steady. I put in a second reef, raise the sail more cautiously, and bear away for Shaw Point, a mile and half away. A few tacks and twenty minutes later, I sail into the lee of the Point and drop the hook close to the beach on the steeply shelving bottom. It is only nine o'clock. I sponge the last of the water out of the boat, change into dry clothes and set the wet ones out to dry. I wasn't aware of being chilled, but it feels really good to be warm and dry.

Now I have time to reflect on what happened. I realize I wasn't actually afraid at any time. I was too busy trying to save myself and the boat to feel fear, I think. I feel a profound sense of relief that comes from having come close to disaster as a result of my incompetence but then having escaped through my own efforts. While it does give me a sense of confidence, it mostly leaves me with a resolve to pay more attention to the details, all the time. Half an hour later Tim rows in and rafts up alongside. He gave up sailing a couple of miles back and rowed the rest of the distance along the shore. He was far enough behind that he didn't see any of my drama. One of the potential benefits of sailing in company with another boat is the ability to help one another. That only works if you are close enough to render assistance. If I was in the water and unable to get back in the boat, I might have been able to radio for help, but in this case I didn't have the radio attached to my person when the boat went over. There are also no other boats in Sunderland Channel this morning. It strengthens my belief that when you are boating solo, you pretty much have to be able to get yourself out of any jams you get yourself into.

The wind in Sunderland Channel is now blowing in from Johnstone Strait about twenty knots, and the whitecaps are marching past the point, just a few boat lengths away. It looks like we are here for the day. The clouds never really clear off but they do thin out in the afternoon. As a result it brightens enough and warms enough that everything that got wet from the knockdown dries out. Just after I arrived in the morning a large black bear came out of the bush down to the beach. Given how near I am to the beach, this is uncomfortably close. I got out my horn and gave him a couple of blasts. He ambled off slowly. He returns a couple of hours later and Tim applies the horn again. This time he leaves more quickly and we don't see him again. Clearly, the neighbourhood is getting too noisy for him. The horn doesn't put off a pair of Kingfishers that live in the bay as they rattle back and forth from one perch to another between fishing forays. There isn't a lot of wildlife otherwise. I saw a Pigeon Guillemot earlier and few gulls and ravens flew over but that is it. Everyone seems hunkered down out of the wind.

I'd underestimated how much time we would have for reading on this trip. I finished the book I have brought with me, Dan Simmon's "Terror," a fictionalized but highly entertaining version of the fate of the Franklin expedition. I trade it to Tim for some copies of The New Yorker magazine that he brought along and I start reading them as we wait. We discuss the challenge for the next day. We are faced with the only section of Johnstone Strait for which there is no alternate back door route. It is about sixteen miles from where we are to the entrance to Havannah Channel, the next alternate route. It will be a long row if there is no wind, or a tough slog if we have to sail to windward. Tim confesses to lacking motivation, after the hard day we had. Since he started in Seattle, he has been out almost a week longer than I have, almost a month in total at this point. I get the feeling that he may have had enough fun for one trip, notwithstanding his initial intention. If he decides to pack it in early, I don't know what I will do. I could continue on my own or I could turn around and run back downwind through Johnstone Strait.

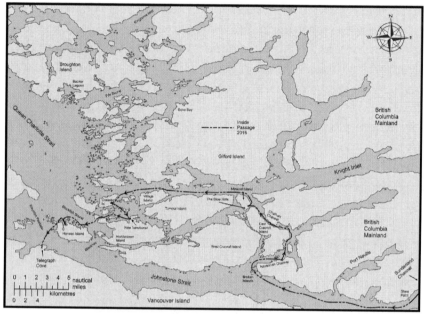

Vancouver Island North and Johnstone Strait

* * * * *

It is six thirty in the morning and it is cool. The sky shows bands of stratocumulus clouds below lighter patches of higher cloud, and the wind is calm in our little bay behind Shaw Point. There doesn't look to be any wind in Sunderland Channel either. Out from behind the shelter of the point, the ebb tide helps us along and we quickly cover the two miles to Gunner Point, where Sunderland widens out at its junction with Johnstone Strait. A light wind comes up, just enough to tempt me into raising sail, but I am not moving any faster than I can row and the wind soon drops off again. I lower the sails and start rowing some distance behind Tim, who wasn't taken in by the fickle breeze. There is still a light headwind, from the northwest, just enough to add to the labour of rowing, but not enough to sail. Meanwhile the morning VHF roundup of weather conditions reports southeast winds to both the north and south of where we are. How there can be contrary winds to what we are experiencing, both north and south of us, is beyond me, but we have what we have so we just get on with it.

Rowing non-stop we cover about seven miles by a quarter to nine, to a point in the Strait opposite Port Neville. This is our last possible bailout point, if we need it. Tim is resting on his oars as I come up and bob alongside him for a breather while we confer. The wind is still light. Tim says, "This might be our best chance to cover this next stretch. It would be good if we could sail it, but the next best thing is rowing while it is mostly calm." I think about it for a minute and say, "You're right. My arm is a little sore this morning, but not enough to stop me from rowing. Let's go for it."

We set off again and settle into a strong, steady rhythm. There are a lot of other boats that pass us, going both north and south, transiting this section of the Strait while the conditions are good, but they are all motoring. We are the only ones rowing and we don't see any kayakers either. The last high tide was higher than usual and it has floated a lot of wood off the shore, everything from small sticks and bits of bark to whole logs and even downed trees, with their root mats sticking up like sails. We have to turn around constantly to make sure we aren't about to run into anything major. The morning seems interminable. Both the Vancouver Island and the mainland shores along this stretch have high forested ridges but are otherwise unremarkable. Even the scenery, normally so entrancing, isn't very distracting today. The Broken Island group at the entrance to Havannah Channel gradually crawls closer and closer until, after three and a half hours of hard steady rowing since Port Neville, we pull in and drop anchor among the islands for a belated but much needed lunch. We have come nearly ten miles since the break and have been rowing steadily, with only one break, for six hours. Everything is hurting, but we have done it.

As we eat lunch and recuperate a little the clouds start dissipating from the north. With the blue sky comes the northwest wind, right down the Strait. It feels like it is going to build as the afternoon thermal effect takes hold. The current is running strongly through the anchorage by this point, and it requires careful timing to get the anchors up, jump to the oars and get rowing before being swept onto the rocks. A few minutes of hard pulling and we are out of the tangle of islands with enough room under our lee to raise the sails. Up they go and we are off on a broad reach, around Domville Point and then up Havannah Channel, running with the wind behind us. After the hard morning, it is a delight to be sitting back in the sunshine with our feet up on the thwarts, surging up the channel. We won't be able to make the afternoon slack in the Chatham Channel narrows, our next gate and we start looking for a place to anchor. On the chart we find a tiny bay on the south side of Havannah Channel, just southwest of Whitebeach Point, and head for that. As we approach the point enclosing the bay, I notice a commotion on the surface of the water near the shore. I pull out the binoculars for a better look.

"Tim," I shout, "There's an eagle over there swimming ashore with a fish!" Tim grab his binoculars and looks. "I've never seen that before!" he says. I reply, "It's only the second time I've ever seen it. The first is probably twenty years ago."

We watch as the eagle struggles to the shore with the fish in his talons and then we sweep past and lose sight of it. We feel privileged to have witnessed this rare sight. The point that forms the bay turns out to be the site of what looks to be a herring spawning pound. There are large floating cage-like structures with suspended nets, but no floating docks. Whatever it is, it isn't in use at the moment. There is enough room inside of the structures for us to anchor our boats in the shallow water, out of the wave action now being driven in by the afternoon wind. It is very pleasant to while away the afternoon in the warmth, with just enough breeze reaching into the bay to keep it from being hot and to keep the bugs at bay. There isn't nearly as much boat traffic in here as out in Johnstone Strait but the *MV Aurora Explorer* comes by. It is coastal freighter/landing craft that serves all the nearby inlets. We have seen it in the distance for the last few days, as it makes its rounds.

* * * * *

The water is billiard-table-smooth as we row out of the little bay next morning under high cirrus cloud that obscures the sun but does not conceal the distant mountains. We're on our way to catch the slack in the narrows. We have about three miles to go. We are a little late leaving but at first it doesn't seem to matter as it is easy, fast rowing. Nearing Hull Island, though, the beginning of the ebb current pouring out of Call Inlet suddenly makes itself felt. I opt for the western shore and Tim the eastern as we look for the back eddies in order to make progress. Half an hour's hard work brings us around to Root Point at the start of the narrows and after that the current is in our favour. After seeing almost no boats in the channel yesterday or earlier this morning, a number of them all show up at once to transit the narrows. There are two sets of range markers on shore at either entrance. The idea is that you get the relevant pair of markers aligned, line your boat up with these markers and keep them aligned as you go through, and you will be in safe water. The narrowest part of the passage is a little more than a hundred yards wide – not wide, but plenty of room for boats to deviate off the line enough to pass each other without danger of running aground. We are following the range markers and boats are passing us, but one large power yacht that is coming up astern to overtake us pulls over alongside. A woman steps out of the wheelhouse, "You should be over by the side, not in the middle of the channel! Leave the middle to the big boats!" she shouts. I am taken aback, but Tim, who is closer, says, "We're just following the rules of the road. You should too!"

The woman replies with something I don't catch and then steps back into the wheelhouse, slams the door and the boat powers on by. The rules of the road clearly state that powered vessels give way to engineless vessels and the overtaking vessel gives way to the vessel being overtaken. We have the right of way no matter which way you look at it. In addition, if they feel that the passage is too narrow, it would only be five minutes, at the most, before we are into the wider part of the channel and they would have more room. Are they really in so much of a hurry that they can't afford five minutes delay? Isn't the point of pleasure boating to get away from the hurry-up mentality that prevails in everyday life?

I am still shaking my head a few minutes later when another, much smaller, powerboat pulls up behind me. The young woman steering it stands up and says, "I know you! You were at Newcastle Island in Nanaimo. Where are you going?" It is the woman who had raccoon trouble on her boat. I reply, "We're heading to Minstrel Island. I understand there is a marina there and we are in need of showers and to do some laundry."

"That's old news" she says, "that marina has been closed for years. I'm the caretaker at a lodge just a mile away around the corner and there is no one staying there. Why don't you come and stay with me and my son and you can shower and do laundry?" "It's a deal," I say, "We'll be there as soon as we can get there." "See you in a few moments" she says, and speeds off around the point.

Soon we are pulling up to the dock of Chatham Channel Lodge. Daphne, as she introduces herself, and her young son Liam, are taking care of the lodge for her friend Jennifer, the owner, who is out for a brief holiday. The place is for sale and it looks to me as if the owner's heart hasn't really been in it lately. Daphne tells us that Jennifer is renowned locally for her baking. She used to sell it at the resort in a cove a few miles ahead but the owner of that resort somehow decided that this represented some kind of competition and put a stop to it. It sounded to me that it was more likely that the baking brought in more business to the other resort, when people stop there for fuel. So, a small but significant source of income was lost for Jennifer, in a place where there are few alternatives. No wonder she is selling. At the lodge, we shower and get the laundry going and sit and talk to Daphne. A family stops at the dock and unexpectedly rents out the cabin, which is a bonus for the business but it relegates Tim and I to a spot on the floor of the main lodge. That is fine with us, as the docks are not well protected from the wakes of passing boats and would be considerably more uncomfortable than a piece of floor. It is great to be clean again and to have clean clothes that have been dried on a clothesline in the sun and the breeze. Daphne makes us supper and we wash the dishes as a very small recompense for the hospitality.

* * * * *

The tide is flooding strongly up Chatham Channel during the first part of the morning, strongly enough that there is no possibility of making headway against it. We depart mid-morning after it finally turns. Yesterday's sunshine has given way to low cloud. We haven't rowed half a mile before the wind picks up suddenly, blowing strongly right from the place we want to go. It is difficult to row at all, let alone make any meaningful headway, and my left hand immediately goes numb. We struggle along painfully slowly and, after taking an hour and half to travel less than a mile, we pull into the old docks at the abandoned marina on the southeast corner of Minstrel Island. The docks are in just enough of a bay to avoid the worst of the winds that funnel in from both Johnstone Strait along Knight Inlet to the north, and from Clio Channel just to the south through the aptly named "Blow Hole." We are safe but stuck there for the rest of the day, as the wind is forecast to rise to gale force later in the day.

Now follows nearly a week of a Kafka-esque nightmare. For the next six days, the winds outside our little refuge don't drop below twenty knots, day or night. We have unwittingly come to rest in one of the windiest spots on this part of the coast. At the beginning of the week, there are continuous northwest gales of thirty-five to forty-five knots in Johnstone Strait. Towards the end of the week, it is sometimes less windy where we want to go, but we can't get there because it is too windy where we are. The early part of the day, when we might have struggled against the wind, the tide is also against us in Clio Channel and Knight Inlet. The weather pattern at Minstrel Island is similar every day. The mornings dawn cool, if not cold, the clouds remain low over the mountains of East Cracroft Island and the mainland shore, and the wind-driven waves march by out of the Blow Hole into Cutter Cove opposite. Some mornings also bring fog and drizzle or rain along with the wind, slanting in and making the wind a solid, visible thing. Afternoons it usually lightens up and warms up, and it clears off, or mostly so, by mid-to-late afternoon. The clearing never stays round long, though, as the clouds usually roll back in after supper.

In compensation for this lesson in practicing the art of patience, we discover that Minstrel Island is something of a crossroads on this part of the coast and the docks become quite a social place. Later on in the morning of the first day after we arrive, a large power yacht pulls in to the public dock. We fall to talking to them, discover that the owner is an ex-Navy man and that he and I briefly served together in the same training ship decades ago. I left the Navy after a couple of years but Richard stayed in the Navy, ending his career as skipper of various ships. Richard and Suzanne invite us for lunch and we sit talking and reminiscing over people we both have known. Later in the day a couple on another boat that has come in, Phil and Betty, come around to the few boats on the docks and offer to host happy hour on their boat. This proves to be the pattern for the week. Next day Richard and Suzanne are still at the dock and host happy hour on their boat. Tim gets out his fishing gear that first day while we are waiting, and fishing off the dock, catches a small ling cod and a flounder to serve as the base for our supper. Fishing becomes a daily routine for Tim and on the second day he catches a couple of greenlings, which we fry in breadcrumbs and bring as our contribution to the happy hour snacks. Tim's fish also contributes to dinner with Richard and Suzanne on the third night. Mornings, since we aren't going anywhere, are quite leisurely and with space on the dock, we make up batches of pancakes for breakfast.

Minstrel Island government dock

On the fourth day, the wind drops just enough for everyone else to decide to move on. It is still too high for us, though, and Tim and I have the docks to ourselves for most of the day. In late afternoon, a couple of sailboats motor in and we help them tie up in the swirling winds. Unprompted by us, Dave and Carol invite us over for happy hour and the next day for supper when we sit in their cockpit while they tell us about their travels as liveaboards, having been to South America and back with the boat. The boat is beautifully set up for offshore sailing. On our second-last day at Minstrel Island, time is beginning to weigh a little heavily on us. We have exhausted most of the possibilities for entertainment on the island, having gone for walks, and Tim isn't catching as many fish. The winds are still high and the forecast doesn't call for them to drop until a couple more days away. We are standing on the upper part of the government dock in late afternoon, watching the passing parade of boats coming up Chatham Channel. Most go through the Blow-Hole to the marina around the corner – the only one in the neighbourhood with fuel and thus somewhat of a magnet. We see couple of sailboats following each other under power and I comment on how the lead boat is a nice-looking yawl. As it gets closer, Tim says, "I think that's Dave and Rosemary's boat!"

I put up my binoculars for a closer look. Sure enough, there is no mistaking the lines and the distinctive colour of the hull. I rush down to my boat and grab the radio and hail Dave. I explain that we are at the old abandoned marina and that we will be delighted to see them. I add that they will get a much friendlier reception here than at the other marina (which has developed a bad reputation). Dave agrees to stop in and in a few minutes we are helping him and his friend Dan in the other boat tie up in the blustery afternoon winds. We have a grand visit with Dave and Rosemary and Dan. Now comes a very great scandal for dedicated, engineless sail and oar aficionados. Since the forecast with respect to winds the next couple of days is still bad, I broach the subject to Dave of potentially getting a tow from them out of the wind trap we find ourselves in. Dave eventually warms to the idea and decides it will be cool to tow all three lapstrake boats (including Dave's peapod that he built) behind his boat. Without further ado, the next morning we swallow our pride and Dave rigs up long tow lines. We pull out into Knight Inlet, and after some adjusting of line length to get the boats riding straight without hunting, we are finally free of Minstrel Island. It is an uneventful trip down Knight Inlet. The morning is its usual cloudy condition although the wind is dropping the further we move away from Minstrel Island to the Broughtons, where Dave drops us off at Crease Island. It really is a very great favour and we are very grateful. After saying goodbye to Dave and Rosemary, we row into shore and have lunch on the beach of small gravel. Over lunch we decide that we will sail down to New Vancouver, where showers are to be had. We have a very pleasant downwind sail in a moderate breeze to the floats at New Vancouver, run by the local First Nations band. We go up and have a shower, our first in over a week. New Vancouver has relatively new government floats, behind a massive floating breakwater. While the floats are exposed to the northwest wind, the breakwater does its job with respect to the waves and the water is smooth behind it. The skies do not clear until late in the afternoon, but while the wind persists, it is never more than moderate, much less than at Minstrel Island.

* * * * *

We aim to catch the last of the ebb current in the early morning to make our way out from New Vancouver and across Blackfish Sound. It calms completely overnight and when we leave the dock at quarter past six, the colour palette for nearly everything we can see is various shades of grey. The clouds are low stratocumulus, the bottoms of the lumpy bits dark grey with lighter grey seams between, shading to almost white. The water is smooth, reflecting the clouds and adding a hint of blue to the dark grey. The low, dark green, forested islands have a grey overlay from the morning haze. It is a morning where the beauty is subtle, compared to in-your-face bright sunshine and vivid colours. We make good time rowing to Mound Island but in the narrow passage alongside it we find the current against us. Not too much to row against, but a surprise when we expected the opposite. Once out into Blackfish Sound, the currents are very confused, swirling us one direction and then another within the space of a few yards. A humpback whale is feeding in the middle of the Sound, diving then surfacing and blowing. We definitely have the feeling of being back in big waters again. We get across Blackfish uneventfully and row along the north shore of Hanson Island until we reach Double Bay, where we anchor for lunch and to listen to the updated forecast. It is discouraging. The winds for the area immediately to the north of us are for more gales for the rest of the week, and it is only Monday. As we eat lunch, low fog blows in with a light north wind and brings the visibility down to less than a quarter mile, but it is obvious that the sun is above it and it will likely dissipate. We discuss our options. The week at Minstrel Island seriously cut into any discretionary time we had in the schedule. Tim has limited time because he has to get back to work in a few weeks. Should we be weathered in again for any length of time he won't be able to get north of Cape Caution and then back again, or to someplace where we can ship the boats home. Already, talking to the locals, we have learned that this is one of the windiest summers at this end of Vancouver Island that anyone can remember. We don't see any prospect for improvement. We don't have much appetite for sitting for days waiting out the wind again. We resolve to get to Telegraph Harbour across Johnstone Strait and make a decision there. Besides, it has a pub.

We raise anchor and row around through the Plumper Islands and into Weynton Passage in time for the afternoon slack current. We find confused but light currents in the passage and as we reach the edge of Johnstone Strait proper, enough of a breeze comes up from the north that we are able to raise our sails and set off on a close reach, pointing directly at Telegraph Harbour. There is lots of turbulence and disturbed water at the exit to Weynton, right where it the disturbance is marked on the chart, and the wind is just enough to push us through. As we get across the strait, the wind begins to pick up a little more and black clouds begin to loom up from the south, climbing higher in the sky. It becomes a race against time as to whether we can get in ahead of the rising wind and rain under the clouds that are now towering over us.

We arrive outside the cove just as the rain begins to fall and we row in and find a couple of slips on the west side. We are the odd men out, as the marina caters mostly to small runabouts for fishing, along with a few larger boats. We get everything secured and go up to the restaurant for supper while it sheets down rain outside. After supper, the rain gets even heavier and we move to the pub for another beer. Talking it over, we reluctantly come to the conclusion that the rest of the Inside Passage will have to await another season. It is a good end to a memorable trip. We didn't travel as far as we thought we might when we set out, but we saw a lot of territory neither of us had seen before. I covered about 300 nautical miles, Tim much more. We saw fine weather and rain, we saw gales and calms. We saw spectacular scenery. We met many genuine people, and were met with much unexpected hospitality. It was a great adventure, a quintessential coastal summer.

Inside Passage North

In the pre-dawn darkness, I listen to the weather forecast, the lighthouse and ocean buoy reports on the VHF as I pack my gear and get ready. I'll move out as soon as even a little bit of light appears. I am the only boat in tiny Jones Cove, north of Cape Caution. It is the nearest protected cove to the Cape to wait in readiness for rounding it. Cape Caution! For the small boat sailor voyaging along the Inside Passage, it's the equivalent of rounding Cape Horn, and frankly, I am very nervous about getting round it safely in *Fire-Drake*.

* * * * *

It has been hard work to get this far. Last year, my friend Tim and I had a go at the Inside Passage travelling from south to north, but we got held up by a week of high winds at the north end of Vancouver Island. That delay scuppered our schedule and caused us to bail out at Telegraph Harbour. The Inside Passage is unfinished business for me and this year I resolved to complete the journey. Despite that resolve, there is the question of whether I should be doing this at all. Over the Christmas period, I had three significant episodes of Atrial Fibrillation[83] ("AFib," as it's generally shortened to by the medical folks). Once I had it diagnosed, I realized in hindsight that I had several other much shorter episodes over the previous three years. At the time I put them down to drinking too much coffee, and had cut back. When I finally got in to see the cardiologist in the spring, he told me that there is a pretty strong correlation between long-term high level aerobic sports and AFib, and pointed me to a couple of studies as evidence. Throughout my adult life, I spent a lot of time every day on the bicycle. I've been a runner for the past twenty-five years, including a few years when I ran marathons.

I've done a fair amount of hiking in addition to all the years of kayaking. So, there was a high likelihood that all of this actually caused the AFib. AFib is not, by itself, that dangerous, although it limits your ability to do things while it is happening because your heart is not pumping properly. The main concern and risk is that the lack of proper blood flow can cause clots to form in the heart, which, if they break loose and travel to the brain, can cause a stroke or to the coronary arteries and cause a heart attack. Treatments vary, but, as you get older, one that is recommended, as a preventive, is to take anticoagulants to reduce the stroke risk. So, I am now on anticoagulants for the foreseeable future. But the question remained: should I do this trip, which will involve a lot of sustained hard work, the very thing that likely caused the AFib in the first place, and which can, in itself, be a trigger? Perhaps I am in denial, unwilling to admit that I can no longer rely on my physical toughness. I learned long ago, in basic officer training when I joined the Navy, that I have more physical endurance than most people. I have always counted on that, have always believed that there is no challenge requiring physical persistence that is beyond me. Perhaps I am simply in denial that my body, which has always been reliable, can no longer be counted on to do what I tell it to. If the only criteria for living your life is risk avoidance, I wouldn't do it. Regardless of how ill-advised this might be from that perspective, I am pressing ahead, I am going to do this trip.

For the beginning of the trip, I face a logistics dilemma. How to get the boat to Ketchikan if I wanted to start there and go south, or how to get the boat back from there if I wanted to end the trip there? I decide to cheat, by cutting out the Dixon Entrance part of the Passage, and start the trip in Prince Rupert, the northernmost part of the Passage that is accessible by road. I persuade my brother Neil to come out and make the two day road trip to Prince Rupert with me, where he will drop me and *Fire-Drake* off and drive the car and empty trailer back to Victoria. We roll into Prince Rupert late on the second last day of June, check in to the hotel and go in search of dinner. We find Dolly's Fish Market, where we not only have an excellent meal of local seafood, I also pick up a couple of packages of their smoked salmon jerky to take with me - ideal journey food. Next morning we get up early, but by the time we get the gear from the car stowed in the boat, stop at the marine supply store to pick up a couple of charts I don't have, get to the launch ramp, wait our turn and get the boat in the water, it is nearly nine o'clock.

The weather is overcast and much cooler than it was through the interior during the drive up. The wind is nearly calm and there is nothing more to delay me.

"Are you sure you really want to do this?" Neil says. "Yep, I'm sure. Well, pretty sure," I say. "Not too late to change your mind," Neil says. "No, I'm committed now," I say, "I'll be fine." "OK, good luck, be careful," Neil says, as we hug and I climb down into the boat. I set off rowing while Neil stands at the end of the dock watching me until I am out of sight. I think he is questioning my sanity a little. I also feel a little twinge of anxiety. BC's north coast is a place of great beauty, but for a solo traveler in an engineless vessel, the reward is hard-won through bouts of adverse weather and sea conditions.

Prince Rupert is primarily a fishing and forestry town. It is also the terminus of CN's northern railway line, which makes it the nearest rail port in North America to Asia. As a result there is a lot of industrial waterfront to pass by before you get to uninhabited countryside. I row past the commercial docks, the BC Ferries terminal, the container ship terminal and, after about three hours of rowing, get to the Ridley Coal Terminal. There, a light wind comes up from the west northwest, not the southeast that I expected. This is welcome news and I raise sail and set off south, but I am soon faced with a choice. The late morning forecast on the VHF calls for strong southeast winds later in the day and even stronger for the next day. Once past Port Edward, there are limited bailout options for the next ten to twelve miles. I decide to make it a relatively easy first day and head into Port Edward for the night. I turn towards the marker light outside the port and the view of the mountains, still snow-topped, enclosing the mouth of the Skeena River, opens up to the southeast. The wind drops away at the entrance forcing me to take up the oars for last the mile and half to the dock. I stop at the first dock I come to, which is the public fishermen's dock. The wharfinger comes by and tells me that normally he would chase me farther along to the yacht dock, but since the fisherman's dock isn't busy, I can stay.

I'm content to have called it a day, as it begins to rain on and off. I talk to a few of the fishermen, who are getting their gill nets ready for an opening the next day. Every one of them tells me fishing has been bad so far this year. The wind comes up in the evening and it rains on and off through the night. I wake in the middle of the night with another of the bad migraines I have been plagued with for the past twenty years. I take one of my abortive meds and go back to sleep. At six when I wake and get dressed, I am still feeling really bad. I take another dose and lay back down again for an hour. When I get up the second time I am marginally improved. I make a pot of really strong coffee and sit drinking it but I still can't face breakfast. I listen to the morning forecast and it still calls for strong southeast winds during the day, associated with a trough moving in from offshore to park itself over Hecate Strait, just offshore from here.

Given the forecast and the way I feel I decide not to travel today. I go in search of the shower and get cleaned up. Around lunchtime the rain stops and I feel a little better. I catch the bus from Port Edward back into Prince Rupert. It will be a chance to take in the festivities for Canada Day 150, this year being the 150th anniversary of the country's official founding. The mood in town is festive, the weather reasonably warm under the thin cloud and the people watching is fun as everyone takes in the music in the park. I visit the local museums that detail the history of this part of the coast and walk around much of the downtown, particularly admiring the colourful flower garden behind the city hall. After supper at the pub, I go over to the bus stop to catch the bus back to Port Edward. After waiting twenty minutes past the time I think it should have come, it dawns on me that the buses might in fact be operating on a holiday schedule, not a Saturday schedule. I check the website with my phone and sure enough, that is the case. I bite the bullet and get a taxi back to the boat. I turn in to the sound of yet another interminably long train rumbling by the port, carrying containers away from the ship at the terminal. As with last night, these trains run continuously until the ship is unloaded, which works out to a train every three to four hours.

* * * * *

I try for an early start next morning, but my routine is always rusty at the beginning of a trip and it is past seven o'clock before I get going. It has been raining on and off since midnight, the forecast is for five to fifteen knots southwest and it is shaping up to be an RDF[84] kind of day. I struggle into my newly-acquired dry suit, as this seems to be exactly the right conditions for it. The day's challenge is to get across Chatham Sound safely and maybe some distance down the east side of Porcher Island, heading towards Grenville Channel. I am worried about the potential to encounter serious weather or a bad sea state in Chatham Sound. The Sound is at least ten miles wide at its southern end, where I will be crossing, and there is an eight mile gap between Stephens Island and Melville Island that leads right from the open Hecate Strait to the west. Should the winds come up from that direction before I can turn south and into the protection of Porcher Island, I could be facing some unpleasant, if not ugly, conditions.

The harbour is narrow and there is both a headwind and a flood current against me when I leave. It is slow rowing to get to the turn at the entrance, where the wind has just enough south in it that I can sail in the direction I want to go. The sky is gloomy with thick cloud, the islands are partly obscured by fog and when I look out to the west it looks even thicker out in Hecate Strait. The wind holds until about a mile past Holland Rock, but when I go on the other tack to try to head south, the wind unexpectedly dies away. I switch between rowing and attempting to sail several times, when a slight sailing breeze comes up, but I'm not making much headway. Between the tide and the outflow from the

Skeena River, the currents are complicated here and I suspect I have hit an adverse patch of it. I shed my dry suit in a surge of overheating during one of the bouts of rowing.

Finally, in the early afternoon, a steady wind comes up from the west southwest, just about the opposite direction from what was predicted. This is a welcome wind that I can use, and I quickly raise the sails and set off south. The wind veers[85] around to the north and blows straight down Malacca Passage. I am now sailing directly downwind. The low clouds get thicker and darker and begin to release the rain that they have been holding, cooling the air and chilling me. I put on my floater coat for warmth as well as additional protection from the rain. The wind continues to build and I turn into Bloxam Passage, hoping to find shelter in a bay on Elliot Island that looks promising on the chart. When I arrive at the bay it is too exposed, with the wind sweeping right across it – there is no shelter at all. I race through the Passage with the wind still behind me, sailing at hull speed now, with the rain slanting down in sheets. By this time the heavy rain and the inactivity are making me chilled again. I know I have to stop and seek shelter soon. If I can get through the narrows of Kelp Passage safely I think I can find shelter just beyond, in the lee of Lewis Island. As I turn the corner, my hope is rewarded. A tiny calm bay opens up, with just enough room for *Fire-Drake* to swing at anchor close in to the beach. Under the steady rain, I drop the anchor, set up the tent and sponge the water out of the interior. I quickly brew up a pot of hot soup and get that down. That makes a world of difference. With hypothermia averted, I change into drier clothes and feel positively comfortable. While it is not that late in the afternoon, the tide has turned against me out in Arthur Passage, and it is another four or five miles to the next possible anchorage. I call it a day and set about making a proper supper.

* * * * *

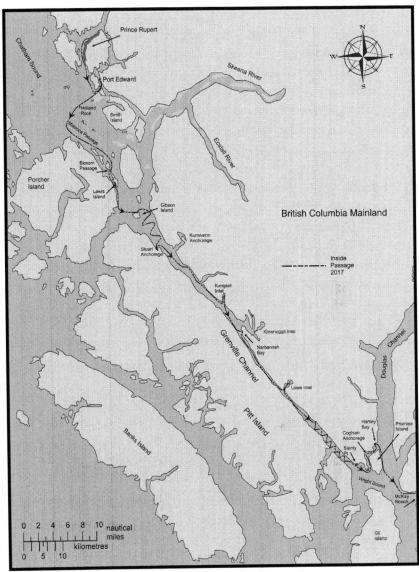

Prince Rupert to Hartley Bay

While it is still overcast this morning, it is not as thick as yesterday and it doesn't look like rain. There is both a light south wind and a current coming into the harbour and it takes me an hour and a half to row out the mile and a half against them to the waters outside. Although I am moving slowly, there are gulls, ducks and other seabirds to look at in the harbour, all just out of identification range. I don't begrudge the time it takes. There is just enough wind outside to sail, slowly. I short-tack about a mile down the shore of Porcher Island, avoiding the current further out, before having to resort to oars again as the wind dies. A half mile later, the wind rises again, from the south as predicted, but by this time I am far enough south that I can head across the channel. The rumpled surface of the sea is grey-green and the tops of the mountains are obscured by the low clouds that have trailing skeins of even lower cloud obscuring some of the hills. This is yet another mood of the coast and it makes the sailing, a close reach in light wind, very pleasant and I feel very mellow. Approaching Gibson Island, the wind strengthens and I decide it will be a good idea to stop, have lunch, and take stock before getting into Grenville Channel. It brightens up a little during lunch and gets warmer, leading me to hope it might clear off. I can see that there is still plenty of wind outside the lee of the island. As a precaution I put in a reef before setting out again.

It is the right thing to do. With the wind now blowing directly up Grenville Channel towards me, I reach the mainland shore quickly. As I tack offshore again, the wind drops enough for me to shake out the reef. Now comes some grand sailing. Tacking upwind, I cross and re-cross from the Pitt Island shore to the mainland, moving steadily up the Channel. I have in mind that I will reach Kumealon Inlet[86] for the night, but about three miles short of the inlet, the wind rises again, necessitating a reef. Now the sea state catches up with the wind and the ride gets rougher. I am proud of the way *Fire-Drake* shoulders aside the waves, powering to windward, not taking any solid water aboard, but with each crash, the bow throws up a lot of spray. I am getting pretty wet and the wind continues to rise. Looking at the chart, I see Stuart Anchorage close by on the west shore. I turn aside and sail into its shelter. The inner part of the bay, where the wave action is least, is shallow to the point of drying at low tide and I'm forced to anchor further out. The wind still blows over the low hills that enclose the anchorage, but the down at water level it doesn't pose any threat of dragging the anchor as the hills take the bite out of it.

Peeling off the dry suit, I realize that my left hand has become swollen. The wrist and neck seals are really too tight, but I am unsure what to do about it. I have never owned a dry suit before and am not sure what is normal. Too loose and the seals wouldn't keep the water out, but tight enough to cut off the circulation is clearly too tight. I send a message to Tim, via my satellite tracker, to ask if he had the same problem. After I get anchored the clouds thin enough that I can feel a little heat from the sun, enough to put out wet clothes to dry. While I'm getting supper, my eye is caught by movement on the beach at the head of the bay, 300 yards away. Even through the binoculars, I can't be positive, but from the size and shape, I think it is likely a grizzly. The bay is also home to a Bald eagle, who makes periodic forays from a perch in the trees behind the beach, around the bay in search of fish. Just before I turn in for the night, I poke my head out of the tent for a look around, just in time to see a pair of wolves silently patrolling the beach alongside me. They move out of sight in less than a minute. I haven't seen another boat since the morning. With the isolation of this little cove and the wildlife, I feel that I am at last truly in the heart of the north coast.

* * * * *

My task for the next few days is to negotiate "The Ditch," as Grenville Channel is known locally. It's a forty-five mile long channel bordered by steep-sided mountains, with limited anchorages for a small engineless boat. Traversing it is a different story if your boat is powered by internal combustion engines fueled by hundred-million-year-old dead-dinosaur swamps. Then you just crank up the throttle and it's only an hour or two to the next anchorage five or ten miles away. If your human-powered speed is two and half to two and three quarters knots in flat water, and a contrary current sets in against you, then it can be five hours away, and the days are long and hard. Grenville Channel for me, then, is all about the currents, and in the absence of usable winds, how to take advantage of them when they are in my favour and how to work around them when they are not.

Six o'clock next morning finds me rowing out of the bay and into the Channel in hopes of catching a boost from the morning flood tide. The cloud thickens and settles low over the mountains, accompanied by some fog but there is no rain. Well out in the channel, I seem to be moving quickly and a check of the GPS shows that I am gaining about a knot of speed from the current. I settle in for a steady row right down the centre of the channel. I am rowing smoothly, in nearly a trance, for over three hours, when it gradually creeps into my awareness that the scenery is no longer moving by as quickly. A check of the GPS again confirms that I have lost a knot and a half and the current has likely turned against me. This reversal of current is a surprise, since it is well before high tide. I am to encounter this significant disconnect between tide height and current direction in these channels for the rest of the trip. I move over to the shore to try to take advantage of whatever back-eddies might be there, or at least get out of the grip of the adverse current. At first it seems to be working somewhat, as I'm making about two knots over ground, but once past Baker Inlet, there is no hiding from the current and my speed drops to about a knot. Working hard, I crawl along the north shore and arrive at the mouth of Kxngeal Inlet[87] just before one o'clock.

Just inside the mouth of the inlet, I rest on my oars and eat lunch. It's been eight hours since breakfast and I'm ravenous. Although it is now only early afternoon, I decide to stay here for the night. I've covered over thirteen tough miles and I am tired. I row into the head of the bay and find anchorage just off a drying mudflat. I worry that it will be too exposed if the south wind gets any stronger, but as it is, a nice breeze reaches into the bay and keeps the biting black flies at bay. The clouds mostly clear by late afternoon, revealing a magnificent view framed by the mouth of the bay. A surprising amount of snow still lingers above the fifteen hundred foot level on the mountains of Pitt Island opposite. There is still wind in Grenville Channel but here in the

Evening calm, Kxngeal Inlet

bay it has gone calm, the water reflecting the mountains and the pale blue sky above. In the bay below the boat I see the first sea stars of this trip, both sun stars and regular sea stars. I feel blessed to have this lovely spot all to myself and feel that the scene is staged just for me.

* * * * *

Next morning, after a quiet night, there is fog and very low cloud obscuring the hills again, but there doesn't look to be any rain in the prospect. It is a little later by the time I leave, but it is flat calm outside the inlet and again there is a helpful current to start. The rowing feels easy, the sun begins to come out after eight o'clock, I see a humpback whale in the distance, and I have the channel to myself. I cover six miles in about two hours and pull into Narbannah Bay behind Evening Point, at the entrance to Klewnuggit Inlet, to wait the turn of the tide. It has turned into a beautiful sunny day and the sky is now almost completely clear. There are only a few puffy clouds caught on the lower slopes of the snow-topped mountains to the north across Klewnuggit Inlet. The green of the low hills enclosing the bay contrasting with the mountains makes a spectacular setting. It is one of those days that you are simply glad to be alive. There is more boat traffic today, passing by as I wait at anchor. According to the guidebooks, Evening Point is the place where the tides from south and north meet in the channel. When I head out after lunch about at the time of the tide change, I find a current that is still in my favour. However, after a couple of miles, the current slackens, the water becomes confused and lumpy and then a slight south-going current sets in again, but not as strong as before. What I was feeling at first was the last of the flood current from the north, which carries on for two miles south of the point. The lesson here is not to put too much faith in guidebooks.

I begin to see some impressive waterfalls along the channel, some which are obviously draining high lakes, tumbling down over the rocks at the shore into the sea. The sound of them comes clearly across the water to me. The afternoon progressively warms up, and there isn't enough wind to sail and I keep rowing. The heat seems to sap my energy today and it slows me down. I wonder if perhaps I might have had some brief episodes of AFib during the day and that accounts for the lack of energy. My heart seemed to be beating faster than it should for the level of effort, but I didn't notice any irregularity. I have become hyper-aware of my heart now, whereas all my life up till now I just took it for granted. I persevere but it seems to take forever to get to my target anchorage, Lowe Inlet. What's worse, the black flies come out and I can't row fast enough to outpace them. First I apply some repellent, but even that isn't enough. I resort to donning my bug net over my hat. It restricts the airflow and cooling around my head, but it is better than being continually bitten.

The entrance to Lowe Inlet finally crawls up alongside me in mid-afternoon and it takes me another hour to get to the head of the inlet, where Verney Falls drains the lake behind. I've covered about seventeen and a half miles since raising the anchor this morning. Verney Falls are an impressive sight, not very wide or very tall, but they drain a significant lake just behind them, and a deep curtain of green water rolls smoothly over the rock shelf of the shoreline before breaking up into foaming white froth where it meets the sea. The volume of water creates quite a current as it dissipates in the bay, strong enough that I can't row up to the falls. I settle for a spot off to one side in shallow water near the south shore. The steady roar of the falls provides pleasant white noise as I set up the tent. The flies followed me right into the inlet and I am afraid I am in for a tormented night. Soon a little breeze comes up and once I am under the tent, it is like I have put on an invisibility cloak as far as the flies are concerned, and I'm not bothered again. A small power boat comes in and anchors on the other side of the current. I realize that this is the first anchorage I have shared during the trip, which gives a measure of how much territory there is on the north coast, compared to the number of people that travel through it, even at the height of summer. In the low evening light, the bottom is visible, and I can see a lot of Brittle stars, some fairly large. Either they have escaped from or are recovering from the wasting disease, which is encouraging. Once more, as I drift off to sleep, I know there is no place I would rather be.

✳✳✳✳✳

I have every intention of having a leisurely morning in Lowe Inlet and leaving on the ebb tide which doesn't start until early afternoon. However, a brisk little breeze coming into the inlet in the morning convinces me to leave early to try to sail instead of row. Alas, the breeze only exists in the inlet. It is possibly only a land breeze caused by the warmer air over the land. Once out in the main channel I figure I might as well carry on rowing the back eddies along shore to see what progress I can make against the flood. I manage to make about three and a half miles before lunchtime. I see a little creek mouth then, that looks like it will offer a bit of shelter. I drop the hook to have lunch, wait for the ebb and watch the passing parade of boats. There are quite a few of them, mostly fish boats heading south, presumably for an opening. I am getting ready to leave when I feel a little queasy. I put it down to some tamari almonds I was snacking on. A little water got into the bag during the rain a couple of days ago. I laid them out in the sun on the back deck yesterday afternoon to dry, but I suspect they have gotten contaminated somehow, so I dump them over the side.

When I leave, a nice wind comes up from the south, right where I am heading. I raise the rig, harden in the sheets and start sailing to windward. I begin to feel better within half an hour of getting underway, so I think the queasiness might actually have been a touch of mal-de-mer caused by the wakes of the passing boats. I'm surprised, since this is the first time I have ever felt queasy on the boat. The afternoon is wonderful, under sunny, hazy skies and a moderate wind with enough power to sail but with only a moderate sea state. I make tack after tack across the channel, paying close attention to the GPS to make the best velocity to windward. The least lapse in attention to the helm and I lose a half a knot to a knot. The sailing is so good that I set my sights on getting to Hartley Bay. I sail hard all afternoon but about seven o'clock, a long mile short of the lighthouse on Sainty Point, the wind dies and I have to take down the rig and start rowing. It is tough work because at this point the channel starts to open up to Wright Sound. The waves and slop in the Sound haven't gone down with the slackening wind. Rowing consistently is almost impossible in the three foot confused slop. The boat is being thrown around so much by the cross swell and chop that it is difficult to get both oars in the water at the same time. I'm catching air on one side then the next moment the oar is buried deep up the loom and I can't drag it backwards. It takes me an hour and a half to work my way the mile and a half around Sainty and Waterman Points into the beginning of Coghlan Anchorage.

Once around Waterman, the water immediately smooths out, thankfully, but it is another couple of miles to Otter Shoals, the likeliest anchorage. It is nearly quarter to ten and beginning to get dark by the time I get there. It is only another few miles to Hartley Bay but I am completely done, as I've been on the water rowing or sailing hard since seven in the morning except for the lunch stop. I'm much too tired to make a proper supper. I settle for a well-balanced meal consisting of a cold beer and a couple of pieces of chocolate. I get the tent set up and get ready to turn in. With a waxing moon following the sunset the pale cornflower blue sky above the distant mountains of Gil Island, it should be a perfectly quiet night. But now the smooth water in the anchorage becomes a little unsettled as ripples and a whisper of a breeze from Wright Sound work their way in. I set the mizzen sail and sheet it in hard, which usually works to weathercock the boat, but there isn't enough breeze for that to work this time. *Fire-Drake* tugs at her anchor first one side and then the other and the ripples set the boat to rocking. It is uncomfortable but I drop off to sleep anyway, consoling myself with the forecast. The wind is due to shift to the north in the night, from over the nearby shore, which will settle the ripples. I wake up within ten minutes with my heart going rapidly and irregularly. I definitely have an AFib episode happening. There is nothing to be done about it though, and I'm so tired I go back to sleep. When I wake at three in the morning for a pee, the Afib episode is over and I'm back to normal sinus rhythm.

* * * * *

In the morning when I wake up, *Fire-Drake* is still rocking uncomfortably to the ripples. I poke my head out and can see that the predicted wind shift didn't happen. Within five minutes I start to feel queasy with the uncomfortable motion. I quickly pack up, pull up the anchor and row out of there as fast as I can. I pass a sailboat anchored nearby and I notice that it is rolling heavily and the mast is gyrating. In a misery-loves-company way, I am glad to see that it isn't just me that finds the anchorage uncomfortable. I pull into Hartley Bay under cloudy skies at half past eight. I figure I need a rest day after the exertion of yesterday. First on the agenda is a good strong pot of coffee, then breakfast. Next is to see if I can find a shower to get cleaned up. Hartley Bay is a First Nations community which turns out to have no amenities for tourists or boaters except the government dock and a fuel dock run by the Gitga'ata nation. It is also the nearest habitation to the site of the sinking of the Queen of the North, the BC Ferry that hit Gil Island in 2006 and sank, with the loss of two lives. The people of Hartley Bay were first on the scene and brought the rest of the people back to the village and provided them with shelter, food and clothing.

I ask a couple of guys at the main float about showers. The younger guy thinks perhaps I might be able to use showers at the gym. The older man thinks there aren't any showers there and my best bet is to follow the boardwalk trail along the river to the swimming hole. I collect my things and walk up the dock to the village. The entire village consists of buildings built on pilings, connected by boardwalks, with the result that the only vehicles in town are bicycles, ATV's and a few motorcycles. At the top of the ramp, I check out the gym, which is open but empty, and it has no showers. From there it isn't obvious which way the river walk is. As one direction is as good as another, I turn left. I wander along for a bit admiring the houses and the unique boardwalk layout and encounter the older man I met down on the dock, sitting in front of his house drinking coffee. "Is this the right way to the river that you told me about?" I ask. "Nah, you turned the wrong way at the top of the dock," he says. "OK, I'll head back down and over to the river," I say. "Hell, I am actually moving out today and I'm pretty much packed up. You can use my shower as long as you clean up when you're done," he says. "That would be great," I say, "I really appreciate it."

When I'm done I sit and yarn with him for an hour. He is a teacher and his two year contract is up and he is moving to a town in the interior. He's enjoyed his time at Hartley Bay but feels it is time to move on. Hartley Bay is his favourite of the several small towns on the coast where he has taught.

After lunch it starts to clear and gets warmer and I go for a walk along the river boardwalk. The river is clear and fast, with small waterfalls, and wildflowers at the mouth. At the edge of town along the boardwalk is a small hatchery and next to it is the village smokehouse. They are preparing for a funeral feast that evening for a member of the community who is being brought back for burial. They are making kippered salmon, which is new to me. Kippering involves soaking pieces of Coho salmon, in this case, in brine, cooking/smoking for a bit over a low alder wood fire, then adding brown sugar and smoking some more. They offer me a piece to try and it is incredibly delicious. I say to the woman putting the pieces in to be soaked, "If you ever want to make a business of selling this to passing boaters, you can make a killing." She immediately says, "In that case, that'll be ten bucks!"

I carry on walking the boardwalk alongside the river, enjoying the dappled shade, the sound of the water and stopping to read the interpretive signs that the village has placed along the trail. The forecast showers for the day never do materialise and it stays warm, at times even hot. I spend the rest of day resting and cleaning up the boat. I'm glad I stayed.

*　*　*　*　*

The morning brings the usual low-hanging cloud caught on the mountains but it is calm as I row away from Hartley Bay. The skies begin to clear after an hour and I have great views over *Fire-Drake's* transom, of the mountains up Douglas Channel, which leads north to Kitimat. There is a current of some kind assisting me as I row under the high cliffs on the east side of Promise Island and across to the south end of Gribbell Island and Mackay Reach. I cover the eight and half miles in about three and half hours of rowing. As I row past the lighthouse at Point Cummings, a favourable breeze comes up from the northwest. I happily raise the sails and set off downwind. With my feet up I eat lunch as *Fire-Drake* charges along Mackay Reach. The BC Ferries vessel that makes the Inside Passage run, the *MV Northern Expedition*, comes up behind me. I hail them on the VHF to make sure I'm not hampering their manoeuvreability in this restricted passage. I have seen them in the distance a couple of days ago and I will see the ship several more times on the trip as they make their way up and back.

It seems to take no time at all to travel the eight or so miles of Mackay Reach, but I worry that the wind might in fact be against me coming up Fraser Reach on the east side of Princess Royal Island. I get out the chart and I begin looking for bailout options

Kippering salmon, Hartley Bay

if that is the case. I needn't have worried, as the wind actually picks up behind me after I round Kingcombe Point I'm moving at hull speed and more. At this rate it won't take me long to get to Butedale, thirteen miles further on. With the bright sky and scenery, the sailing is terrific. I start seeing some of the waterfalls that Princess Royal is famous for. I think perhaps this channel might be the waterfall factory for the world, with waterfalls small and large, some cascading down smooth walls, others tumbling noisily down jumbled rocks. As I get a little further along, I seem to be outpacing the wind. The wind will drop, I will slow and the wind will fill in behind me again. It also begins to cloud over and then to rain. Along about half past three, the wind really picks up and off I go again. I have the GPS on and I find my average speed is about six knots. At one point, I glance down and see that the boat is doing seven point seven knots, which is about two and half knots more than theoretical hull speed. I really should reef the main sail, but Butedale seems so close and I really want to get there before the weather gets any worse.

I discovered this morning that I don't have detailed charts for the channel down the east side of Princess Royal Island.

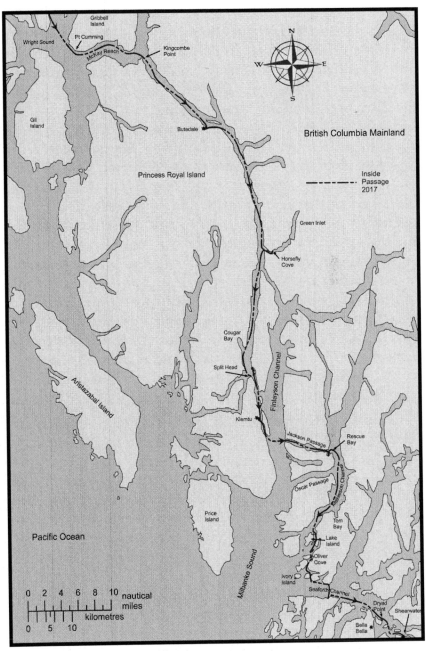

Hartley Bay to Shearwater

I only have the marine atlas for that area, which doesn't give any detail about Butedale Harbour at all. It really only shows its location but doesn't give any indication of how sheltered it is. On the edge of control in the rising, gusting wind, I surf in on the building swell around the corner to Butedale. The swell curves around the entrance and follows me in to the dock. I put the tiller over, round up into the wind with the sails cracking and slatting furiously, drop and secure the rig and row into the dock. Butedale is an abandoned canning factory and is slated for re-development by the current owner. In the meantime, the owner has not put any money into existing facilities, including the dock, which is one of the most decrepit I've seen, and is a use-at-your-own-risk proposition. However, any port in a storm. It is late in the day, it is blowing hard by now and I am going to stay here. I am pretty sure the dock will stay above water one more night, which is all I need. The swell causes *Fire-Drake* to bounce and chafe alarmingly at the outside of the dock, but I spy a short stretch at the end, on the inside of the dock, where I figure a boat of shallow draft can sneak in. I move there and tie up and it is indeed much quieter, although still not exactly calm. I put up the tent in a light drizzle, sponge out the boat and go up to see if anyone is about.

The sight that greets me from the top of the ramp at Butedale is one of decay and ruin. The buildings and machinery are all pretty much returning to the high entropy state of the raw materials they were made from. I walk up to the caretaker's cabin and spend some time talking with the caretaker, Corey, about the site and the plans for it. Standing on his porch looking out and listening to the rain he outlines how the current owner, who bought the site in 2013, has a plan to turn the place into an eco-resort. Apparently the previous owners let go the water lot and foreshore leases that were associated with the cannery. The current owner spent the past four years buying them back and pursuing planning permissions. The plan includes installing breakwaters from both sides of the harbour mouth to better protect the new docks from just such swells as are now rolling into the bay. Not much can be salvaged from the current site. Perhaps the water-mill-powered compressor for the cannery's refrigeration plant, a wonderful piece of industrial engineering, will be cleaned up and put on display. The old bunkhouse has pretty much had it, but the dinner triangle from it that is hanging on Corey's porch will assume pride of place in the new development.

We discuss the wildlife that frequents the place. I comment on the Swallows swooping about and on the hummingbirds that are working over the foxgloves. Corey says that he used to have a Hummingbird feeder up but that he had to take it down, as the male Rufous hummers kill the Anna's hummers. He saw them do it and went out and picked up the bodies afterwards[88]. I hoped to catch a sighting of a female Kermode[89] bear that often comes to the beach at the head of the cove, but she doesn't put in an appearance while I am there. The lake water is so clear and clean it is not treated at all, and at present some is piped down to the dock and runs continuously. It tastes wonderfully pure and I fill up my water containers when I go back down to the dock. The day ends with continued strong wind and a steady rain that persists into the night.

* * * * *

When I leave the next morning, the rain has mostly stopped, and a leftover breeze carries me the two and half miles to the kink in the channel at Red Cliff Point, where it goes calm. I take to the oars and begin to work the back eddies along the shore. It is to be another rowing day, except for a brief one-reef wind that rises out of nowhere for about twenty minutes off Griffin Point, briefly raising and then dashing my hopes for another good sailing day. The rest of the day alternates between sun and showers as I labour along the shore. I make surprisingly good time in the back eddies. The waterfalls that I started to see yesterday are even more numerous along this stretch. It seems I don't go more than 200 yards without encountering another one. Some are from the marked major streams on the chart but others are nameless but delightful little splashing rills that would make world-class

Princess Royal Island - nameless waterfall

water features in any landscape architects plan. Travelling close to shore in the eddies I'm also close enough to appreciate the sounds of the land. Swainson's thrushes call with their plaintive clear notes and the Pacific Wrens trill their complicated songs. I wouldn't be able to hear either of these while rowing out in the centre of the channel or being propelled by a motor.

I arrive at the entrance to Green Inlet at about four o'clock, having rowed more than eighteen miles today and having sailed another three. I come around the corner to Horsefly Cove, intending to anchor there rather than farther in so I won't have as far to row out in the morning. I'm met there by a woman who is out rowing her dinghy. She is from a powerboat that is tied between a small island and a rock at the entrance to the cove. 'Where have you come from and where are you headed?" she asks. "Prince Rupert," I say, "and I'm headed for Victoria."

"Did you row all the way?" she asks. "I sailed when the wind was right, but I've done a lot of rowing in Grenville Channel," I say. She says, "I like rowing and I've always wanted to do a big rowing trip, but I am not sure I could do something like that."

"You do have to have the right boat for it but once you get going it's really just putting one day in after another," I say. She says, "If you are planning to anchor in the cove, the bottom is not good holding. That's why we're tied between the rocks and the little island." "I'll give it a try," I say, "I can usually find a place shallow enough," I say. "Well, if you can't get safely anchored, you are welcome to tie up to our transom for the night," she says.

I go in and try several places and it is either too deep or too uncomfortably close to shore in any place where the anchor will reach. I go back and take them up on their offer. Bill and Joka, as they introduce themselves, generously invite me for supper. We sit talking after supper and we have a good visit as they tell me about various places on the coast they have been in their previous sailboat and present powerboat. Once again, the ready hospitality amazes me and I am grateful. I check the tide tables before turning in and see that if I want to get a boost from the ebb tide down Tolmie Channel in the morning, I will have to get a very early start.

* * * * *

Trying to be quiet and not disturb Bill and Joka as I untie *Fire-Drake* from their transom, I ship the oars and row out of the inlet half an hour before sunrise. It is a beautiful morning. The usual low cloud is hanging around the mountain tops but only in clumps, with patches of clear sky showing between, promising sunshine once the sun comes up. As soon as I get out of the inlet I find the looked-for boost from the current and the first few miles feel like they fly by. This early I seem to have the inlet to myself and no other boats pass me in either direction. The cloud gradually evaporates in the increasing sunshine and all feels right with my world. I row steadily and strongly for four and half hours with only one short break and arrive at Cougar Point by nine thirty. The scene that greets me as Tolmie Channel opens up into Cougar Bay is incredibly peaceful and benign. The few remaining puffy white clouds contrast with the washed-out bluebell colour of the sky. The low mountains at this end of Princess Royal Island still have snow on their tops above patches of bare rock and the lower slopes are covered with forest. The whole is reflected in the smooth water and there is no hint of wind. Even the fish farm pens and structures that block most of the Bay don't seem as obtrusive as these structures usually do.

Rowing a little more slowly now, it seems to me that I have all the time in the world to get to Klemtu, now only nine miles away, as I have already come twelve miles. The tide turns to flood and I think I might face a bit of a struggle to make progress past Split Head but I hope to be able to work the back eddies beyond it, as usual. When I get around the point at Split Head, the flood current is so strong I can't make any headway at all. I crab across to the east shore of the channel, thinking I can work the back eddies there. I struggle past the first few small points jutting out, but get to one larger point I just cannot get around. Rowing as strongly as I can, which gives me about four and half knots in flat water, I just can't make any headway. Skunked. I retreat to the nearest rocky nook out of the tide, and sit there, waiting for the tide to turn. I sit there spinning in circles in the eddy, eat lunch and watch the passing boat traffic. Once the tide rise a couple of feet and covers the rocky points that form my protected nook, it shrinks in size and I'm no longer in a backwater. It is now untenable and, reluctantly, I bite the bullet and retreat down-current a mile to a beach in a cove behind Waterfall Point.

It turns out to be a perfect spot to wait, with a tree to shade me from the hot sun, a cool breeze to keep the bugs off and a small stream at the end of the beach to go and have a wash. Even more unexpectedly, I find I can get a cell signal from Klemtu, which is about six miles away and I am able to check in with home. The tide finally turns mid-afternoon and I push off the beach and set off rowing towards Klemtu. I think, given the strong flood current of the morning that I should also have a big ebb current in the afternoon to carry me south, but it never materialises. I am doing alright for the first half hour but then the wind begins to play havoc. Extremely gusty and fluky in both direction and strength, it is mostly on the nose, but not reliable enough to sail. I grind along up the channel under oars and it is hard labour right up to the public dock at Klemtu, where I arrive about six o'clock. I have rowed for about nine and a half hours and traveled nearly twenty-four miles. I am completely done in and grateful to be tucked up for the night.

* * * * *

I was very tired when I turned in and I barely wake up around midnight when I hear a boat come in and tie up on the float ahead of me. I wake later to find that I am having another AFib episode, but I don't stay awake long and when I wake once more two and half hours later, it is over. When I get up in the morning, I'm rather surprised to find in the morning that it wasn't just one boat that came in, it is actually five fish boats belonging to a group of Vietnamese Canadians, rafted up together. All the noise they must have made, and I barely registered it. I talk to them as they are getting a communal breakfast and they tell me that the fishing so far this season has been terrible even though they are rigged for both gill netting and trolling. I hear this story about the fishing season all down the coast as I travel south.

There is about ten knots of south wind in the morning, with a forecast of twenty knots by mid-morning. It will be a little too much wind for me to comfortably sail against and a lot of wind to row against and I'm tired. I declare a rest day. I explore the town and have a good long talk with Brent, the operator of their small salmon hatchery, which was built nearly thirty years ago mostly with local materials, and is still a going concern. Brent tells me they run on a nineteen month cycle, from eggs to release and that I have caught them at a quiet period in the cycle. There is only a single thirty gallon tank in use at the moment, with coho fry in it. I completely underestimate the number of fry in the tank, thinking there are perhaps a thousand, when in fact there are about six thousand. As well as keeping an eye on the fry, Brent is doing maintenance to get ready for the next parts of the cycle. I go in search of a shower in the afternoon but two likeliest possibilities, the bunkhouse for the fish farm, and the fishing lodge, both turn me down. I come back to the river that the hatchery is on and find a quiet out-of-the-way pool and have a good wash and shave.

Coming back along the road from the river, I see a familiar looking boat at the dock, tied up across from me. From a distance it looks like a Pinky and as I get closer I can see the boat is the *Grace B*, of Port Townsend. She is clearly returning from Ketchikan after completing the Race to Alaska. As I walk up to the head of the dock, I see a man I know coming up it. "Sockeye!" I say, greeting him by his nickname, "how are you doing?" "I never expected to run into you here," John says. "What are you doing?" "I'm doing the Inside Passage, north to south," I say. "I launched at Prince Rupert about ten days ago." Johns says, "We're returning the boat to Port Townsend after finishing the Race to Alaska in Ketchikan." "I thought you might be," I say, "Who else is with you on Grace B?"

Johns says, "There are three of us, me, Ernie, the owner and skipper, and the other crew member is Carol. Have you met them?" "I haven't met Ernie before, but I have met Carol, years ago," I say.

We sit in their cockpit, eat cherries I bought at the band store, and yarn for an hour. John points out a better route south from Klemtu than the one I was contemplating. I am grateful for the tip as it will keep me out of potentially rough seas, although it will add a few miles. They decide to push on, and since they have an outboard motor for the return journey, they think they can cover a fair distance before dark. I watch them motor out of the harbour into the strong wind and am happy to have had this chance meeting with them. The day ends in drizzle and increasing rain and wind.

* * * * *

The alternate route that John suggests is, rather than sail or row straight down Finlayson Channel and Milbanke Sound and turn left at Ivory Island to get to Seaforth Channel, to go across to Jackson Passage and then south along Mathieson Channel and so reach Seaforth that way. This should work well, especially as the flood tide in Jackson Passage will coincide with my arrival there if I time it right. I leave Klemtu about quarter to eight in a steady drizzle and fog and row south directly into the wind alongside Cone Island. This south wind is just right for sailing on a reach once I turn the corner into Finlayson Channel. I sail the short distance across the channel but the wind heads me just as I get to Jackson Passage. I have to tack a few times to get in to the entrance, where the wind dies away altogether. As I row into the Passage, the weather gets thicker, to the point where the cloud and fog obscures Cone Island right down to the shoreline, only two miles behind me. Half a mile in to the passage, I hear a float plane behind me. I turn around and there is a De Havilland Beaver, flying no more than a hundred feet up (I'm not exaggerating) as the ceiling is that low, heading for Finlayson Channel. I think to myself, "This guy is insane!" As I know these planes don't carry radar but instead operate on Visual Flight Rules. He disappears into the murk, and leaves me shaking my head, but, five minutes later, he appears around the corner, down on the water, taxiing in to Jackson Passage, where he anchors. I suspect he put down onto the water in a hurry and I can't imagine what his passengers thought.

About halfway through the passage a light wind comes up astern from the west. It isn't strong, but it is enough to push me faster sailing than I can row. As a bonus it begins to get brighter and warmer. I pump and sponge out the rainwater and the boat begins to dry out. The wind drops and switches direction again as I approach the narrows at the east end of the passage. There is not enough power in the wind to sail and I drop the sail rig to row through. The tide is still flooding and it feels like a downhill ride as the boat accelerates in the strong current. Pulling hard first on one side and then the other to keep clear of the powerful smooth flow bending around the submerged rocks, I hit seven and half knots over the ground in the narrowest part. Safely through the narrows, another half mile of rowing brings me to Rescue Bay, a provincial marine park and popular anchorage. It is early in the afternoon and I have only come about eleven miles, but the tide is due to change shortly and the wind is against me up Mathieson Channel. Rather than struggle against that all afternoon, I decide to spend the rest of the day here. I anchor in about twenty five feet of water, which is quite a distance from shore in this shallow bay.

It starts to drizzle again before I have the anchor down and the boat, which pretty much dried out, gets thoroughly wet again. Tent up, I sponge everything out and struggle out of my dry suit. It kept me dry in the rain but is not that comfortable for sitting around in. As the afternoon progresses, more and more boats come in, but there is lots of room. The low land to the south shelters the bay very well from the waves, but not the wind, which is barely impeded. It sets all the boats in the bay to shearing about at the ends of their anchor lines. The rain continues on and off the rest of the day. Between the wind and the rain, the bay, which is probably quite attractive in sunny weather, has a rather dreary aspect today and I notice that nobody, including me, is going ashore.

* * * * *

The forecast for the next day is for south winds of about fifteen knots by noon and the ebb tide is early, ending by about half past ten. This dictates an early start. I set the alarm for quarter past four. I make a batch of porridge to put in the thermos with the insulated cover, in order to as to have it ready in the morning without having to take the time to cook it. The night is quiet and I get up, make coffee, eat my porridge, pack up and row away from the anchorage at half past five. Nobody else human is stirring as I make my way out through the shallow shortcut at the northeast corner of the bay but the hundreds of seabirds there are well into their day, already busy diving, fishing and circulating about. Although I can't travel as fast without a motor, having shallow draft allows me to use shortcuts like this and to see things in them that powered boats miss.

This morning the wind is calm and there is low cloud and fog around. It is very peaceful and once again I feel that I have this part of the coast to myself. It only takes me fifteen minutes to row out of the bay and around the corner into Mathieson Channel. There is a little bit of current in my favour, but as I row by the open entrance to Oscar Pass a couple of miles south, that dissipates and my speed drops. Once past Dowager Island south of the pass, the current becomes noticeable again and my speed goes back up. It remains calm but periodically I'm inundated by short-lived drenching showers. I can see them coming. The visibility underneath them is nil although you can see to either side of them. The mist gets thicker, the mist turns to drizzle, the drizzle to light rain then the light rain to thick small raindrops, drenching everything, before the whole sequence reverses itself as the showers move off. There is a lot of wildlife around, seals sticking their heads up inquisitively, seabirds flying and floating and then a breaching whale off in the distance near Tom Bay. Rowing alongside the Don Peninsula, between the showers, the water is as smooth as a newly Zamboni-ed ice rink. The higher, darker hills in the distance, the closer green hills near the water and the rocky fringe of the shoreline below the overhanging tree branches are perfectly mirrored in the water, like some gigantic horizontal Rorschach test. As I near Hyde Point, I keep hearing a whale blow, and I turn my head every time to look, generally only to see disturbed water where it has been. Finally it surfaces only a hundred yards away and reveals itself to be a minke whale[90]. This is the first of that species I have seen on this trip.

Most boats take Perceval Passage south from Mathieson Channel, but on the chart I see a possible small-boat back door to the beginning of it, behind Lake and Nathan Islands. Rowing in north of Nathan Island, it looks at first as if I won't be able to get through, but it opens up just enough through the thick kelp for a shallow draft boat. The current is against me, which I don't expect, but it is not too strong to row against and there is no wind. There are lots of black flies behind the islands though, and I have to resort to the bug net again. Coming out from behind Lake Island the wind starts up from the south, and there is a swell from Milbanke Sound, which isn't that far away to the southwest.

A power boat comes up from Perceval Passage, stops alongside me and hails me. It is Brian, who I met and talked to in Hartley Bay. He recognised my boat and came over to see if I need anything. This is kind of him but as I had a chance to pick up a few things in Klemtu and am only about a day from Shearwater, for once there is nothing I am in need of. I thank him, he pulls away and I carry on. I am only a little over a mile to the entrance to Reid Passage, which completes the protected alternate route to Milbanke Sound. I stop at Oliver Cove, just into the Passage, and drop the anchor. There is plenty of daylight left, but I've managed to come nearly fifteen miles and have had enough for the day, with my early start. Oliver Cove is another popular marine provincial park and in late afternoon several other boats come in and anchor as well. Reid Passage is also busy with boats transiting both north and south. It brightens up in the afternoon enough to be able to dry things out from the morning's rain and it is quite pleasant to lounge the rest of the day away, reading and playing my harmonica.

* * * * *

Overnight is quiet except for a tug and tow coming through Reid Passage about midnight, which sends a wake into the anchorage, briefly rocking me awake. In the morning, I figure if the weather gods smile on me, I might be able to make it to Shearwater today. I am packed up and rowing by quarter to seven and although there is cloud, it is not thick and it is apparent it is going to be a much brighter day than the last few. I encounter a little bit of contrary current in Reid Passage and it slows me down just enough for the bugs to find me. Once out of the passage I leave them behind and I row across to the narrow pass east of Watch Island and out into Seaforth Channel. At this point I am less than two miles from where, almost exactly nine months ago, the articulated tug-barge Nathan E Stewart ran aground in the middle of the night on Edge Reef, on the south side of Seaforth Channel[91], and subsequently sank. Although the fuel barge the tug was pushing was empty, the tug spilled about one hundred ten thousand litres of diesel fuel and twenty two hundred litres of lubricants into the sea. Less than one percent of all that was spilled was recovered. It was and is a disaster for the Heiltsuk people of the nearby first nations community of Bella Bella. This area is one of their most productive harvesting areas for clams and other seafood, and the spill contaminated it all. It is not known when, if ever, it will be safe to harvest again. Thinking about this as I row, I mourn for yet another piece of the coast despoiled by our collective addiction to fossil fuels.

In Seaforth Channel the swell coming in from Milbanke sound makes itself felt and it combines with the west-going ebb current in the channel to make rowing hard and slow. It is an especially hard pull getting around the first part of the south end of the Don Peninsula, but then there are some back eddy breaks until Bush Point. I creep along slowly until I get to the corner where Spiller Channel meets Seaforth. There my forward progress is stopped dead by the current coming out of Spiller Channel. There is no point in fighting it and I have to cross Seaforth Channel anyway, so, in less than half an hour of rowing, I cross over to the south side. I come alongside a tiny shallow quiet cove just short of Idol Point, and tuck in to wait the turn of the tide. It is a delightful little place, the sun is now out and it is no hardship to wait here. The shore is covered with grapefruit-sized cobbles but the shallow bottom is white sand covered with sparkling water the colour of pale jade. The rocks that enclose the cove are covered in seaweed and mussels, providing good foraging for a pair of resident Oystercatchers. Seaforth Channel is busy with transiting vessels going both north and south and there are many recreational fishing boats, no doubt from Shearwater and Bella Bella, only a few miles away.

The tide finally bottoms out. My rest period is over and I pull out into the channel and head east. There is a light east headwind and the ebb current has disappeared but the flood current hasn't really started. I think, given the amount of sunshine, that there is a good possibility that the large islands to the east will heat up enough to create a sea breeze in the afternoon. Sure enough, after rowing for a couple of hours, enough wind comes up from astern I'm able to sail. At first it is only a little faster than rowing, but it feels good to have a significant break from rowing, the first in several days. At the speed I usually travel, I rarely overtake any other boats, but today is an exception. I catch up to, and eventually pass, a medium-sized trawler towing several large logs that are rafted together. Since towing is not what the boat is designed for, it is heavy going, and he is only making about a knot and a half. It isn't clear from the size of the logs whether they are salvage, destined for a mill, or whether they have been collected for some personal project. Either way, it is a good example of the way people on the coast turn their hands to whatever brings in extra income or avoids expense by doing work themselves.

It is a great downwind sail past Dryad Point. The Point is the site of another of the iconic weather reporting light stations and to see it feels like meeting an old friend, although I have never seen it before. The wind strengthens as I bowl along to Saunders Island, where I make the turn towards Shearwater. The wind slackens in the lee of Saunders but retains enough poop to carry me to within a couple of hundred yards of the dock at Shearwater, before dying away altogether. I row in and the harbourmaster assigns me a space on the dinghy dock. I've covered more than seventeen miles and I'm grateful to be in ahead of forecast strong winds for tomorrow. I'm also glad to be in a place where I can get a shower, do my laundry and replenish the stock of beer, which is getting dangerously low.

Shearwater is a full-service marina and resort that includes docks, accommodation, showers, laundry, coffee shop, grocery store, pub/restaurant, boatyard and fishing charters. Because of the amenities it's a major crossroads for boaters heading north or south and it's a lively place. It's built on the site of a World War Two float plane base, which was established here to counter the threat from Japan after 1941. The first planes based there were Supermarine Stranraers. The current owner commissioned a large model of the plane, which is mounted on a swivel pedestal at the head of the dock ramp where it serves as a windvane. It is good to see that the local waters are very clean, judging from the tubeworms and other creatures that I notice are growing on the float next to my boat. After doing the chores and buying supplies, I chat with a couple of kayakers who are making their supper at the picnic table. Paul and Kelly are a couple who started in Skagway and are heading south. With them at the table is Kai, a solo kayaker from California who is heading north, and resuming his journey after taking a couple of weeks off to recover from a wrist injury. I go up to the pub for supper and catch the last three innings of a Blue Jays ball game on the pub TV. It is a bit of culture shock after many days of quiet and usually solitary anchorages.

There is rain overnight but it stops by the time I wake at seven. The wind is not yet up but I listen to the forecast while I have a slow breakfast and pot of coffee, and it hasn't changed from yesterday – strong south winds later in the morning. It is a day to stay put and wait for the weather to change for the better. I idle away the morning, drinking coffee and socializing with staff and visitors to the marina. I head over in the water taxi to Bella Bella to see what, if anything, has changed since I was last there with my kayak twenty years ago. What I see are a number of new public buildings, including a significant addition to the school. Not yet completed is a nice new building that will house a larger version of the Band store, I am told. I find a poster that celebrates the recent discovery by Simon Fraser University archaeologists, of 14,500 year-old charcoal and bone tools on Triquet Island, not far away. The discovery aligns with local oral tradition. I camped on that island years ago with my kayak and had no idea then that it has been occupied by humans for that long. This discovery definitively predates Clovis culture and may be the earliest site in North America for which there is hard evidence of human presence.

It is kid's fishing derby day, in spite of the increasing wind, thickening cloud and occasional shower. Everyone is out on the public pier and the kids are totally focused on the fishing. I have a few minutes of panic as I search for my Newfoundland baseball cap, which I thought had blown off my head. The wind was strong enough that I thought it blew off of the pier, but I find it later. It was right where I must have dropped it when I took it off to take a picture of the strong wind funneling up Lama Passage under threatening skies. Back at Shearwater, the Stranraer windvane, and the resident Bald Eagle that occupies the dead tree next to it, are both facing southeast, showing how the wind has switched. I have supper at the pub again, this time with all three of the kayakers, and end up shooting pool and shooting the breeze with them the rest of the evening.

* * * * *

Attractive as the charms of Shearwater are, I can't stay forever if I want to get south. I set my alarm for quarter past five, wanting to take advantage of the ebb current in the morning, and turn in. I wake briefly at ten o'clock when the pub closes and the locals all jump in their power boats and disperse, but the disturbance doesn't last long. It rains pretty steadily overnight and it is raining hard when the alarm goes off. I am snug and dry in my sleeping bag and don't really feel like getting-up-and-at-'er. I listen to the forecast and it sounds like it will be alright later on, with maybe even a shift to following northwest winds in the afternoon. I get up but am slow to get organized and don't leave until half past seven.

It is still raining and I'm wearing my dry suit as I row out of the marina towards where Lama Passage turns south. The ebb is in my favour and there is a little bit of headwind, but not enough to sail. I don't have the GPS on this morning but judging from the rate the shoreline is moving past me, I am making about three knots over the ground with not a huge effort and it is a pleasure to row. There is lots of traffic in Lama Pass as I turn at Bella Bella and continue rowing south. At the light on Denny Island opposite Hunter Channel, about where I am due to turn east, a southwest wind pipes up out of Hunter Channel. This is perfect and it allows me to raise sail and set off on a close reach. The close reach soon turns into a broad reach as I get around the corner. I stick close to the north shore of Lama Pass

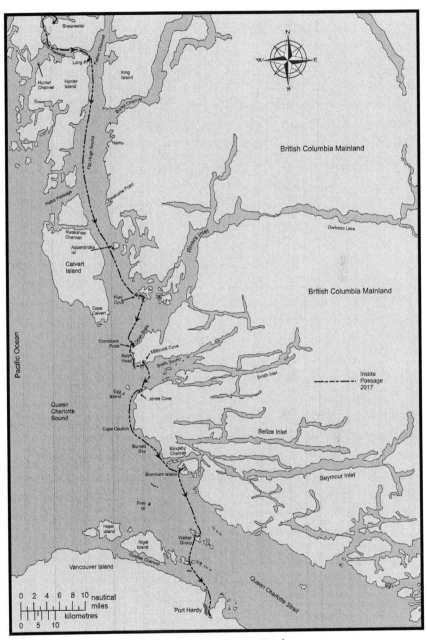

Shearwater to Port Hardy

to avoid a large tug which is coming straight down the middle of the channel behind me towing a barge piled high with logs. It is good to be sailing, although I'm getting cool in the rain now that I am no longer rowing, but the rain goes from steady, to on and off, to just showers, to stopping altogether. With the cessation of the rain also come the cessation of the wind. I take up the oars and I soon warm up again. The wind saved me from rowing for about six miles. I'm not too far from the east entrance to Lama Pass by then and the ebb has ended.

I come round the corner out into Fisher Channel and encounter a light headwind from the south together with the flood current setting against me. I decide to tuck into a harbour behind Long Point, about a mile south of the Pass and wait to see if the promised northwest wind will develop. I think myself very clever for discovering my own private harbour, not mentioned in the cruising guides, but shortly after I drop the hook at the head of the bay, a fish boat shows up. The afternoon is really brightening up and I have hopes for a favourable wind with the clearing of the clouds. It is sunny enough to get things dried out and to put my feet up and take a nice little nap. The only drawback to this little harbour is that I am having trouble pulling in the continuous marine weather broadcast for the forecast on my handheld VHF. I resort to tying it to the end of my boathook, cranking up the volume and holding it extended over my head. It improves reception enough that I can just make out the forecast. The northwest wind that is forecast for later in the day never does show up and the wind continues to blow from the south, but I'm not too fussed about having to spend the night here as I have come nearly fourteen miles.

I always carry a large golf umbrella on the boat, one with fibreglass poles that don't corrode in the wet. An umbrella is surprisingly useful on a small open boat. When at anchor or when you have the boat pulled up on the beach, it can keep you dry in brief showers and it can provide useful shade on hot days. The umbrella got very wet at Shearwater and I open it up to dry in the sun. A sudden gust lifts it and, seemingly in slow motion, tumbles it overboard as I lunge for it, just failing to grab it as it goes over the side into the water. I watch as it sinks, just out of reach. I get out my small spare anchor and cast around the boat with it, hoping to snag the umbrella and bring it up, but, after half an hour's fruitless effort I resign myself to doing without it. By the time I turn in, there are twelve fish boats in the little bay. Clearly, they have their own network of anchorages and hidey-holes. This one is handy for fishery openings in Fisher Channel. Most of the boats that are here leave at three in the morning, amidst great rumblings of diesel engine and clanking of anchor chain.

* * * * *

The start of the ebb tide is of course getting later every morning, as the moon moves across the sky in its retrograde arc, but I want to get going early. If there is no sailing wind I reckon I can work back eddies at the end of the flood, in order to take full advantage of the entire ebb. When the alarm goes at quarter past five, I am excited to feel a light northwest wind coming into the bay – a full sailing day at last! I get underway at quarter to seven and row out of the bay only to find that the wind is only in the bay and that it is calm in Fisher Channel outside. No matter, I had originally counted on rowing anyway. The tide must have turned early because when I check my speed over ground it is three and a half knots. The sky is covered with low marine cloud when I start but within an hour it starts to burn off. At one point there are three fuzzy points of bright light shining at me over my transom from the northeast; the low sun itself, a bright spot from the sun shining on some thin low cloud that hasn't yet dissipated and a final bright spot from the sun reflecting off some fog trapped in a bay to the east. It is another fabulous morning and I'm glad to be alive and to find myself in such a magnificent place.

About half past eight a breeze comes up from the north so I put up the sail rig and speed off downwind. I sail in beautiful sunshine the rest of the day. The wind strength is variable all morning, including half an hour before lunch where I have to put in a reef. There is lots of traffic in the channel, including where Fisher Channel transitions to Fitzhugh Sound at Burke Channel. I see a sailboat coming out of Burke Channel, which is actually sailing to windward, instead of motoring, as nearly every other sailboat I have seen on the Inside Passage. It is such an unusual sight I'm moved to take a picture. There is a lot of commercial traffic as well, including the Central Coaster, a double-bottomed 150 foot long, 350 tonne general cargo ship owned by Shearwater Marine, which carries general cargo for customers between Port Hardy and Hartley Bay. I intended on stopping at Namu, the site of an old abandoned cannery and the site of a first nations village for at least ten thousand years. However, the sailing is so terrific and I am making such good time that I can't bear to stop and I carry on right past it. Opposite Kwakume Point, the wind dies away again and I drop the rig and begin rowing. Within an hour, I am abreast of Kwakshua Channel, which separates Hecate Island from Calvert Island, and row into a strong northwesterly breeze blowing out of it. I put up the rig and immediately am doing five knots on a broad reach. It doesn't take long to reach Addenbroke Island, another of the major reporting light stations on the coast. The conditions are such a contrast to the last time I came this way, going north in my kayak twenty years ago. Then it was in a calm with the weather closing down and drizzle setting in. This time, the lighthouse and associated buildings are a wonderfully colourful and picturesque sight in the sunshine as I sail past.

The wind moderates a little past Addenbroke and the water becomes quite lumpy, as by now the tide turns to flood, opposing the north wind. It begins to smooth out a little as Fitz Hugh Sound widens. All day I've been seeing salmon jumping and now I start to see whale spouts over along the shore of Calvert Island. As I get further south there are protracted bouts of tail slapping and I can see that they are orcas. I presume that this is some kind of hunting behaviour, but I'm not close enough to see exactly what is happening. The wind increases again to the point where I consider reefing, but I'm getting close to Fury Cove, which will be a fine destination for the day. It is a beautiful spot and popular with boaters. It is close to supper-time when I come abreast of the tip of Penrose Island, which encloses the cove. I round up into the wind and drop the rig to row through the chop into the anchorage. Once inside I count a dozen boats already at anchor in the warm calm waters and sunshine. I find a smaller inner cove, too shallow for bigger boats, and have it all to myself. The white shell beach that I camped on all those years ago is opposite my anchorage. I am well content with the day. I covered thirty six miles since leaving Long Point Harbour, my highest mileage day to date. I celebrate with an oversized beer for supper. The night is quiet and clear when I turn in.

* * * * *

Before me is the potentially riskiest section of the whole trip. From Cape Calvert on the southern tip of Calvert Island, to the north end of Hope Island, Queen Charlotte Sound is over thirty miles of open coast. It is not protected by the islands to the north and south that make the Inside Passage inside, not outside. It's exposed to the full impact of swell, wind and wave from the open north Pacific. There are major outflows of tidal current from Rivers Inlet, Smith Sound, Queen Charlotte Strait and Slingsby Channel. If these currents oppose the wind, they create nasty and dangerous conditions for all boats, not just small boats. You're not out of danger once you enter Queen Charlotte Strait either, as the north end is very open to the ocean to the northwest, and it's nearly forty miles from Cape Caution to the relative shelter of Malcom Island. For an engineless boat, if the wind is not in your favour, you need to plan carefully and keep a close eye on the weather. I set objectives to cover the section in shorter stages: getting by Rivers Inlet, getting by Smith Sound, finding a staging spot for Cape Caution to wait for a favourable weather and tide window, getting by Cape Caution and getting by Slingsby Channel.

My first task from Fury Cove this morning is to get by Rivers Inlet. I get up early, in order to get past the inlet on the last of the flood and to avoid the wind, and begin to row out of the cove at quarter to six. It is calm and clear, with the moon rising above the eastern horizon while the sun is not yet up. Outside the cove, the swell from the open Pacific, while not high, is enough to slow my speed over ground to less than two knots. There are a number of sport fishing boats out early, likely from the lodges in Rivers Inlet, speeding to various fishing spots. As the sun comes up I row by a small raft of half a dozen sea otters, the first I've seen on the trip. The sight of them always brings joy, watching as they roll and groom their fur, dive and surface with a shellfish and crack it open on the anvil rock they carry. Further out a humpback whale blows and later a Harbour porpoise surfaces near me. I may be the only person in a boat for miles around, but I am certainly not lonely.

As I get past the small islands southwest of Walbran Island, which form the northwest shore of the entrance to Rivers Inlet, I begin to feel a light breeze from the northeast coming out of the inlet. I think at first it is the last of the nighttime land breeze, which hasn't yet succumbed to the rising sun. It gets strong enough at about eight that I can raise the sails and begin sailing. Instead of dying away, which I expect, it becomes stronger and veers to the south. The south wind carries in a thick fog from offshore, which wasn't forecast. Visibility quickly deteriorates to less than a hundred yards. Although my GPS gives me my position, I figure it is too dangerous to sail in this, as I can hear the fishing boats going by at high speed. I suspect most of them don't have radar and I'm not sure how well my small wooden boat with wood masts would show up on radar even if they do have it. By this time I'm only a mile off Kelp head, which offers shelter. I set a course for Cranstown Point at the end of Open Bight. The fog is not deep and the sun above it makes it glow to the point where it erases the boundary between air and water. It's beautiful, but it is dangerous. It is eerie, charging along at four knots with wisps and knots of fog streaming past but very little sense of motion unless I look down at the water. I can see the point getting closer and closer on the GPS, but there is no sight of it, until suddenly, the cliffs of the Point resolve above me out of the fog about a hundred yards away. A last minute minor course correction and I am around the Point and into the calm waters that front the beach behind it.

Rowing this morning I feel sharp pains on the points of my butt where it contacts the thwart cushion. This is more than just the soreness from long days rowing - it feels like being stabbed with needles. I take the opportunity during the forced stop to get out the mirror from my toiletries bag to awkwardly peer at my butt, where I discover patches on both sides where the skin has chafed right way. I can't let this go untreated. I apply some antibiotic cream, a couple of bandaids over each spot and then cover the bandaids with patches of ancient, but still serviceable moleskin that I have. Thus repaired, it is much less painful, although not exactly comfortable. The joys of self-propulsion.

As the morning wears away, although it is bright at the beach, the fog keeps blowing in overtop the point from the southwest. The shorebirds are busy working the tideline along the half-mile sweep of sandy beach, using the calories to pack on fat reserves ahead of the fall migration. It begins to look like one of those days where the fog will persist all day. I don't hear any more fishing boats motoring by, so when the fog thins a little at half past twelve, I am sure that I can safely creep around Kelp Head. I think I will be able to reach Millbrook Cove, which will be more sheltered for the night. Rowing out around the point, the swell increases, if anything, rebounding off the rocks, making rowing difficult, but I plug away until I come opposite Bay Point. Here the wind starts up from the southwest, enough to raise the sails. At first I'm not moving any faster than slow rowing. The wind gradually increases and I'm moving at a little over three knots as I go past Extended Point. The fog begins to lift then and I can see up Smith Sound to the east but it is still foggy over toward Cape Caution and I can't see it. I decide to stick with the plan to head for Millbrook Cove, because of the fog and of the rising southwest wind. By the time I make the turn northeast toward the cove, the sun is fully out and it becomes a pleasant sunny downwind sail. I run through the narrow pass north of Shield Island at five knots, round up just outside Millbrook Cove and drop the rig. I row in and see a large sloop at anchor, the only other boat in the cove. I go past him to the northwest corner and find a shallow spot to anchor. The wind comes in strongly over the land ahead, but the fetch is short. I set the mizzen and sheet it in to weathercock the boat and prevent it from sheering about on the anchor line.

I sit in the sunshine with a beer, gaze at the prospect in the bay and ponder my mortality, it being my birthday. I have just turned sixty-five, the official old-age pension age. I don't feel that old. I once had a conversation with my mother when she was about the age I am now, in which she said that she really didn't feel any different inside than when she was sixteen. Thinking about it, I decide that I don't feel like I did at sixteen, but maybe at twenty or twenty-one, except with a lot more mental scar tissue, perhaps. However, although I have always believed that age is just a number, I can no longer avoid acknowledging that I have many more years behind me than are likely to be ahead of me. That has been true for some time, really, but it is still a hard thing to come to grips with. I can't complain at all about my life so far. I've been privileged to have led the life I have and especially to have been able to experience as much of the coast as I have in this self-propelled fashion.

* * * * *

I set the alarm very early, half past three, to get up and get rowing before any contrary breezes start, with a view to maybe getting around Cape Caution. When the alarm goes I look out and see fog and I turn over and go back to sleep. I wake again at five and look out to see that the fog has gone but it has left behind low cloud. I decide to get up and go, to Jones Cove at least, and see what conditions are like for progressing further once I get there. Most of the other boats in Millbrook are either leaving or have left, presumably to get around Cape Caution. I am rowing by six on the dot and very shortly a light breeze suckers me into raising the sails. My speed rarely exceeds two knots under sail and most of the time is nearer to one, forcing me to finally give up and go back to the oars. I find that, even with the swell, I am making a little more than two knots over ground. The mouth of Smith Sound is pretty much devoid of boats this morning, but there are a fair number of seabirds about. I row by a group of Phalaropes, doing their spinning vortex thing to feed. I try to get a picture of them doing this, but only get a rather fuzzy image of them flying away. The rowing gets harder as I approach Table Island in Alexandra Passage, as the swell increases from offshore. I labour into the shelter of the Turner Islands and the swell drops there but increases again in the gap between the islands and Jones Cove. While it is still mid-morning, I judge that with the difficult rowing, it is too risky to try to get around Cape Caution today – it's just too far. I opt to spend the rest of the day in Jones Cove. It is a good staging spot for the Cape, and pretty much the last place north of it that I can wait.

As I approach the cove, a fifty foot power boat that went ahead of me to look into the cove comes out and passes close to me. As they do, they slow down and ask if I need anything. As it happens, I am a little short of fresh water, as one of my water bags sprang a leak and drained its contents into the bilge. I yell out, "I could use a couple of gallons of water if you can spare them!" and one of the crew goes below and comes out with two jugs of bottled water and tosses them over. We have a short chat about the weather and strategies for getting round the Cape. I am grateful for the water as it saves me a couple of hours of hard rowing to the nearest stream and back.

As I drop the anchor in the tiny cove, the sun begins to peak through the clouds. I make a pot of coffee and sit back to take in the scene. Behind me at the head of the cove is a sandy beach, shelving out to a shallow sandy bottom interspersed with patches of various kinds of seaweed. Steep rocks, topped by cedars and firs toughened and gnarled in the winter gales, enclose the bay. Out the open end to the northeast I can see past the Turner Islands to the Barrier Group in Smith Sound. Beyond them are the mountains of the mainland, separating Smith Sound from Rivers Inlet. There is cloud over the mountains but the open patches of sky above me are a clear pale blue and the ruffled water that morning is the dark blue of a new pair of unwashed Levis. To complete the picture, an immature Bald eagle seems to make the bay his base for foraging forays, and a resident Kingfisher rattles around the cove, diving for small fish. I can't imagine a better setting to wait for a chance to get around the Cape.

I spend the rest of the morning doing boat chores, having a seawater wash and programming in GPS waypoints for the days ahead. The wind picks up briskly in the afternoon from the southwest, which would be dead on the nose for sailing around the cape, validating my decision to go no further today. The water in the shallow cove is very clear and I can see that the bottom is mostly sandy, with some patches of seaweed. I can't see any fish but, finding myself with the leisure time and a sandy beach adjacent, I think I'll try fishing for my supper. I'm no great fisherman and on previous trips I unashamedly sponged off the efforts of my sailing partners. However, for this trip I thought it was finally time I made an attempt at becoming fully coastal by fishing. I bought a cheap rod and reel and a few lures for the trip. On the first four casts, I bring up weed, but on the fifth cast, I feel tugging, and after a short tussle, reel in a modest-sized greenling of some sort. Into the bucket it goes and within five minutes I catch a somewhat larger rockfish. I am amazed that a neophyte like me can manage this. I probably can catch more but I'm just looking for dinner, not bragging rights. I immediately go ashore, fillet them and pan fry them with a little oil and spice. Sitting in the warm sun on a beach rock, eating the freshest of fish, is the best meal I can imagine. Maybe I'll become a fisherman after all.

* * * * *

"In the pre-dawn darkness . . ." it is cloudy at quarter to four when I get up. The four o'clock lighthouse reports at Egg Island, just off the Cape to the northwest, West Sea Otter buoy offshore, and Pine Island further south in Queen Charlotte Strait all indicate calm or very light winds and low seas. The forecast is favourable for the early part of the day. If I get under way soon I will have a little bit of ebb to help me the last little couple of miles out of Smith Sound. I am still a little nervous, as Cape Caution isn't really a single landmark. It is only the southernmost point of a four-mile long headland that includes Milthorpe Point and Neck Ness before you come to Cape Caution, where the light is situated. From my anchorage in Jones Cove it is about six miles to the Cape and about nine miles to the nearest plausible cove to duck into should the weather deteriorate.

I dig out my battery-powered running lights for the first time in the trip and clamp them on bow and stern. I raise the anchor, ship the oars and start rowing by quarter to five. It is very sloppy rowing in the confused, rebounding swell in the open, but I get the expected boost from the tide, averaging a little over two and half knots. Abreast of Milthorpe Point, I'm able to turn from west to southwest, and just then a west wind comes up. I put up the sails and set off on a reach, doing four knots. I have visions dancing in my head of a monster mileage day, but a mile short of Cape Caution the wind dies away and I have to take to the oars again. By this time the tide has switched to flood and is helping me along as I row south. I soon pass the storied Cape where the swell diminishes somewhat and it is a bit of an anticlimax. The Cape itself turns out to be a rather undistinguished low point of land, but I imagine it would be all the more dangerous in thick weather because it would be hard to see. There are no pleasure boats to be seen at this hour, which surprises me as I thought that any other boats wanting to get around the Cape would be out early to take advantage of the calm. I do see, picked out against the cumulous clouds offshore, a tug and barge several miles out, heading south. It is reassuring, as tugs tend to wait for a favourable weather window.

At the cove north of Wilkie Point, my first possible bail-out option, I'm doing well and I keep going. Across Burnett Bay, the current alternately helps then disappears. A little wind comes up from the southwest and I am afraid that it is the southerly gale predicted for later, come early. I decide that the next bail-out option, the cove at Buccleugh Point, will be where I'll stop. As is often the case, what looks good on the chart doesn't pan out in reality. While the cove is sheltered from the southerly winds, it is wide open to the northwesterly swell that is setting strongly into the bay when I get there and it clearly isn't going to work. With no choice, I push on, now targeting Miles Inlet on Bramham Island. While this will carry me past Slingsby Channel, the timing is right for this as it is still flood tide. The rowing now is very difficult and it is not just the swell and current around the point. The area is now thick with sport fishing boats coming and going at high speed, with their usual disregard for the consequences of their wake. The current is very confused, but not dangerous, off the mouth of Slingsby and it seems a long, long slog to get to Miles Inlet. I finally pull into the inlet, and drop the anchor at quarter past eleven, in a very small rocky-sided cove a little over half a mile in on the south side. I've been rowing hard and sailing, mostly rowing, for six and a half hours. I am tired, but I've done it, I am safely past both Cape Caution and Slingsby Channel! I feel like I should rush to get my left ear pierced for a gold earring[92].

Over lunch at anchor I get out the chart and review my progress since leaving Jones Cove this morning. I calculate I have come sixteen and half miles, not much of it under sail, under difficult rowing conditions, so I think I have a right to

Rocky nook in Miles Inlet where I waited out a gale for 48 hours

feel tired. I listen to the updated forecast to hear that a southeast gale is forecast for all three forecast areas near me, with the only difference between them being how strong the peak winds will be and when the gale will arrive. The prediction is that it will start to get strong sometime in late afternoon, will blow overnight and through the next day, and then will be back to northwest winds the day following.

Where I am seems to be as good a place as any to hunker down and ride out the gale. There is probably more shelter further into Miles Inlet, in one of the side arms, but maybe not, as the whole of Bramham Island is pretty flat. I am tucked up near to high rock walls, which should block the worst of the wind. In addition, it will be an additional mile and a half to row to get out when I want to leave, and I'm not keen on the extra distance. I do think I can take steps to better secure the boat, though. I raise the anchor and run lines first to one shore, then across to the other and re-set the anchor. This should prevent the boat from swinging too far or dragging at anchor if it should blow hard in this little pocket. In the afternoon, the sun that came out for a while when I arrived disappears and there is actually a little northwest wind that find its way in, but that dies away by early evening.

* * * * *

It is calm when I turn in at quarter to ten, and I must have been more tired than I thought, as I don't wake up until quarter to eight next morning. At first this morning I think that the gale has been cancelled, it was so quiet overnight, with so little wind in my protected corner. But the nearest station, Pine Island, is reporting southeast winds of ten knots already. The forecast is still calling for a gale, but the prediction is that it will arrive later and depart later.

It starts drizzling on and off about dawn and as the day progresses this thickens to become rain off and on. I have a bit of a panic around noon when I try to listen to the updated forecast and can get nothing on any channel. Nor does anyone respond when I broadcast an any-station request for a radio check. I think my radio has gone on the fritz and go so far as to take it apart to see if it has a reset button. I can't see one, so I put it back together. Along about one o'clock, the continuous marine broadcast comes back on. It turns out they have been offline. The incident does tell me that if I have to call anyone, I will have to move out of the cove. After supper, the winds at Pine and Herbert Islands are southeast twenty four knots. This is not yet the forecast gale, but it is a stronger wind than I want to be out in. I turn in but it is a restless night, with gusts rattling the boat and every noise magnifies into some kind of problem in my half-asleep imagination. In the morning, winds are southeast fifteen at Pine and southeast twenty at Herbert. The predicted wind shift hasn't happened yet. The rain, which stopped overnight, starts up again. I'm getting a little stir-crazy, as by this time I've been cooped up in the boat, mostly under the tent in a space about the size of a double bed, for nearly forty-eight hours. While the vertical rock walls of the cove are dramatic, the view palls after a while, and anyway, it is raining much of the time, keeping me in the tent.

As the morning wears away, the wind seems to be dropping, and at the ten-forty reports, Pine is southeast two and Herbert northwest four. I decide to go for it and start for Port Hardy. Even if I have to row all the way, it is only ten and half miles to the first bail-out point in the Walker Group. I put on the dry suit, both because of the rain, and because I am heading out to fairly open waters. Out of Miles Inlet into Queen Charlotte Strait, there isn't enough wind to sail but I am making good speed rowing, three-plus knots. I can't account for this speed as the flood current should have ended by now. The weather begins to thicken, the visibility reduces to exactly two miles (I know this because there is a small island two miles away just on the edge of visibility) and it begins to rain again, fine, drenching sheets of water. I'm glad I have the dry suit on and am thankful for the new sou'wester hat I bought for the trip (after failing to locate my old one).

After a couple of hours of rowing, the northwest wind finally fills in and the cloud begins to lift. I raise sail and there is enough wind to push me along about four knots, sometimes a little more sometimes a little less. Once again, visions of sugarplums dance in my head and I start calculating how much distance I will make in how short a time. Such foolishness is always punished of course, and as I approach the Walker Group, the wind begins to die away and the tide starts to set up a funny chop, hobby-horsing the boat. I take this as an omen and decide to not push my luck, but to duck into the anchorage formed by the space between Kent and Staples Islands in the Walker Group. I come to anchor at about four o'clock in shallow water in an indent on the Kent Island side. I've come eleven and a half miles according to my GPS. I sponged off the rainwater while we were still sailing and the boat is nearly dry when I put the tent up. It is good to get the dry suit off and into dry clothes. It is a quiet evening, with entertainment provided by the many Pigeon Guillemots actively feeding in the bay.

* * * * *

I wake at twenty to five and listen to the forecast and the light station reports. It is already blowing ten knots northwest at Herbert Island. I know I have to get my skates on, as the British say, before the wind builds up. It stayed cloudy overnight and my tent is dry this morning for once, without condensation, and I don't have to pack it away wet. I have only twelve miles to go to Port Hardy. It shouldn't take long with this good wind. I am out into Bolivar Channel west of the anchorage by seven and I raise sail. Immediately the GPS shows three and a half knots over ground. My speed is more than that through the water, but the ebb tide is against me. There are some pretty strange wind-over-wave patterns and currents in the channel. I note on the chart that there is an Alex Rock in the channel up ahead, and I think that some time I will have to come back and have a look at my namesake. Be careful what you wish for. The tide is stronger than I think, and although I am sailing at a good clip, it is setting me sideways and I get a much closer look at Alex Rock than I want to. The seas are breaking with a tremendous noise on the Rock. I'm glad I have the sail power behind me to push me past and am not relying on muscle power alone to escape. The seas begin to flatten out as I approach the Gordon Islands, the last obstacle before Hardy Bay. My speed picks up to five knots as I fly through between the islands on a broad reach.

The seas get lumpy again past the islands but the wind strengthens some more and my speed is up too. Now I also have to dodge literally dozens of sport fishing boats in the channel and off Duval Point at the entrance to the bay, trying their luck on this sunny Saturday morning. Once past the point and into Hardy Bay, the water flattens right out, the wind shifts forward and I am sailing on a beam reach. I rocket down the three mile length of the bay, hitting six and half knots in the gusts, with the bow wave creaming up and alongside. In less than half an hour I round up outside the last light before the marina breakwater and stow the sail rig. I pull in to an empty slip at half past ten.

I go up in search of a shower, do laundry and to think about re-supply for the rest of the journey south to Victoria. While I'm sitting looking at the washing machine, I realize I have zero enthusiasm for continuing on. In hindsight, I focused all my energy on getting to Cape Caution and getting around it. I don't have an appetite to re-cross, in the opposite direction, ground I covered last year. The fact that the winds are forecast to be strong for the next week, albeit in a favourable direction, causing me to likely have to sit them out for some days, also plays a part. I decide to pack in the trip at Port Hardy.

I am well content with what I saw, with the interesting people I met and with what I accomplished. I officially became an old-age pensioner on this trip and although I retired from my business, I have not yet retired from an active life. This trip may well have been a sort of magnum opus of single-handed sail and oar cruising for me, but I feel that the end of the composition is yet to be written. I look forward to seeing how it will turn out.

Fire-Drake at rest in Port Hardy at journey's end

Endnotes

1   A nautical mile is, by definition, the distance subtended by one minute of arc of latitude of the earth's surface at the equator. One degree is 60 minutes or 60 nautical miles. A nautical mile is about 6,076 feet long, compared to a statute or land mile, which is 5,280 feet. Any distances on the water in this book designated in miles will mean nautical miles.

2   Eel Grass *(Zostera marina)* is the most common of several varieties of seagrass found on the Pacific Northwest coast. It is a perennial aquatic flowering plant that send up new leaves every year from rhizomes. One source says that Zostera marina is the dominant species in terms of biomass and habitats on the Pacific coast where it grows in the lagoons, estuaries and fjords. Seagrass habitats are important as food and shelter for many animal species, including as spawning sites for herring. Also, many First Nations made use of it. The Kwakwaka'wakw, Haida and Makah ate the rhizomes in various ways. The Makah used the leaves in basketry and the Chumash of California fashioned seagrass skirts.

3   Grey Whales have come close to extinction at least twice in the last 150 years but began making a spectacular comeback in the late 1980s. They are baleen whales, i.e. whales which take in large volumes of water, and in this case bottom mud, and then expel it through the sieve-like baleen, and eat what remains. Adults range from 35-45 feet in length and are mottled Grey in colour. They have no dorsal fin and generally are covered with clumps of barnacles. They winter and calve off the coast of Baja, California and migrate north along the entire west coast of North America in the spring to feed in shallow water just offshore.

4   The Chocolate Lily *(Fritillaria affinis var. affinis)* is widely distributed along the coastal areas of BC, from sea level to sub-alpine. The bulbs were eaten by the Coast Salish first nations people, after being steamed in pits or boiled in pots.

5   Notwithstanding the lyrics of the chorus of the Tom Lewis tongue-in-cheek shanty - *The Last Shanty*:
"Don't haul on the rope, don't climb up the mast,
If you see a sailing ship it might be your last,
Just get your civies ready for another run ashore,
A sailor ain't a sailor, ain't a sailor anymore."

6   About 45-50 degrees Fahrenheit

7   I did go on to take current and surf lessons later that spring and to make the required modifications to the boat.

8   The island is named after Juan Francisco de la Bodega y Quadra, who was a colonial Spanish naval officer, based out of San Blas, Mexico, and who had made several earlier voyages of discovery to the Pacific Northwest. He was sent in 1792 to resolve the Nootka Crisis, in which Britain and Spain disputed the ownership of this part of the coast. George Vancouver was sent out from Britain to act on Britain's behalf. Both parties neglected to consult the First Nations people living here at the time. The two men met in Nootka Sound and, while they failed to resolve the crisis, they personally got on very well. Vancouver thought so highly of Quadra that he named Vancouver Island Quadra's and Vancouver's island on his charts. That name remained for many years until Quadra's was dropped by the British Admiralty in the 19th century.

9   This name is a measure of how different our late twentieth century worldview is from that of Europeans in the late eighteenth century. Whereas we look at the wild scenery and

setting and see great beauty, Captain George Vancouver, who bestowed the name Desolation Sound on this area in 1792, did not. Beauty for him was a tamed, settled, civilized and pastoral land. He wrote in his journal *"Our residence here was truly forlorn; an awful silence pervaded the gloomy forests, whilst animated nature seemed to have deserted the neighbouring country, whose soil afforded only a few small onions, some samphire and here and there bushes bearing a scanty crop of indifferent berries. Nor was the sea more favourable to our wants, the steep rocky shores prevented the use of the seine, and not a fish at the bottom could be tempted to take the hook."*

10   The explanation for the warm water can be found in the fact that the tidal streams from the open Pacific that sweep around Vancouver Island meet about here, so there is very little flushing by cold water. The summer weather is predominantly sunny so the water in these protected inlets can get very warm by Pacific Northwest standards.

11   The Vellela is a type of hydroid polyp, which lives its entire life at sea, generally in warmer waters, unless driven ashore by storms. The most fascinating thing about the transparent sails of these creatures is that they come in two orientations in relation to the body. They are northwest to southeast on animals found in the eastern north Pacific, and northeast to southwest on the western side of the ocean. In each case, the prevailing winds tend to push the animals offshore. I am always amazed at what tricks and adaptations that evolution produces, and here is another example.

12   A knot is a unit of speed used by mariners. It is one nautical mile per hour. One nautical mile is equal to one degree of latitude at the equator. A knot is therefore very useful for navigation, since it directly relates speed to the latitudes and longitudes shown on nautical charts. The correct usage is knot, not knots per hour.

13   Bligh was the sailing master aboard Captain James Cook's sloop Resolution when he put in here in the spring of 1778. Both Resolution and the other ship of the expedition, the sloop Discovery, commanded by Lieutenant Charles Clerke, were desperately short of water after crossing from Hawaii. They had sighted the coast off Cape Foulweather in Oregon and had been driven south by bad weather before being able to sail north again, past the entrance to the Strait of Juan de Fuca, which they sighted but did recognize for what it was and not enter. Both ships also needed repairs that required the calm waters of a harbour. When they made landfall, it was at the entrance to these inlets, which Cook named Saint George's Sound at the time (only later to be changed to Nootka by the British Admiralty). As they anchored, they were met by the local Nuu-chah-nulth people, sent out in canoes by their Chief Maquinna, to see who these people were and what they wanted. Relations were cordial for the four weeks the ships lay at anchor re-fitting and exploring and there was much trading between the Nuu-Chah-Nulth and the British. Because of the friendly relations, Cook gave the name Friendly Cove to the village near their anchorage, which of course already had its own Nuu-Chah-Nuth name of Yuquot.

14   Sitka Spruce *(Picea sitchensis)* is one of the iconic trees of the BC Coast. It has sharp, flattened needles that are quite prickly to encounter. It can grow up to 300 feet tall in the right circumstances. It prefers wet coastal and river valley habitats. First Nations peoples used many parts of the tree, not just the wood. It is particularly prized for its lumber, which has a high strength-to-weight ratio. This property was why it was used in World War Two to construct de Havilland Mosquito fighter-bombers, many of which were built using wood from Haida Gwaii. In fact, so much Sitka Spruce for this purpose was taken out of the north end of Moresby Island that the lake there was named Mosquito Lake, after the airplane.

15   The Osprey, *(Pandion haliaetus)*, is found throughout North America, in both fresh and salt water. It is about the only raptor here that feeds exclusively on fish. One of the cool things to watch is how they line up a newly caught fish fore-and-aft in their talons,

which reduces the aerodynamic drag for flying. While they favour large old-growth trees for nesting sites, they have also adapted to using man-made structures. In Victoria, a pair frequently nests on top of the light pole of the baseball stadium, unperturbed by the ball games below.

16   Whales were an important food source for the first nations of the coast and they never took enough to threaten the population. Whales are not found in abundance on the coast all year round. We now know that the North Pacific population of humpbacks come to our coast to feed in the summer and then head back to the warmer waters around Hawaii to breed and bear their calves in the winter. Commercial whaling reduced their numbers to a few thousand before whaling ceased in British Columbia in the late 1960s.

17   Pretty much all the bears on Vancouver Island are Black Bears *(Ursus Americanus)*. An adult Black Bear will range in size from 24 – 36 inches high at the shoulder and weigh 175 – 650 pounds. The population of Black Bears in British Columbia is estimated at 120,000 – 150,000, some of the highest density in the world. Black Bears that are not habituated to human garbage are generally considered to be reasonably wary of human contact. While Grizzly Bears have been spotted from time to time on northern Vancouver Island, they are thought not to be regularly reproducing there.

18   The diminutive Pacific wren, (which has the delightful Latin name of *Troglodytes Pacificus* – meaning "cave-dweller of the Pacific"), is now known to be a sub-species of winter wren. It must have the most song for the least amount of bird on the coast, taking from five to ten seconds to complete.

19   After the trip, on consulting my plant book at home, I figured that the plant that most likely matched what I saw was an Entire-leaved Gumweed, a member of the Aster family. An unlovely name for a beautiful and hardy little plant.

20   The Swainson's Thush *(Catharus ustulatus)* is widely spread throughout British Columbia, but there are two groups and six sub-species. The coastal group is known as "russet-backed." They winter in Central America.

21   Sea Otters don't have blubber to keep them warm in the cold waters where they live but instead rely on the densest fur of any living mammal, with over 250,000 hairs per square inch. The otters continually groom the fur to keep it clean and work air into the fur to act as insulation. This wonderful fur was used by the first nations peoples, but they didn't seriously impact the populations. When Vitus Bering arrived in the mid-eighteenth century in the waters that were later to bear his name, he brought back some pelts. This started a period of commercial exploitation of the otters that lasted more than 150 years. James Cook and his crew, during his 1778 visit to Nootka Sound, acquired some sea otter pelts there which were later sold in China for what were, to the Englishmen, astonishing sums. When word of the finding of Sea Otters on the British Columbia coast got back to England, the rush was on there as well. It is now estimated that there may have been as many as 300,000 Sea Otters before the fur trade started. In 1911, when a treaty banning the trade was signed, there were as few as 1,000 left, mostly in Russia and Alaska, and they were extirpated in Canada.

22   Science may not be able to explain such things at present, but that is not to say they have no rational explanation. At least not yet. I believe that eventually an explanation will be found. Maybe there is such a thing as a biological field that living things tap into, which we don't yet know how to measure. After all, who in the 18th century would have guessed the existence of electromagnetism and predicted the development of radio, let alone radar or lasers?

23   I always find shorebirds among the hardest birds to identify. They're invariably always on the move so it's hard to get a good look at them. Several species resemble each other

with only minor distinguishing marks differentiating them, for example Killdeer and Semi-Palmated Sandpipers. The former have two neck stripes and the latter only one, but that is often hard to see if you just get a quick look. And that's just in their summer plumage. When they have molted to their non-breeding plumage, they look completely different.

24   The Round-leaved Sundew is one of two carnivorous, or to be more precise, insectivorous plants found in British Columbia. The Sundew grows in bogs and other nitrogen-poor habitats and gets its needed nitrogen from hapless insects which it traps on reddish sticky hairs that grow on its egg-shaped leaf ends. The sticky fluid also digests the insects which are absorbed for their nitrogen. They are no threat to unwary humans, however, as they rarely grow much more than a couple of inches tall. Rather, they have medicinal value. First nations peoples along the coast used the leaves to remove corns, warts and bunions.

25   Fairly recent research, including genetic testing, has revealed that while the coastal wolves are a form of American Grey Wolf *(Canis Lupus)*, they have distinct genetic differences from inland wolves. The coast wolves have a diet centred around seafood, including salmon in season, and inhabit the coastal zone which is ecologically and geologically different from the interior. This is something the local first nations have always been aware of.

26   The logging company planned to use the bay as the log sorting area for the planned logging, which is why it was the location for the centre of the protest. The Tla-o-qui-aht quickly built the cabin with help of the locals from Tofino and declared the island a Tribal Park. There was a tense stand-off between the protesters and the logging company who were accompanied by the RCMP. The issue went before the courts, who declared in 1985 that no logging could take place until the Tla-o-qui-aht land claims were settled. It was a historic victory for the first logging blockade in Canadian history.

27   The Common Merganser is a little larger than a Mallard and is common in our coastal bays and estuaries in summer. They make their living by diving for fish and aquatic insects. They nest in tree cavities, although I've never managed to see such a nest.

28   The hypothesis goes something like this: if you don't have enough of the important mood-regulating neurotransmitter serotonin in your brain, you are likely to become depressed. Serotonin in the brain largely comes from converting it from the amino acid tryptophan, which requires adequate water to process. Dehydration can also decrease production of energy needed by the brain, which also can contribute to depression. As if those aren't enough, dehydration can cause stress and stress itself can cause dehydration, an unwanted feedback loop. When you are exercising hard, especially in cool weather, it easy to overlook the fact that you are using water at a greater than normal rate and so it is not difficult to become dehydrated. The cure is simple - drink more water.

29   Also known as Northern Rice Root, these are similar to Chocolate Lilies but are darker purple in colour. Also the flowers are pollinated by flies that are attracted by the colour and the smell, which is of rotting meat or feces, but they are pretty, nonetheless. The bulbs of this plant were also a food source for the First Nations people.

30   Marbled Murrelets (Brachyramphus marmoratus) are smallish, rather compact diving seabirds. They are remarkable for their nesting habits, making their nests on the mossy tops of very large branches of inland old-growth trees. The first Marbled Murrelet nest was only discovered in 1974.

31   Although no one knew it at the time, Triquet Island is the place on the coast that holds the record for the longest period of human habitation. Recent (published 2017) work by researchers at Simon Fraser University has found evidence of human occupation at least 14,500 years ago. This is a remarkable date, preceding the earliest known Clovis sites by at least 1,500 years.

32 "Tending the Wild," M. Kat Anderson, University of California Press, 2006

33 Haida Gwaii, meaning "Islands of the People," is the name the First Nations Haida people who live there have for the island archipelago that lies off the north coast of British Columbia formerly known as the Queen Charlotte Islands and it is now (as of 2010) the official name. The first European to visit the islands was the Spaniard Juan Pérez, in 1774. The islands were formerly named the Queen Charlottes by George Dixon in 1787, captain of a ship of the same name. Dixon had served as armourer with Captain James Cook on his final voyage but Cook never stopped at the islands. The islands are separated from the mainland by Hecate Strait, with the nearest point being about 30 nautical miles offshore in the north and the furthest point, Cape St. James in the south, being about 80 nautical miles.

34 How clever do you have to be to catch an oyster, which is fixed to the sea-bottom? Despite the goofy name, Oystercatchers are medium-sized shorebirds of very striking appearance. Their plumage is all black and they have long, bright red-orange bills and a red eye. My bird book describes their call as "loud, ringing yelps." They make their living by winkling out small shellfish from cracks in rocky shorelines.

35 Pigeon Guillemots are smallish seabirds. They are mostly black with a white patch on their sides and distinctive red feet. When foraging in shallow water, they swim along the surface, sticking their heads under water every few seconds to look for fish and dive to catch them.

36 There are many species of Sculpins (family Cottidae) in BC waters, ranging from the very small (an inch or so) to medium size (fourteen inches). I didn't know enough about them then to know what kind it was.

37 Gwaii Haanas, meaning "islands of beauty" in Xaad Kil (the Haida language), is the protected area in the south of Haida Gwaii, designated the Gwaii Haanas National Park Reserve and Haida Heritage Site and co-managed by the Haida and Parks Canada.

38 These are the smallest cetacean found in BC waters, with the adults not exceeding five feet in length and two hundred pounds in weight. They are easy to miss as they are dark grey in colour, which blends in with the dark water, and their blow is very small and doesn't make much noise.

39 Haida have always had watchmen, whose role it was to warn of the approach of an enemy or of any other happenings that the people should be aware of. This role was recognised in the 1993 Gwaii Haanas Agreement, by which the Haida and Parks Canada co-manage the area. The three figures often seen on the top of Haida totem poles symbolize the Watchmen.

40 As it turned out, I made the most significant career move in my life exactly two years later, to the day.

41 Killer Whales (Orcinus orca) are often referred to as just Orcas. They are black with quite distinctive white patches. Adult males can be 25 – 30 feet long and weigh up to 5½ tons. Their tall narrow dorsal fins are unmistakable at 5 feet tall. Females are a little smaller and have much shorter dorsal fins. There are three types of Orcas found in BC waters, residents, transients and offshore. Residents tend to keep to known areas and eat exclusively fish. They live in matriarchal family groups called pods, of up to 50 whales. Transients, as the name implies, don't have defined territories and eat other marine mammals. They travel in much smaller groups. Not much is known about the offshore whales.

42 Western Grebes are largish diving water birds, about the size of a Loon. They are an unremarkable grey and white in colouration. They nest in the interior and come back out to coast once breeding season is over.

43 Hlk'yah GawGa was one probably the most important site of the protests in 1985 by the Haida to the logging planned in nearby Sedgewick Bay. This was the last intact old-

growth valley on Lyell Island. The longhouse was built to house the protesters during the standoff. The standoff lead to the historic agreement to create Gwaii Haanas co-managed protected area.

44   It is hard to overstate the importance of Western Red Cedar (Thuja Plicata) to the economies, cultures and lives of both First Nations and Europeans on the coast. It is not a true cedar but a type of cypress. It can grow to 70 metres in height and live more than a 1,000 years. First Nations used nearly every part of the tree; the bark, the wood, the roots, the young branches. The fashioned clothing, ropes, baskets, boxes, canoes and houses from the tree. Ceremonial masks are most often carved from Cedar. So important, materially, culturally and spiritually is Cedar to the Haida it is called by them "The Tree of Life." Its wood is naturally rot-resistant, which means it is terrific wood for buildings and boats. This property makes it valuable to our European civilization to this day and over-harvesting has led to many conflicts between traditional users and loggers.

45   "Gale" is not just a figurative term in the nautical world. It describes a specific range of wind speeds, from 34 – 47 knots. It is also described as Force 8 on the Beaufort Scale. This scale, which assigns numbers and descriptions to escalating ranges of wind speeds, was first devised in 1805 by Royal Navy officer (later Admiral) Francis Beaufort in an effort to bring objectivity to reporting of weather conditions by ships. The scale was adopted officially in the 1830s and at first had no absolute wind speeds associated with it, but instead described the amount of sail that could be carried by boats and ships. Only later were wind speed numbers associated to the descriptions and Force numbers. Further up the scale, a "Hurricane" is Force 12, with wind speeds greater than 64 knots.

46   Klepper is a popular brand of German folding kayak. While Johannes Klepper did not invent the concept of a folding kayak, in 1907 he developed an improved design along with mass production and marketing techniques. They have been popular ever since.

47   I learned when I got home that these were Lion's Main Jellies (Cyanea capillata) a jelly common in BC waters. The ones I saw had bells of more than a foot in diameter. They have tentacles up to 100 feet long that can deliver a painful sting. They catch zooplankton, small fish, and other smaller jellies.

48   Copper use has a long history among the first nations of the coast. Foremost was the making of shield-shaped objects known simply as "coppers." These embodied great wealth and prestige, with their value derived from the inherent worth of the metal, the skill with which it was made, the amount of use they got and how often they were given as gifts.

49   The deer are not native to Haida Gwaii. They were introduced in the 1880s and have spread, as there are no cougars or wolves, their main predators elsewhere. They have drastically altered the character of the forests. In many places there are no understory plants, just mosses and ferns. There is, as of 2017, a plan to eradicate the deer from the southern islands, in an attempt to restore the forest ecology.

50   A broach is when a boat or ship travelling downwind is forced side-on to the waves by the action of wind or waves and subsequently heels over and fills with water or capsizes. It is a very dangerous condition.

51   Also known as Antony Island, SGang Gwaay means Wailing Island, and is one larger island and number of small islets. Its location, southwest of the exposed outer coast, meant that it was hard to get to and so its rich collection of totem poles was not taken by outside "collectors" decades ago when most of the totems in other villages were removed. The village, SGang Gwaay Llnagaay, is sited on a beautiful little bay on the east side. It is a UNESCO World Heritage Site.

52   German for "crooked wood," it describes trees growing near the treeline that have been stunted by the wind.

53   Dall's Porpoises (Phocoenoides dalli) are the other porpoise found in BC waters. Fully-grown adults are about 7 feet long and fairly chunky, weighing as much as 475 pounds. Despite that, they are one of the fastest of swimmers among the dolphins, porpoises and whales. They are mostly black with white side markings. They are often found playing in the bow wakes of boats.

54   The BC coast does not have Blue Jays. That ecological niche is instead filled by the Steller's Jay (Cyanocitta stelleri) another member of the crow family. It gets its name from German naturalist Georg Steller, who was the first European to see the bird during a 1741 Russian expedition that briefly stopped in Alaska. The Jay is a beautiful glossy indigo blue with a black crested head and cape. It is omnivorous and it has a variety of calls, none very musical. It is the provincial bird of British Columbia.

55   The Common Murre (Uria aalge) is a medium sized diving seabird, rather handsome in its breeding plumage of black head, back wings and tail, with a sharp dividing line between the black and the white underparts. Their croaking call is distinctive and on shore, their upright stance resembles that of a penguin.

56   Insect Island, neighbouring Fly Island and a host of other small islands in the area are also part of the modern Broughton Archipelago Marine Park. xoxop'a village was a site for harvesting clams, fish, timber and a base for hunting and trapping.

57   From the markings, which we could see quite clearly as they swam and flew, we could tell these were Red-necked Phalaropes (Phalaropus lobatus). They are a small-medium sized bird about 10 inches longs but with long necks and long legs. They nest in the Arctic and are done early in the season, so that the ones we saw in August were moving south again. They practise a role reversal during nesting season, with the males raising the chicks.

58   Black Swifts (Cypseloides niger) breed along the north coast of Vancouver Island, nesting on small ledges or crevices in steep canyons, often behind waterfalls. At first glance they may appear to be swallows, but they are larger, with more curving wings and have more rapid, nearly flickering, wing-beats.

59   The Great Blue Heron (Ardea Herodias) is the largest of the wading birds that are found in BC, being 4 feet tall and with a wingspan of 6 feet. They are a beautiful blue-grey in colour with a long wicked-looking yellow beak. They have an elegant black-capped head that trails feather plumes. They nest in the tops of trees in large communal colonies the length of the BC coast and interior.

60   This system starts with setting the anchor out a ways from the beach, and buoying the anchor line to a fender that has a large metal ring tied to it. A long continuous line is run through the ring to a similar ring tied to a line on the beach. The bow eye of the boat is fastened to a point on the continuous line, so that boat can be brought in to the beach to put gear in and out or it can be run out to the buoy to avoid grounding at low tide, by hauling in and out on the line, like a clothesline on a couple of pulleys. Hence the name for the system.

61   Point the bow in the direction the wind is coming from.

62   A displacement hull is a hull that is limited in speed, in theory, by the length of its hull and hull shape. It basically just pushes the water aside and can't, for technical reasons, go much faster than the speed of the longest wave it creates while doing so. For *Hornpipe*, that maximum theoretical speed is about 5.4 knots. A planning hull, on the other hand, is flatter and so can produce lift so that, with enough power, it can ride partially out of the water and go much faster than the wavelength would suggest.

63   Sailor's language is full of words not used by the general populace or by familiar words that have a different meaning. Fetch is one of the latter. It is commonly used in a couple of ways. The first is to indicate the length of a stretch of water over which the wind has been blowing without being interrupted by land. At Cape Mudge on Quadra Island a southeast

wind blowing up the Strait of Georgia has a fetch of nearly 125 nautical miles from Lummi Island in the south. The second meaning is how I have used it here, which is when a sailing vessel can point to and arrive at a destination to windward on one course without changing tack.

64   Weatherly means a boat that can point closer to the direction that the wind is coming from when sailing to windward. Sailboats can't sail directly against the wind but can sail about 45-60 degrees to either side and must tack, or change direction, from one side to the other. Some boats can sail more directly, or closer, to the direction of the wind than others, and so travel less distance and get there sooner.

65   James Island is the former site of a dynamite factory and is now owned by Seattle billionaire Craig McCaw. It comes complete with its own golf course.

66   Following up on this later, I find there is surprisingly little known about their habits. They may make summer inshore and winter offshore movements, but it is more likely they simply follow prey. It is known that mothers with young seek more sheltered coves and bays.

67   A little research when I get home reveals that they are likely to have been Pacific White-sided Dolphins. Once considered a pelagic species and largely absent from the BC coast for much of the 20th century, they have been increasingly making a comeback since the 1980s.

68   Musgrave Landing is where Miles and Beryl Smeeton, famed sailors and circumnavigators, had the farm they came to on emigrating from England, and the cove is where they kept Tzu Hang, their boat.

69   There are 5 species of Salmon endemic to the BC Coast; Sockeye (Oncorhynchus nerka), Coho (Oncorhynchus kisutch), Chinook Oncorhynchus tshawytscha), Pink (Oncorhynchus gorbuscha) and Chum (Oncorhynchus keta). They vary from each other in appearance and habits, but they all hatch from eggs laid in freshwater stream beds, migrate to sea to mature and return as adults to spawn in the streams of their birth, after which they die. This cycle is critical both as a food source for many other species and as a key source of nitrogen and other nutrients from the sea. Many are caught by bears, wolves and eagles as they migrate upstream. The uneaten remains of their carcasses are eaten by progressively smaller scavengers, down to the insect level, so that the fish ultimately return to fertilize the forests alongside streams and rivers. The work that uncovered this intricate interdependency between fish and the coastal watersheds happened only relatively recently.

70   Weather helm is the tendency for the boat to turn up into the wind if you let go of the tiller. It feels like the tiller wants to pull away from you and requires you to counteract it by pulling the tiller towards yourself to stay on course.

71   Tombolo is an Italian word that has migrated into English. It describes a spit of land, usually gravel or sand, that connects an island to the mainland or another island. They are formed by wave refraction and diffraction, which slows the speed of the water so that sediment drops out and builds up into a tombolo.

72   The Fox Sparrow (Passerella iliaca) is described in my field guide as a "bulky, plain-faced sparrow" (who knew bird books could be so judgmental?) "With chevron-shaped spots on whitish breast, reddish-brown tail, yellow bill." There are a couple of forms, but they all tend to be pretty dark coloured. They forage on the ground, kicking forward with both feet to scratch at the detritus and uncover seeds, insects and fruit.

73   Rockweed is one of 530 kinds of seaweed found on the BC Coast. All seaweeds are a type of marine algae. They have no roots but have holdfasts, which are attached to the bottom or to rocks in the intertidal zone. The many varieties of Kelp belong to this group.

Rockweed is a short seaweed found in the intertidal zone and has CO_2 filled bulbs that buoy them up when submerged.

74   Whether this is actually true, I was never able to discover, and I have never encountered this ban elsewhere. However, the marina believed it at the time.

75   Pacific White Sided Dolphins (Lagenorhynchus obliquidens) are described as an average-sized oceanic dolphin of the North Pacific, with males weighing up to 440 pounds and measuring up to 8 feet long. Females are a little smaller. They are generally found in large groups of 10-100 individuals and not uncommonly in much larger groups like the one I saw. They were a traditional food source for the First Nations people of the coast, but were not seen on the BC coast in the 19th and early part of the 20th centuries. They started to re-appear in the 1950s and have become more common ever since.

76   Nanaimo is one of regrettably few places on the BC Coast where the original, First Nations, name associated with the area prevailed over the European name first assigned. The bay in front of area where the city is now located was named Bocas de Winthuysen (after a Spanish Rear-Admiral) by the Spanish explorer Lieutenant Commander Francisco de Eliza y Reventa and his navigator Jose Maria Narvaez, the first Europeans to see the area in 1791. Despite that name appearing on official charts, it was more commonly known by everyone locally as Nanaimo, an Anglicisation of the name of the Snuneymuxw First Nation who lived in the area. The original settlement in the early 1950s that later became the City was first called Colville Town, after a Hudson's Bay Company Governor, but that was short-lived – becoming Nanaimo in 1860.

77   Relations between the various First Nations before the Europeans arrived were not all sweetness and light. Although they traded with one another, warfare was common as was the taking of slaves from other tribes to enhance one's own status. The north coast people, the Haida and the Tlingit, raided as far south as Puget Sound. In one documented incident, a party of over 100 people, said to be Haida or Tlingit, landed at Port Gamble in Puget Sound in November 1856 with the intention of raiding the settlement. The US Navy steam packet USS *Massachusetts* arrived, shelled the camp and landed a shore party, killing 26 people, while 1 US sailor was killed. The sailors burned the camp and the raider's canoes. Stranded, the remaining indigenous people surrendered a couple of days later and were eventually taken back to the mainland of southeast Alaska.

78   In the 18th century Royal Navy, and also many merchant vessels, sailors were not issued uniforms but made their own clothes from cloth purchased from the ship's purser. A day was set aside, usually Sunday, when regular ship's maintenance was suspended, for the off-watch crew to make new clothing and mend their old clothes. The ship still had to be sailed and so the crew stood their regular watches, in rotation. The make-and-mend term survived in the Canadian Navy at least into the 1970s when I served.

79   Yuculta is a word derived from the Kwak'wala language. It is thought to refer to the Laich-kwil-tach or Southern Kwakiutl First Nations people of Campbell River and Quadra Island. Another spelling for it is Euclataw, which survives in how the locals actually pronounce Yuculta, namely: Yew-cla-ta

80   Sound travels roughly 1,100 feet per second in normal atmospheric conditions. So the lightning was less than 1,100 feet away – whether it was horizontal distance or vertical was impossible to tell, but it was much closer than I was comfortable with.

81   Sea star wasting syndrome is the name that has been given to the large-scale die-off of sea stars on the west coast, from California to Alaska, that started to show up in 2013-14 and which is not completely over yet, at the time of this writing in mid-2018. While there have been previous sea star die-offs in the 1970s, 80s and 90s, they were not on this scale. Researchers have not been able to pin down any one cause, although warming waters due to

a prolonged El Nino event and a Densovirus have been implicated. Many species have been affected but mortality seems highest among the sunflower star (Pycnopodia helianthoides) and the ochre/purple star (Pisaster ochraceus). The effects are dramatic and rapid, leading to death with a few days after the first symptoms appear. As sea stars are a keystone species, there will likely be changes in the intertidal communities where they were found.

82   On my return, I looked up this place name on the BC Geographical Names website and learned that it had been so named by William Bauer, BCLS, a native of Australia, who practised in BC until 1929 and who died in 1932. It was first a village near Sydney, Australia and is now a suburb of that city.

83   Atrial Fibrillation (AFIB) is defined by the Mayo Clinic as "... an irregular and often rapid heart rate that can increase your risk of stroke, heart failure and other heart-related complications. During atrial fibrillation, the heart's two upper chambers (the atria) beat chaotically and irregularly — out of coordination with the two lower chambers (the ventricles) of the heart. Atrial fibrillation symptoms often include heart palpitations, shortness of breath and weakness."

84   Rain, drizzle, fog - as they say in Newfoundland.

85   Veering and backing are terms used by weather forecasters to describe directional wind changes. The definition according to NOAA is "Backing winds are winds which shift in a counter-clockwise direction with time at a given location (e.g. from southerly to southeasterly). The opposite of veering winds."

86   Also known as West Inlet

87   Also known as East Inlet. I have no idea how the name is pronounced.

88   I had never heard of such a thing before but I checked it out when I returned home at the end of the trip and apparently it is not uncommon.

89   The Kermode, or Spirit bear, is a melanistic white variant of a sub-species of Black Bear, Ursus americanus kermodei, found on the mainland mid and north coast and adjacent islands. It is thought that the white colouring makes the bears less visible to fish in the streams where the bears hunt them, so the white bears are more successful and the colouration persists and spreads in the population.

90   The Minke (Balaenoptera acutorostrata) is a baleen whale and the smallest and most common of such whales. They are not easily seen as they spend so little time on the surface, have a very small blow and they are fast, not reappearing where you expect them to even if you do catch a glimpse of them. Like other baleen whales they feed by scooping water that includes their prey into their expandable mouths and then filter the food through the baleen by expelling the water.

91   Nineteen months after the sinking, the Transportation Safety Board of Canada released its report into the investigation of the sinking. The weather was reasonable and basically, the second mate, who had the navigational watch, fell asleep and failed to make a required course correction. The investigation found that the crew had been working a 6 hours on – 6 hours off watch schedule for the previous two days while they had been in port. This schedule, in addition to not providing rest of sufficient duration, means that the same people are on watch at the same time every day and night, crucially, in the middle of the night, when alertness and cognitive function are at their lowest. The report "estimated that the second mate's performance at the time of the grounding was equivalent to a normal nighttime sleeper who had missed 1 night of sleep."

92   In the days of commercial sail, where square-riggers generally made the passage around Cape Horn from west to east with the prevailing winds, a sailor who had done so was entitled by custom to wear a gold hoop earring in the left ear, the one that had faced the Horn during the passage.

Bibliography

The works of a number of authors and scholars informed me not only before and during the journeys chronicled in this book but especially later during the writing of it, as I reflected on what I had seen and experienced. Their data, findings and thinking, while not always acknowledged explicitly in the text, contributed, I hope, to the accuracy and clarity of any observations I made.

Anderson, M. K. (2006). *Tending the Wild*. Berkeley, CA: University of California Press.

Archer, C. I. (1997). Book Review of Leland Donald. *Aboriginal Slavery on the Northwest Coast of North America*. Berkeley: University of California Press. BC Studies.

Blood, D. A. (1993, October). *Sea Otter Brochure*. Victoria, BC: Wildlife Branch, BC Environment, Ministry of Environment, Lands and Parks.

Brownstein, D. (2011, Oct 06). *The Tree of Life: A History of the Western Red Cedar on Haida Gwaii*. http://niche-canada. org/2011/10/06/the-tree-of-life-a-history-of-the-western-red-cedar-on-haida-gwaii/.

Cannings, R., Aversa, T. & Opperman, H. (2005). *Birds of Southwestern British Columbia*. British Columbia: Heritage House. Surrey.

Graham, K. *Heiltsuk village site on BC's Triquet Island is 14,000 years old*. http://www.digitaljournal.com/tech-and-science/ science/heiltsuk-village-site-on-bc-s-triquet-island-is-14-000-years-old/article/489190.

Hampton, D. (2016, August 28). *How Dehydration Contributes To Depression*. https://www.thebestbrainpossible.com/how-dehydration-contributes-to-depression/.

Hayward, B. (1981, No. 50, Summer). *The B.C. Salmon Fishery: A Consideration of the Effects of Licensing.* BC Studies.

Huang, A. Cedar. https://indigenousfoundations.arts.ubc.ca/cedar/.

Hunt, H.F. (1918-10-10). *Slavery Among the Indians of Northwest America.* The Washington Historical Quarterly, Volume 9.

Iredale, J. & Pfahler, U. *Community Involvement in the Nomination and Management of SGang Gwaay World Heritage Site.* Heritage Branch, Ministry of Forests, Land and Natural Resource Operations, Province of British Columbia, undated.

Luca, B. G., Johannessen, D. & Lindstom, S. (2007). *Ecosystem Overview: Pacific North Coast Integrated Management Area (PNCIMA)* Appendix E: Marine Plants. Canadian Technical Report of Fisheries and Aquatic Sciences 2667.

Macann, C. (2007). *Being and Becoming Overview.* Philosophy Now magazine. Issue 61.

MacKechnie, I. (2015, No. 187, Autumn). *Indigenous Oral History and Settlement Archaeology in Barkley Sound, Western Vancouver Island.* BC Studies.

Nelson, S. & Turris, B. (2004, December). *The Evolution of Commercial Salmon Fisheries in British Columbia.* Report to the Pacific Fisheries Resource Conservation Council.

Scagel, R. F. (1961). *Marine Plant Resources of British Columbia.* Fisheries Research Board of Canada, Bulletin No. 127.

Sheldrake, R. (1995). *Seven Experiments That Could Change the World.* Rochester, VT: Park Street Press.

Stokes, D. & Stokes, L. (1996). *Field Guide to Birds: Western Region.* Boston, MA: Little, Brown and Company.

Wyllie-Echeverria, S., Olsen, A. M. & Hershman, M. J. (eds). (1994). Seagrass Science and Policy in the Pacific Northwest: Proceedings of a Seminar Series. (SMA 94-1), EPA 910/R-94-004.

General Internet Resources Without Individually Identifiable Authors.

Battle of Port Gamble: http://www.historylink.org/File/5505; http://tinyurl.com/y6ffab4k; http://tinyurl.com/y6hr4xz9.

BC Cetacean Sightings Network: http://wildwhales.org/speciesid/dolphins-and-porpoises/pacific-white-sided-dolphin/.

E Fauna BC: http://linnet.geog.ubc.ca/efauna/.

E Flora BC: http://ibis.geog.ubc.ca/biodiversity/eflora/.

Gwaii Haanas Indigenous Land and Rights Advocacy and Activism Blog: https://blogs.ubc.ca/indigenousactivism/gwaii-haanas/.

Pender Harbour History: http://www.sunshinecoastmuseum.ca/pender-harbour.html.

Port Moments in Time Brochure. (2017). Nanaimo Port Authority,

Printable Identification Guide. British Columbia: Cetacean Sightings Network.

Sea Star Wasting Syndrome: https://www.sciencedaily.com/releases/2018/03/180320141317.htm https://www.eeb.ucsc.edu/pacificrockyintertidal/data-products/sea-star-wasting/ https://www.ocregister.com/2018/04/02/sea-star-wasting-disease-is-still-a-mystery-but-csuf-researchers-are-on-the-case/.

Yuculta: https://en.wikipedia.org/wiki/Yuculta.

Author

Alex Zimmerman is an adventurer, boatbuilder and writer, occupations which paralleled his mainstream career as technologist, executive, environmentalist and consultant in the green buildings industry before his retirement, and which occupations he now can afford to indulge full-time.

Alex got a basic grounding in seamanship, navigation and sailing as a junior engineer officer in the Canadian Navy and continued it by teaching in the Canadian Power Squadron after he left the Navy. He did a lot of big-boat sailing in other people's boats before downsizing to kayaks and small open boats. He built all his own boats; his three kayaks and both of his sail and oar boats. He used his decades of experience to also design his latest sail and oar boat, the eighteen foot lug yawl that he named Fire-Drake.

Alex has long been fascinated by the marvelous coast of British Columbia, its natural wonders, its people and its history. Alex has put several thousand self-propelled miles under the keels of his various boats over the past two and half decades exploring that coast. The culmination of that exploration was the successful and safe solo completion of British Columbia's Inside Passage in 2017 in his boat, Fire-Drake.

Alex lives in Victoria, British Columbia with his wife, and, between injuries, maintains the fiction that he is a still a runner and an athlete. He says he can stop boatbuilding any time he wants to.

Made in the USA
Columbia, SC
24 December 2019

85529401R10191